MENTAL HEALTH, RACE AND CULTURE

Mental Health, Race and Culture

3rd Edition

Suman Fernando

First edition 1991
Reprinted eight times
Second edition 2002
Reprinted four times
Third edition 2010
published by
PALGRAVE MACMILLAN

Palgrave Macmillan in the UK is an imprint of Macmillan Publishers Limited, registered in England, company number 785998, of Houndmills, Basingstoke, Hampshire RG21 6XS.

Palgrave Macmillan in the US is a division of St Martin's Press LLC, 175 Fifth Avenue, New York, NY 10010.

Palgrave Macmillan is the global academic imprint of the above companies and has companies and representatives throughout the world.

Palgrave® and Macmillan® are registered trademarks in the United States, the United Kingdom, Europe and other countries.

ISBN: 978-0-230-21271-8

This book is printed on paper suitable for recycling and made from fully managed and sustained forest sources. Logging, pulping and manufacturing processes are expected to conform to the environmental regulations of the country of origin.

A catalogue record for this book is available from the British Library.

A catalog record for this book is available from the Library of Congress.

10 9 8 7 6 5 4 3 2
19 18 17 16 15 14 13 12 11 10

Printed and bound in Great Britain by
CPI Antony Rowe , Chippenham and Eastbourne

1006686268

To the memory of my father and mother

Contents

Tables

Acknowledgements

I am indebted to many works of scholarship in the fields of psychiatry, psychology, anthropology and religion, especially those works that cut across these disciplines. However, this book would not have been possible without the stimulation I derived from discussions with numerous colleagues of various disciplines, the insight I gained through talking to people I have met as patients or clients, and, most of all, the support of friends and my immediate family.

In revising the book for its third edition, I drew on material in recent publications and also discussions I have had over the past ten years with users of mental health services and workers in the field of mental health; people in the fields of mental health, community development and psychosocial support in Sri Lanka; and colleagues in social and cultural psychiatry in Canada, the Netherlands and England. I am most grateful, too, to Kate Llewellyn and Catherine Gray of Palgrave Macmillan Publishers for their support and help in developing this third edition.

Introduction

At the start of this millennium WHO (2000) defined the objective of good health as twofold: 'the best attainable average level – *goodness* – and the smallest feasible difference among individuals and groups – *fairness*' (p. xi, italics in original). Eight years later, WHO (2008), stating that 'mental health is crucial to the overall well-being of individuals, societies, and countries', points to the negative cycle between poverty and mental ill health (p. 6). The issue of fairness is about justice and human rights not just *individual* rights as embodied in current international conventions – the United Nations first adopted its Universal Declaration of Human Rights in 1948 (United Nations, 1996) and the European Community adopted a similar convention in 1950 (Council of Europe, 2003) – and in British law as the Human Rights Act (1998), but rights of groups of people, communities, cultural groups, nations, or whatever, who wish to maintain their ways of life, their cultures, their inheritance and their futures; and the rights of groups of people seen as 'races' covered, for example, in British Race Relations Acts of 1968 and 1976 and the Race Relations (Amendment) Act 2000.

Health care in the world today is characterized by a number of paradoxes impinging on human rights and fairness. Intensive care units in hospitals in western cities struggle to save individual premature babies using all the techniques available to modern science, while hundreds of healthy children in Asia, Africa and South America die from the lack of basic health care. European doctors try to combat the diseases of overeating while relief workers in some parts of Africa try to combat starvation. The western diagnosis of depression is promoted in Africa and Asia along with antidepressants manufactured by the pharmaceutical industry, while Indian mysticism is marketed in North America. From 1970s onwards we have seen a plethora of social and ethnic conflicts, frequently traceable to the ravages of colonialism during the heyday of European imperialism; and imperialism seems to have taken a new form through economic exploitation in the name of free trade (Smith, 2005) and military interventions justified on the grounds of human rights and humanitarian causes (Bricmont, 2007). The decades since 1980 have seen massive movements of people across continents, many seeking asylum from areas of conflict and sometimes persecution and others looking for a better life. Europe, which had been a continent of emigration for centuries, has become a continent of immigration. It is on this world stage that the current meaning of mental health has to be worked out.

1

In the West, the high value given to wishes and desires of the individual human being, in terms of a self-centred, self-conscious entity, leads to a narrow view of mental health; materialism and distaste for spiritual considerations further limit the perception of what constitutes the person. Awareness has grown recently that mental health is not restricted to separate aspects of individual behaviour and experience but rather involves the functioning of human beings as whole individuals, family groups and communities. Approaches to ill health, such as 'holistic medicine' and 'systems theory', indicate dissatisfaction with the traditional reductionist approach in the West to health, illness, psychiatry and psychology. The West prides itself on its scientific sophistication and an advanced system of medical treatment to combat ill health; but the question of mental health is somewhat different, especially when considered cross-culturally.

Western psychology and psychiatry are rooted in worldviews, attitudes and beliefs characteristic of western culture; they have not been influenced to any significant extent by non-European cultural traditions and so remain ethnocentric disciplines with a limited perspective. Once this assumption was questioned in the early part of the twentieth century, movements developed within psychiatry – called cross-cultural or comparative psychiatry, cultural psychiatry and transcultural psychiatry – incorporating anthropological and psychoanalytic viewpoints. In the past twenty or so years transcultural psychiatry has explored the influence on western psychology and psychiatry of beliefs and myths about 'race' present in European culture, and the impact of racism on service provision for people suffering from mental health problems. The context in which this has been done is significant: In many ways, mental health systems in the western, developed world are in a state of indecision if not crisis; the disciplines that inform them are far from clear as to direction or strategy for service provision. New discourses are being pursued but do not seem strong enough at present to shake traditional western ways of thinking about mental health, linked to diagnosis in a biomedical model of illness. But the movers and shakers of power are complicated and diffuse; so the direction that mental health services will eventually take in the future, taking psychiatry and psychology along with it, is far from clear.

The first and second editions of this book developed and broadened the fields of study around mental health that address issues of 'race' and culture. This third edition has the same basic structure as the second, but has been revised and updated throughout with some reordering and re-titling of chapters and the addition of several new chapters. The concept of identity is combined with that of ethnicity, thus adding to the scope of the chapter on race and culture. Western psychology and psychiatry are explored in greater depth by tracing their philosophical and historic roots to form a background to discussions of racism, updated to address the current political scene and mental health issues. New chapters address discourses in mental health that are relatively new at least to the UK; issues around trauma; mental health in developing countries; and mental health of refugees.

The first part of this book considers theory and tradition. Chapter 1 (*Race and Culture; Ethnicity and Identity*) discusses meaning of the concepts that are referred to in many of the subsequent chapters and, appropriately, racism is also discussed here. A major theme of the book is that culture plays a large part in how mental health is understood across the world. In Chapter 2 (*Traditional Approaches to Mental Health*) the western tradition that underpins the understanding of mental health in a biomedical mode is explored, pointing out areas where it differs from non-western traditions and medical belief systems. Here too stigma is discussed, the outmoded concept of culture-bound syndromes is explained, and diversity in the expression of emotions is considered. This leads on to Chapter 3 (*Background and Culture of Psychiatry*) which delves further into history in order to elucidate the culture of psychiatry and (western) psychology. In this chapter, some aspects of the nineteenth-century scientific paradigm that underpins these disciplines are explained and the background to current psychiatric practice briefly covered. Chapter 4 (*Racism in Psychiatry*) traces the way in which racism has permeated psychiatry and, to some extent, clinical (western) psychology, right up to the present time where people seen as culturally or racially different – 'the other' – are faced with serious disadvantages when they access mental health services. Chapters 5 (*Changing Discourse in Mental Health*) and 6 (*Trauma and Post-traumatic Stress; Suffering and Violence*) are entirely new to the third edition of the book. The first describes some of the more important new discourses in mental health looked at from a 'race' and culture perspective. The second discusses the discourse on trauma, with the subtext of suffering and violence, that has made a big impact on discussions around mental health although it is still unclear how useful that will be in the long run.

The second part of the book addresses practice and innovation. To start with, Chapter 7 (*Application of Psychiatry; Bias and Imperialism*) considers the universal application of biomedical psychiatry both in its traditional home within largely western societies and in non-western settings. The words bias and imperialism give an indication of the practical problems that have resulted, but the chapter also shows how they may be addressed. Although systems of therapy and healing indigenous to Asian, African and pre-Columbian American cultures have been seriously underdeveloped – and still marginalized or even suppressed as a result of psychiatric imperialism – they still function albeit under adverse conditions. Chapter 8 (*Asian and African 'Therapy' for Mental Health*) discusses some of the 'therapies' (as seen in a western idiom) and underlying theoretical concepts that derive from non-western traditions, touching on possibilities of cross-cultural collaboration. The next two chapters are entirely new to the third edition. Chapter 9 (*Mental Health in Low- and Middle-Income Countries*) draws on personal knowledge of the author to bring to a wider audience the serious issues being faced in the process of developing mental health services in parts of the world that have been exploited and impoverished in the process of developing the West, and are still being neglected not least in cultural development. The plight of refugees who have made their way to the West – especially their resilience – has affected the discourse around mental health in western locations. The issues that the UK is trying to confront in understanding mental health needs of refugees are set against the global scene in Chapter 10 (*Mental Health of Refugees in High-Income Countries*). Some of the insights developed in the previous three chapters are brought together in Chapter 11 (*Prospects for Plurality in Therapies for Mental Health*) in considering ways in which East and West, North and South may meet in the field of mental health. And the speculations are taken further in a final Chapter 12 (*Mental Health for All*) where the author goes further towards a vision of mental health that is universally applicable, suggesting some ways forward.

In attempting to cover a wide field, this book necessarily is limited in the depth of discussion of any one aspect of it; also, it is selective in the material and views that are presented. Although his roots are in an Asian cultural tradition of Sri Lanka, and he has been taking an interest in mental health development in that country, the author's personal experience of work in the mental health field is restricted to that of a professional psychiatrist and researcher in the UK – albeit with a strong bias towards social psychiatry and community work – and a participant in the transcultural, anti-racist movements in the mental health field in Britain and elsewhere. More recently he has been advising on – and learning from – research into mental health of people caught up in war and natural disaster and in capacity building in a low-income country, namely, Sri Lanka. The literature covered in the book is confined to that in the English language available in the UK. The word 'western' that is used to qualify cultures, thinking and so on refers to 'the West' meaning countries *traditionally* European although the people currently inhabiting them reflect many non-western traditions too – especially traditions emanating from Asia, Africa and the Caribbean. The language used in the book tries to avoid phrases and descriptions that may be offensive because of their racist implications; but the words 'non-white', 'non-European' and 'non-western' are used in order to emphasize differences between dominant and non-dominant 'races' and cultural traditions. Technical or mystifying terms from both social and biological sciences are avoided – except to make a special point – because the book itself is aimed at a wide readership.

Part I

Theory and Tradition

Chapter 1

Race and Culture; Ethnicity and Identity

The discourse around race and culture in the mental health field has undergone complicated manoeuvres over the past twenty years, bringing to prominence two ideas related to race and culture, namely ethnicity and identity. This chapter discusses all four concepts before exploring the meaning of 'community' in relation to the primary concepts of race and culture and examining racism both in historical and current perspectives, mainly from a practical point of view.

Table 1.1 summarizes popular perceptions and realities in the current socio-political scene in the UK. In short, race is perceived as physical, culture as sociological and ethnicity as psychosocial. Identity is different to all these in being an entirely subjective psycho-personal concept. But it should be noted that popular perceptions change; the description of terms in the table are merely guides to thinking about the concepts rather than strict definitions. A major problem arises from the conflation in popular perceptions of culture and race, discussed later as the muddle between race and culture.

Concept of 'race'

The term 'race' entered the English language in the sixteenth century at a time in Europe when the Bible was accepted as the authority on human affairs; and it was used originally in the sense of lineage, supposedly ordained at the creation of the world (Banton, 1987). A rather vague racial awareness of, for example, Jews and Muslims as non-Christian 'other' evolved into the modern conception of race with the rise of European power and its conquest of the Americas (Banton, 1987). Major figures during the (European) 'Enlightenment', expounded racist opinions: 'The numerous writings on race by Hume, Kant and Hegel played a strong role in articulating Europe's sense not only of its cultural but also racial superiority... "reason" and "civilization" became almost synonymous with "white" people and northern Europe, while unreason and savagery were conveniently located among the non-whites, the "black", the "red", the "yellow", outside Europe' (Eze, 1997, p. 5). David Hume (born 1711, died 1776) reasoned that 'there never was a civilized nation of any other complexion than white, nor even any individual eminent

Table 1.1   Race, culture, ethnicity and identity

	Characterized by	Perceived as	Assumed to be	In reality
Race	Physical appearance	Physical, permanent	Genetically determined	Socially constructed
Culture	Behaviour, attitudes, etc.	Social, changeable	Passed down by parents/parent substitutes	Variable and changeable blue-print for living
Ethnicity	Sense of belonging	Psychosocial, partially changeable	How people see themselves in terms of background and parentage	Culture-race mixture
Identity	Subjective feelings	Psycho-personal, several parts, each fairly fixed once formed	Formed through upbringing and experience	Feelings about heritage; personal choice

either in action or speculation. No ingenious manufactures amongst them, no arts, no sciences'. And Immanuel Kant (born 1724, died 1804) reasoned that the 'difference between these two races [white and black]...appears to be as great in regard to mental capacities as in color' (Eze, 1997, pp. 33–55).

Later, as Darwinian concepts were accepted in European thinking, race was seen as subspecies on the basis of which scientific racism developed (Chase, 1997; Graves, 2002); finally sociological theories of race led to the notion of races as populations, where 'race', a social concept rather than a biological one, continued to play a fundamental role in structuring the social world of humankind (Omi and Winant, 1994). Today, all these ideas exist together, giving rise to considerable confusion in current thinking about race since the corollaries of these various notions are very different. For example, race as lineage may be a satisfactory explanation of physical differentiation of populations that are relatively isolated from each other, but cannot interpret differentiation in an increasingly globalized 'mixed' world, except by assuming that ecological forces determine behaviour of human beings in the way they determine social life of domesticated animals whereby, for example, different breeds of dogs persist.

One consequence of the confusion about what is meant by 'race' is that two seemingly opposite tendencies are evident – 'the temptation to think of race as *essence*, as something fixed concrete and objective...[or] as mere *illusion*, a purely ideological construct which some ideal non-racist social order would eliminate'. Both approaches are faulty. Racism continues to be a powerful force albeit in changing guises; biologically based human characteristics ('phenotypes') are invoked by the concept but these have been – and continue to be – selected by social and historical processes. So 'race' may be defined as 'a concept which signifies and symbolizes social conflict and interests by referring to different types of human bodies' (Omi and Winant, 1994, pp. 54–5, italics in original).

Culture

One of the original meanings of culture was husbandry – the verb 'cultivate' derives from this meaning. But over the years, culture has been transformed from being an activity to become an entity – almost an abstract concept. At one time 'being cultured' was synonymous with being civilized, but then anthropology, in association with nineteenth-century colonialism, gave culture its modern meaning of 'a unique way of life' (Eagleton, 2000, p. 26). During the past thirty years, 'cultural studies' have widened their scope to such an extent that the word culture has almost lost a specific meaning. This section will attempt to bring some coherence to its use with reference to the main subject of the book – mental health.

The term culture applied to an individual usually refers to a mixture of behaviour and cognition arising from 'shared patterns of belief, feeling and adaptation which people carry in their minds' (Leighton and Hughes, 1961, p. 447). The allusion to family culture or the cultures of whole communities or even nations extends the meaning of the word 'culture' further. Therefore, referring to a multiplicity of cultures – for example, in a multicultural society – implies differences between groups of people with different backgrounds, traditions and worldviews. Apart from the use of culture in this broad sense as a shorthand for a sort of explanation of the way people live, we often refer to cultures of institutions or occupations/professions – for example, to police canteen culture, the culture of psychiatry or social work. In all these situations, culture means the ethos or the intangible underlying determinants of people's behaviour in a particular context. We could call these organizational cultures as distinct from culture as the way people live. Finally, we tend to speak of the cultures of people identifiable by particular characteristics such as age (e.g., youth culture), experience (e.g., culture of the aristocracy, the oppressed, the poor) or some habit or predilection (e.g., drug culture, gun culture, paedophile culture). We can call these experiential/situational cultures.

Culture as the way people live

Here culture refers to a way of life common to a group which may or may not be defined as a 'community' (see later for discussion of community). It represents conceptual structures that determine the total reality of life within which people live and die, and of social institutions such as the family, the village and so on. It may go on to subsume all features of a person's environment and upbringing, but specifically refers to the non-material aspects of everything that they hold in common with other individuals forming a social group – child-rearing habits, family systems, and ethical values or attitudes common to a group. In anthropological literature, the idea of culture as a body of knowledge held within a group (Goodenough, 1957) gave way to culture as 'something out there', a social concept, and later as something 'inside' a person – a psychological state (D'Andrade, 1984, p. 91).

The past thirty years have seen major changes in the way culture is applied to the way people live and behave. First, following on the writings of Foucault (1967, 1977, 1988), there was an increasing awareness of the relationship between discourse – fields of knowledge, statements and practice, including those in medical, psychiatric and psychological practice – and power. Hence, categories which lump peoples or experiences together have become suspect. Second, the idea of culture as something that individuals or groups take on passively has been superseded by the idea of culture being *made* by people, both as individuals and groups – cultures as 'products of human volition, desires and powers' (Baumann, 1996, p. 31). In fact, culture is beginning to resemble its original meaning as husbandry.

Since the late twentieth century, culture is understood on a postmodern terrain as something variable and relative depending on historical and political viewpoints in a context of power relationships. *The Location of Culture* (bhabha, 1994) emphasizes the hybridity of cultural forms and behaviour in today's world; *Culture and Imperialism* (Said, 1994) unravels the intimate connections between the understandings of culture presented in Anglo-American literature and European domination – nowadays called globalization. Culture is seen now as something that cannot be clearly defined, as something living, dynamic and changing – a flexible system of values and worldviews that people live by, and through which they define identities and negotiate their lives. Although this postmodern concept of culture cannot be captured properly in terms of polarities such as East and West, or traditional and modern, it is the view of the author that broad categories, such as Eastern, Western, Asian, African and European, have to be constructed and used in the interests of brevity, not in a reductionist frame of reference but in order to clarify what culture means in practical terms. Hence, these rough categorizations are used in discussing cultural variations throughout the book.

Organizational cultures

The report of the inquiry into the way the Metropolitan Police dealt with a racist murder in 1993 (Home Department, 1999) referred to racist attitudes that underpinned police activity as institutional racism defined in the report as:

> The collective failure of an organisation to provide an appropriate and professional service to people because of their colour, culture or ethnic origin. It can be seen or detected in processes, attitudes and behaviour which amounts to discrimination through unwitting prejudice, ignorance, thoughtlessness and racist stereotyping which disadvantages minority ethnic people. (p. 28)

Since the report came out, there has been considerable argument as to whether Macpherson, the Chairman of the Inquiry, pointed to the culture of the Metropolitan Police as racist or just to racist attitudes within it. For many years the mental health system itself has been hailed as institutionally racist (discussed further in Chapter 4) and the question arises as to whether the culture of psychiatry is racist – the term culture being used as indicative of the ethos of the discipline. This is a loose use of the word; speaking more strictly, it is preferable to limit the term culture to describe a way of thinking or operating that emanates from, or is created by, a group of people working in fairly close association with each other. A situation in other words that gives rise to a more-or-less common way of doing things *by people* adhering to a tradition, acting in unison for a particular purpose. So racist attitudes within a system may, if pervasive among the group, constitute a *racist culture*. In other words, it is necessary to be careful in speaking of culture in relation to organizations or systems. Culture is about people not about bricks and mortar, even when attached as an adjective to the words 'institution' or 'system'.

In a study of black people's experience of being compulsorily detained under the Mental Health Act, Browne (1997) found that although social workers knew that racist stereotyping of black people as dangerous was a major factor in police involvement in the admission of black people, this bit of information, usually handed out during training and accepted by social workers as valid, had no effect on their day-to-day activities. It could be reasonably deduced that the culture of social work practice in the area that Browne researched was racist although the culture of the system of training may well have been anti-racist. The underlying ethos of the system as a team or group of people working together had perhaps negated the effect of training. But the research quoted did not mean that all social workers behaved in this way or that social work practice as a whole was racist; social workers do not work *as a whole,* they work in teams or as individuals.

Consider now the training of professionals as a system of training. In the case of psychiatrists, training is overseen by the Royal College of Psychiatrists, through committees under its Dean. Training systems throughout the country are examined by the College although organization of training at grass roots is left to tutors in each training site. It would be accurate to speak of a culture of psychiatric training, seeing the training system as an organization, because there is a particular way of doing things that is promoted across all training. It is well known that psychiatric training perpetuates biomedical ways of diagnosis and treatment; social perspectives and ideas of health and illness inherent in non-western systems of medicine such as Ayurveda are not included in the training. In such a situation, one could say that there is a culture of training that is at least ethnocentric, possibly racist, in being oblivious to ways of thinking that are not derived from western traditions.

Situational/experiential cultures

The concept of culture applied to people who are grouped together for no other reason than their age or predilection to indulge in some habit is of dubious validity or usefulness. Consider the term 'youth culture'. Clearly young people may show similar types of behaviour because they are passing through similar experiences, especially if they are (say) from similar backgrounds. But unless they are involved with each other *as people*, for example, by being members of groups such as 'gangs', social clubs or sports teams, it is misleading to attribute a 'culture' to them, however similar their behaviour, views or appearance as individuals may be. Admittedly, people who use drugs or resort to using guns may well associate with one another because they have to procure their supplies (of drugs or guns) through centres or agents, or live in a particular part of a city. In doing so, they may form personal links and develop a common way of seeing the world, behaving, and so on, in which case they may be properly seen as having a culture. But if this is not the case, it would be incorrect to attribute 'culture' to a class of people merely because they use illegal drugs or guns.

Muddle between race and culture

It would be seen from earlier paragraphs that the term 'culture' lacks precision and its meaning is both variable and dynamic. As a result, culture is often confused with race. The question on ethnicity in the British Census (2001) under the heading 'What is your ethnic group?' asked about *cultural background* not 'race' reflecting this on-going confusion. And national statistics about ethnic groups are interpreted both as differences in culture *and* differences in 'race' – something that may be used to promote racist political propaganda. In the public media, people seen as being *racially* different are assumed to have different cultures; and value judgements attached to 'race' are transferred to culture. Another problem is that when people are identified in ethnic terms – ethnicity containing both cultural and racial connotations that are not clearly differentiated – there may be a tendency to impose culture on people because of the way they look ('racially') instead of allowing people to find their own position in the stream of changing and varied cultural forms. This creates resentment against the concept of multiculturalism itself. Even more importantly, some aspect of culture, like religion, may be taken as a marker of racial difference in the way Jews – and more recently Muslims – are sometimes seen as belonging to a specific 'race'.

Another problem that arises from this muddle between the understandings of race and culture is that ethnic designations (at least in the UK) are seen as concerning non-white people alone; cultural diversity remains a minority issue; and a multicultural society is a place where minority issues are given primacy. To complicate the race and culture discourse even further, racism undermines multiculturalism by introducing the idea, not necessarily expressed openly, that cultures are on a hierarchy of sophistication, some being less 'developed' than others, feeding on the negative aspects of a discourse where industrially underdeveloped or developing countries are seen as 'primitive' in all respects, including their cultures.

Ethnicity

Ethnicity overlaps in meaning with both race and culture, encompassing both, yet the common features of people in an ethnic group are often not clear-cut in terms of physical appearance (race) or social similarity (culture) alone or in combination. Subjective feelings too come into play represented by a sense of belonging to a group – an ethnic group – where cultural or racial similarity, real or imagined, plays a part. Yet, this sense of belonging may well arise not because of self-perception but because of the way *other people* see a person. Thus, a racist society could promote an ethnicity based primarily on race *as perceived by society at large*, rather than culture as experienced by members of an ethnic group. Further, a sense of belonging to a particular religious tradition or some other aspect of culture may override all others promoted either by other religiously committed people (perhaps in the family) or by the way society at large perceives people. Which particular idea is dominant in popular discourse depends largely on context. Sociologist Stuart Hall (1992) states: 'The term ethnicity acknowledges the place of history, language and culture in the construction of subjectivity and identity, as well as the fact that all discourse is placed positioned, situated, and all knowledge is contextual' (p. 257). Ethnicity may be useful for identification but should not be confused with the sense of identity (or identities) that reflects how a person sees himself or herself as a unique individual (see below).

In a multiracial and multicultural society, categorization in ethnic terms emerges in complex ways through various pressures: social, political, economic and psychological. Perceived or strongly felt cultural ties and/or perceptions of being part of a 'race' may occur – and the strength of any of these may be influenced by a variety of pressures. The pressure arising from racism in society may drive together people perceived by others as being racially similar. The ethnicity that is promoted and crystallized by social forces has been called an emergent ethnicity (Yancey *et al.*, 1976). Thus, sociologists refer to 'new ethnicities' having emerged in British society during the 1980s and 1990s (Cohen, 1999) as a result of African, Caribbean and Asian cultures being perceived as 'different' to the majority 'white' culture and, more importantly, people seen as belonging to these cultures being perceived as 'different' racially. Thus, the extent to which ethnicities are culture-based or race-based in British society, and possibly all western societies, is largely dependent on the significance of racism; if racism diminishes, cultural diversity – or more likely cultural hybridity (where society as a whole becomes culturally mixed) – is likely, rather than a race-based ethnic diversity. But while racism continues, as it does in most western societies, racial difference plays an important part in determining ethnicity.

However, there is another side to the way ethnicity plays out in the British socio-political scene. Baumann (1996) argues against what he calls (British) 'ethnic reductionism' whereby individuality gets submerged in ethnic identity. In his research in London's Southall district he found that 'Whatever any "Asian" informant was reported to have said or done was interpreted with stunning regularity as a consequence of their "Asianness", their "ethnic identity" or the "culture" of their "community"' (p. 1). Also, Baumann observed that in Southall the patterning of connections between culture and community was complex, each being largely determined by personal experiences and histories. Cultural boundaries were fluid; new communities were being constantly created and re-created. The concept of 'community' in this context is discussed later.

For practical purposes, such as ethnic monitoring or census designation, ethnicity is taken to mean – at least in Britain – a mixture of cultural background and racial designation, the significance of each being variable. A British government paper about collecting health statistics designated ethnicity as a mixture of culture, religion, skin colour, language and family origin (NHS Management Executive, 1993: Appendix D 1). The main broad ethnic groups that are now recognized in British health surveys and research are African Caribbeans, Africans, Asians and whites, the two largest minority ethnic groups in the UK being South Asians and African Caribbeans. In Britain, the term 'black people' quite often means all ethnic minorities or more specifically Africans and African Caribbeans, but in other places, such as the USA and Canada, the term 'people of colour' or 'visible minorities' is preferred and in many European countries the pejorative term 'migrant' is still used (Fernando, 1991). The most recent trend in the UK is to refer to 'black and minority ethnic' (BME) people sometimes even as 'communities'. It should be noted that the meaning of ethnicity (as described above) – and so the ethnic categories for the census and for ethnic monitoring – may change from time to time. A recent development in the UK has been the recognition of 'mixed race' as an ethnic category in the latest British Census (2001), although there is no suggestion yet of referring to 'mixed-race' communities.

In collecting statistics for the census or for ethnic monitoring, the choice of one ethnic category for identifying each person as a member of an ethnic group is often pushed onto people as representing an overall self-perception indicative of their personal identity; but most people tend to identify psychologically in much more diverse ways in a variety of categories (see below). This forced choice of one ethnicity may have a very practical purpose of obtaining clear-cut statistics, but may lead to problems in cooperation and indeed errors in statistics. It is important therefore that, in requesting a self-designated ethnic categorization, the purpose of the exercise is made very clear – namely that the categorization is required for identification rather than personal identity. Issues around identity are discussed in the next section.

Identity

The term 'identity' refers to a person's distinctive sense of uniqueness – of knowing who one is or is not. It represents the importance given in western culture to the individual as distinct from – perhaps opposed to – the family or community and so identity usually emphasizes individuality. But it is often assumed – and this is an ethnocentric assumption – that identity is a basic 'fact' about a person; and the development of a stable sense of personal (usually individual) identity is central to personality development usually envisaged as taking place during childhood and adolescence.

In western psychology, identity is thought of as something more substantial than a concept – as a sort of 'thing' within the psyche; cultural influences from Asian and African traditions which place much less importance on the individual than they do on the collective (see Triandis, 1995) and perhaps the calamities of genocide and war in Europe, seemingly related to strongly held ethnic identities, have induced a rethink of sorts. Amartya Sen (2006), the Indian Nobel Laureate and ex-Master of Trinity College, Cambridge, bringing some eastern ideas into western thinking, criticizes the idea of identity being fixed or destined (that is evolved early in life). He maintains that identity has several traces – several connections or influences generating it. An alternative way of conceptualizing this state of affairs is to consider each person as holding several identities simultaneously, each being generated through a variety of influences from various sources.

The approach of seeing identity as being represented by multiple identities is analogous with seeing the godhead, God, as being composed of (or seen through the manifestations of) many gods. In other words, it means switching from the mode of thinking in the monotheist, Judaic-Christian-Muslim tradition to a polytheist, Vedantic-Hindu one or the atheist Buddhist tradition. A person's racial, cultural and ethnic identities are some of the manifestations of their inner essence, but there are many others. How and why they are constructed would vary but the antecedents may be held in common (to some extent) in people with a common heritage or history of common experiences. A practical consequence of deconstructing the single identity into many identities is to enable open-ended adaptation for people living in a diverse society. It addresses the fact that human beings derive their sense of who they are from a variety of sources and their loyalties are equally varied. So they could have two or more 'ethnic' identities held together; a person can be (say) Indian or Jamaican *as well as* English or Canadian or whatever. How much of this flexibility could spill over into 'racial identity' (discussed below) is moot point; the question is whether one can be 'black' as well as 'white'. And the increasing numbers of people identifying as 'mixed race' in the 2001 census in UK is indicative of this very change taking place. However, it should be noted that nominal ethnic identity given for practical purposes such as census or ethnic monitoring may not necessarily indicate one's *personal* identity.

Although the Eurocentric view of identity embodied in western psychology refers to a unique quality, a less individualistic worldview would see identity as a part of group solidarity – implying that there is a political dimension. The growth of identification as Serbian, Bosnian and Kosovan in the former Yugoslavia, as the monolithic state itself disintegrated, had obvious political dimensions, although based on historic identities, family ties and religious affiliations. The culturally hybrid population of Sri Lanka, separated into linguistically defined 'race' groups by political forces during and after British colonial occupation, now presents as self-identified ethnic groups (Gunaratne, 2002). In modern societies, identity that is of importance to the person concerned could be best seen as divisible into many 'types' of identity, drawn from a variety of sources. Clearly, there are a large number of such identities of importance in the mental health field – one could think of sexual identity, faith (religious) identity, occupational/professional identity – but this section is limited to discussing identities of relevance to the subject matter of this book namely racial, cultural and ethnic identity. Hence, these are listed with the

Table 1.2   Varieties of identity

Types	Sources/influences
Cultural Racial	Community (and family)
Ethnic Occupational/professional	Individual (personal choice)
Sexual Experiential	Contextual (pressures in society)

main sources or influences they derive from in Table 1.2. The latter may be expanded into the following.

Community (and family)-based sources connect with:

- relationships (e.g., in a family, community, country)
- parental ('nominal') religion
- 'racial' background or appearance
- historical background (imagined or real lineage)
- allegiance (e.g., to profession, work-place or family)

Individual-based sources relate to:

- own (chosen) religion/belief in God/supernatural beings
- sexuality/gender (e.g., 'gay'/heterosexual, female/male)
- body (e.g., disability, illness, size or 'race')
- loyalties (e.g., occupational, family, country)
- values ('good' or 'bad')
- sense of belonging to place, land

Contextual influences determined by:

- forces in society at large (e.g., racism)
- categorization by authorities (e.g., poor, middle-class, schizophrenic)
- occupational allegiance (e.g., type of worker, professional)
- place of residence or birth

Cultural-racial-ethnic identities

Although physical difference, skin colour in particular, is the basis of perceived racial difference, culture is probably more important for most people for distinguishing themselves from others. However, some people may prefer to use 'race' because culture is such a variable matter to define; then greater emphasis may be placed by them on having a racial identity. Also, if a person feels and recognizes the effects of racism, a racial or ethnic identity as 'black' may be strengthened; while, if family, community or subgroup (such as a religious subgroup) pressures are strong, cultural identification as, for example, Indian, African, Jewish or Muslim may be strengthened; and a historical sense of colonial imperialism in Europe may strengthen Irish identity among people in the UK who are of Irish ancestry; and so on.

The 1960s saw positive aspects of black identity being emphasized in the USA and UK as a counterbalance to the harm that was perceived as having been done to black people as a result of their identifying with white norms and thereby internalizing racism. The classic studies were the doll-preference studies (Clarke and Clarke, 1947) that seemed to identify black self-hatred; although these studies were criticized for methodological faults, the thesis of black self-hatred became widely accepted because it resonated with the discourses of the civil rights movement that was then emerging (Mama, 1995). The 'black is beautiful' cultural movement (Docarmo, 2008) came about in the 1960s and the term 'black' itself changed in its meaning – at least for many black people. The psychological insights of Frantz Fanon, accessible in the English language through translations of his main works as *Black Skin, White Masks* (Fanon, 1952) and the subsequent *The Wretched of the Earth* (Fanon, 1961), are crucial for understanding the impact of colonization and slavery on both black and white people.

For Fanon, the internalization of a belief system imbued with racism damages the psyche of a black person causing alienation; but the process of alienation is inextricably linked to, and arises from, a socio-economic political system that denies black people the opportunity to confirm their self-worth: The freedom from oppression is equivalent to the freedom to develop self-worth and hence overcome alienation. And (for Fanon) both the imposition of oppression and the retrieval of freedom are violent processes; they cannot be given but must be taken. Fanon's work highlights the connections between the psychological and the political; the struggle that black people must go through in order to divest themselves of the violence of racism is thus not just within themselves but intimately connected with the political world around them.

Problems of ethnic identity

The practical importance of ethnic classification for mental health service planning is its contribution to anti-discriminatory practice. Yet, serious problems must be recognized. When someone says they are from a particular ethnic group or is perceived as such, the fact denotes a sense of belonging and/or similarity to certain other people. But the meaning attached to this contention is often contaminated by popular misconceptions and institutionalized attitudes as well as political expediency and historical prejudice. It is sometimes unfortunate that a person categorized as belonging to a particular ethnic group for (say) service planning is labelled and may be seen henceforth, not as an individual, but as a carrier of various qualities assumed to be inherent in the particular category of people. This is the danger of stereotyping and labelling. Therefore, however useful ethnic/racial/cultural categorization may be – not least for identifying racial discrimination in service provision – one important fact must be borne in mind at all times: Individuals within a particular category are all different and individual differences may outweigh group differences in extent and importance. Another problem arises from ethnicity slipping into being seen as race whereby ethnic designation (say for monitoring) is perceived as indicative of ancestry alone. But ethnicity (as opposed to 'race') covers background including, for example, a history of oppression. Thus 'black' people within the BME classification may include people of varying skin colours or degrees of pigmentation; some may indeed appear to be lighter skinned than people who may be included in a 'white' group. The statement about them is essentially political and historical, not just biological-inheritance. As Noel Ignatiev (1995) argues in *How the Irish became White*, the Irish who were the blacks of Europe became 'white' in the USA.

The concept of an 'identity crisis' has been used to explain various diverse problems among people seen as being from disadvantaged positions in society. An unfortunate consequence of a person in crisis being seen as 'different', because they are 'from' an ethnic minority is that the crisis is attributed to problems located within their 'identity' and not in society, in social-political experiences and so on. Thus, the concept 'identity crisis' may not be a helpful way of seeing a problem and is a misapplication of the identity concept.

Issues around sexual identity have so much baggage connected with culture (especially through organized religion) that it sometimes complicates ethnic identity in practical ways. Basically, discrimination against people who identify as homosexual (or 'gay') is a matter of human rights, similar to that in discrimination on grounds of race. But the history is different. Homophobia is often embedded in many cultural systems – and continues to be; more importantly, such discrimination has not been challenged in many settings. The unfortunate reality is that many minority ethnic cultural traditions, especially those where organized religion plays a leading part, tend to defend homophobia as legitimate *cultural* difference that they are entitled to practice. Clearly, the struggle against homophobia, as with the struggle against racism, is one to be pursued by society as a whole. In a multicultural society, the struggle may well be represented by those who oppose the struggle as an attack against a 'culture' but this should be seen for what it is – a weapon being used to prevent free expression of difference in sexual orientation.

Communities

There is a tendency today to think of people as belonging to communities without much clarity as to the meaning of 'community'. In a seminal book

Imagined Communities, Benedict Anderson (1991) states: 'Communities are to be distinguished, not by their falsity/genuineness, but by the style in which they are imagined' (p. 6). The creation of communities with meaning for the people who are involved may have little to do with geographical contiguity of residence or even actual person-to-person contact. Yet, once someone identifies as belonging to a community – for example, a nation – there is an almost irrational attachment 'for the inventions of their imagination' (p. 41). So it is important to be careful in designating the term 'community' in any given instance.

The tendency in UK to move very quickly from identifying racial, cultural or ethnic categories for practical purposes into designating racial, cultural and ethnic *communities* raises important issues of social and political nature. Baumann (1996) points out that the division of people to be governed into communities is a 'time-honoured colonial strategy' (1996, p. 29). Many people identified as BME are disadvantaged in various fields of life in British society (Chapter 4), including mental health service provision (Bhui, 2002; Fernando, 2003; and Chapter 7). Designating them as *communities* tends to shift the focus, and hence responsibility for redressing disadvantage, from society at large onto these 'communities'. In other words, postulating the existence of such communities provides a get-out. Thus, a government action plan to deal with injustices in the mental health system suffered by BMEs, *Delivering Race Equality* (Department of Health, 2005), identified 'action to engage [BME] communities' (p. 60) as being required, implying that their failure to 'engage' was the issue (see Fernando and Keating, 2009b). Terrorist activity by people claiming to be 'Muslims' is attributed to the 'Muslim community' and this 'community', rather than society as a whole, is called upon by government to control its extremists. There may well be a need to identify people in terms of their race, culture or ethnicity if they need particular attention because of commonly held disadvantage. But seeing them as communities avoids the issue of redressing disadvantage by obscuring the reasons for it.

The previous paragraph contesting the reality of communities defined by racial, cultural or ethnic words does not mean that group identity is not important. The sense of belonging to a group may be particularly important when there is group-based discrimination. For example, cultural identity as 'Asian' generates a sense of affinity with other Asian people. Similarly with 'African Caribbean' or 'black' but that does not necessarily mean that communities of Asians or African Caribbeans or blacks exist as social or political realities, that such communities can act together in order, for example, to redress injustices or access services. The warning here is for the careful use of the term community in the field of race, culture and ethnic politics.

Most people in the UK who identify as BME on the basis of real or imagined ethnic *differences* from the majority, tend to live in areas with mixed populations, identifying also in a variety of non-ethnic ways – as residents of an area, as workers, professionals, and so on, or in terms of roles they fulfil, for example, as mothers, doctors or office workers. They do not necessarily form ethnic *communities*. Therefore, this book does not refer to racial, cultural or ethnic communities, unless there is good evidence that people so designated themselves have a sense of belonging to an ethnic community or have structures to bind them together as such.

Racism

The doctrine of racism developed in western culture in conjunction with ideas about race. Today, racism is fashioned by racial prejudice and underpinned by economic and social factors; when implemented and practised through the institutions of society, it is called 'institutional racism', referred to earlier in the discussion of organizational cultures. Although race prejudice and racism are related concepts (Table 1.3), they should be distinguished from each other. Basically, race prejudice is a psychological state, a feeling or attitude of mind, felt and/or expressed as 'an antipathy based upon a faulty and inflexible generalization' (Allport, 1954, p. 9); at a deeper level it may be likened to a superstition (Barzun, 1965). Racism, however, is a doctrine or ideology – or dogma. Race prejudice and racism often go together but racism, unlike prejudice, is recognized by the *behaviour* of an individual and/or the way an institutional system works in practice, although (racially prejudiced) attitudes of mind that are recognizable and consciously held may be present also. And racism is associated with power – the power of one racial group over another. Further, Wellman (1977) argues that an attitude such as prejudice must be seen within its structural context – the distribution of power within the society, political

Table 1.3   Racial prejudice and racism

	Basic definitions	Likely associations	Possible causes
Racial Prejudice	Feeling	Misperception Personal antipathy	Malevolence/ immorality
	Attitude	Rejection of outsider	Insecurity/illness
	Belief	Racism Ignorance	Human nature/ instinct
Racism	Ideology	Assumptions about inferior/ superior races Value judgement about people	Political/economic advantage
	Dogma	Power/domination	Social conditioning
	Political stance	Racial prejudice	Tradition/history

constraints arising from external influences, rivalries between social classes and so on. And once racial prejudice is embedded within the structures of society, 'the determining feature...is not prejudice towards blacks, but rather the superior position of whites and the institutions – ideological and well as structural – which maintain it' (pp. 35–6).

History of racism

The classifications of races devised in Europe in the eighteenth and nineteenth centuries were largely based on skin colour. They occurred in a context where the words 'black' and 'white' were associated in the English language with heavily charged notions of good and bad and went hand in glove with race prejudice from the very beginning. Then came the Atlantic slave trade. As Winthrob Jordan (1968) states in *White over Black*, qualities associated with black skins which 'had for Englishmen added up to *savagery*' denoted that 'sense of difference which provided the mental margin absolutely requisite for placing the European on the deck of the slave ship and the Negro in the hold' (p. 97, italics in original). Together with colonialism, slavery based on racial characteristics became a bedrock of European society and an axiom of western culture (Kovel, 1984). Slavery and colonialism fed into racial prejudice and vice versa; the result was the emergence of a consolidated dogma of racism.

Anatomists, biologists and physicians joined in with 'proof' of the superiority of white races over all others. The writing of history was distorted in line with racist notions of black inferiority. Bernal (1987) shows how the Afro-Asiatic origin of Greek civilization (accepted as historical fact until the nineteenth century) was replaced by the myth of a migration into Greece of white people from the north of Europe; and after repeated attacks on China caused social breakdown and opium was forced on Chinese by western nations, the image of China was changed from 'being a model of rational civilization...[to] a filthy country in which torture and corruption of all sorts flourished' (p. 238). The continuity of ancient Egypt with the rest of Africa was denied and Egyptian civilization was downgraded; theories about 'Aryans' and 'Semites' as superior white races emerged. The achievements of African cultures were sidetracked by, for example, attributing the twelfth-century ruins in Zimbabwe (central Africa) to white non-Africans (!) or ignoring the 'glowing accounts' of material culture carried by Portuguese explorers of central Africa and sailors shipwrecked on the coast of South Africa (Fuller, 1959).

The application of 'Social Darwinism' led to the eugenic movement later taken on by European fascism in the 1930s. Physical anthropology was 'inextricably linked to the functioning of empire [and] its efforts were chiefly devoted to a description and analysis – carried out by Europeans, for a European audience – of non-European societies dominated by the West' (Kabbani, 1986, p. 62). Fryer (1984) observes that 'virtually every scientist and intellectual in nineteenth-century Britain took it for granted that only people with white skin were capable of thinking and governing' (p. 169). And this applied to the whole of Europe and white America. Just as the wealth extracted by slavery and colonialism enriched all social classes and nations of Europe and white America, racist ideology pervaded all their political and social systems.

With the breakdown of direct racial domination and physical oppression in the USA during the 1960s, racism became institutionalized through techno-cratic means so that the economic position of black Americans in relation to that of their white compatriots actually dropped between 1970 and 1980 (Kovel, 1984). And the trend has continued so that many American cities now have a black underclass that is increasingly criminalized (through racism) (Goldberg, 1997; Hacker, 1995; West, 1994). The association of blacks with falling educational standards, a decline in moral values and street crime had found a place in popular thinking in Britain even before the so-called riots erupted in various British cities in the 1980s (Ben-Tovim *et al.*, 1986). On both sides of the Atlantic, vicious circles have developed with myths about degeneracy of blacks becoming 'facts' of diagnosed psychoses through the collaboration of psychiatry (see Fernando, 2003; and Chapter 7).

Although the first half of the twentieth century gave little cause for opti-mism, the social and political changes that took place after 1945, namely decolonization of many parts of Asia and Africa, the American civil rights movement and the overthrow of apartheid in South Africa, should lead one to expect the demise – or at least the serious containment – of racism. But, a decade into the twenty-first century, racism continues although its manifest-ations have changed (Ture and Hamilton, 1992); but hopefully the swearing in of a black man, Barack Obama, as President of the USA, the most power-ful country in the world, on 20 January 2009 is a symbol of attitude-change, particularly among the younger generations of the developed world (Miah, 2009). Major demographic changes expected to occur in the twenty-first century may well have a significant effect on racism. The UN's *State of the World's Population 1999* quoted in the British newspaper *The Observer* (Browne, 2000) predicts that 98 per cent of the growth in the world's popu-lation by the year 2025 will occur in the less developed regions, principally Africa and Asia: 'In 1900 Europe had a quarter of the world's population, and three times that of Africa; by 2050 Europe is predicted to have just 7 per cent of the world's population, and a third that of Africa' (p. 17). And the balance of power may also shift as a result of the economic rise of China, India and Brazil. All this may result in a shift in the scene with regard to 'race', perhaps eroding the current colour-based racism – even the dimin-ution of race-thinking itself.

Explanations of racism

Racism is often confused with racial prejudice and, when this happens, it may be attributed naively to a mere personal quirk or ignorance; or it may be seen simply as a mistake made in European history and perpetuated by misinformation and ignorance. When socially unacceptable as a form of behaviour, racism is seen as crime, immorality or sickness (Watson, 1973). Robert Ardrey (1967), arguing that 'aggression' is '*innate*', postulates that its exhibition towards outsiders is a natural condition because 'the biological nation is the supreme natural mechanism for the security of a social group' (p. 253). And Richard Dawkins (1976) writes that 'racial prejudice could be interpreted as an irrational generalisation of a kin-selected tendency to identify with individuals physically resembling oneself and to be nasty to individuals different in appearance' and that this tendency 'could have positive survival value' (p. 8).

Racism is sometimes seen as having originated in an economic capitalist system of exploitation (Cox, 1948) in particular the exploitation of labour during slavery and colonialism (Williams, 1944). Although there is no doubt that political and economic factors reinforced racism, they are insufficient explanations for the strength of racism in the present day. Constructed over hundreds of years, its origins linked to 'race thinking' (Barzun, 1965) are embedded in the history of western culture, although this is not to say that there are no racisms in other cultural traditions too.

Anti-Semitism, discrimination against Muslims – 'Islamophobia' (Casciani, 2004; Halliday, 1995; Seabrook, 2004) – and that against 'untouchables' and other castes in India (Berreman, 1960) are all clearly underpinned by the tendency to think of people in terms of their 'race' – 'discourses which (mistakenly) interpret socially constructed groups [of people] as the product of biology' (Miles, 1993, p. 86). Even conflicts between groups of people in various parts of the world, such as Tamils and Sinhalese in Sri Lanka, Catholics and Protestants in Northern Ireland, or Serbs and Bosnians in former Yugoslavia may stem from perceptions akin to racial ones. But the racism that is based on skin colour and power relationships where white people dominate others, either as individuals or as groups, overrides other forms of racism in its importance across the globe. This is referred to generally in this book as racism, although wider definitions made clear by reference to context may sometimes be used.

An analysis of racism must address several interrelated issues. First, the fact that it is based on a delusion embodied in popular ideas about race classification referred to earlier. Hence, 'race' should not be accorded identical analytical status with factors such as class or gender (Miles, 1982); 'race relations' is not analogous with class relations, or sexism with racism. The subject matter of 'race relations' is the nature of relations between people of different physical appearance and diverse ancestry in a setting where social significance is attributed to physical appearance – and the problems addressed in 'race relations' are to do with racism (Dummett, 1973). Second, the contention that racism is essentially about value judgement about people based on an *a priori* basis; the doctrine that people of a certain 'race' are inherently different from others in qualities that are ordered hierarchically leads to the assumption that some races as a whole are superior to others. Third, the issue of the close involvement of racism with power. It is the association of value judgement with power that is fundamental to racism. Hence, racism is a means of domination, exploitation and enslavement, at a personal, political and economic level. Finally, although racism was created by, and is perpetuated by, various psychological, economic and political factors, it has to be understood as an integral part of the history of Europe (Banton and Harwood, 1975).

Modern manifestations of racism

Current racism in the USA, drawing from its tradition of slavery, affects mainly descendants of African people who were taken there by force – the present African Americans. The racism in the genocide of Native Americans and the suppression of their cultures have changed into racist derision towards the 'American Indians', associated in the northern part of the American continent with colonial-type paternalism. But in South America, a new spate of near-genocidal racism was evident in the late twentieth century with the connivance of the USA through its economic interests and its missionaries (Lewis, 1989). The pride in a tradition of being a land of (voluntary) immigrants from many parts of the world promotes an attitude of respect towards 'Oriental Americans' – for example, people from Japan, China, India and Vietnam – who are seen as no different in terms of status from other (immigrant) Americans. But a diverse group of peoples who speak Spanish called 'Hispanic Americans' – a linguistically defined 'race' (see Goldberg, 1997) – appear to face considerable racial hostility.

The background to British and European racism is different from that in America. Although traditionally welcoming some European refugees fleeing persecution, the British – and many European countries – have never held very favourable attitudes towards the immigrant. Racism is often expressed and felt today in the derision implied in the term immigrant or migrant often used to describe all black people irrespective of where they have been born or brought up. In analysing the historical representations of European racism, Pieterse (1995) states: '"Race" discrimination has increasingly yielded to discrimination along cultural lines, bringing with it different sets of images and discourses' (p. 14). Gilroy (1993) believes that racism now 'frequently operates in Britain without any overt reference to "race" itself or the biological notions of difference which still give the term its common-sense meaning' (p. 23). 'Culture', seen as an immutable, fixed property of social groups has become confounded with 'race' (see 'muddle between race and culture'), and racism is articulated in cultural terms.

Summary

The classification of race based on visual observations of people, particularly their skin colour, has a long history in western Europe but is discounted today from a scientific perspective: 'Human "racial" differentiation is indeed only skin deep. Any use of racial categories must take its justification from some other source than biology' (Rose *et al.*, 1984, p. 127). Osborne (1971) summarizes the scientific findings as follows. First, differences *within* races are greater than the differences *between* races on important physical characteristics apart from those used to define race. Second, there is no evidence for designating any race(s) as 'superior' or 'inferior' in terms of ability in any particular sphere or in adaptability to environment. Third, there are no 'pure' races that have unique genetic characteristics. Fourth, 'primitive' (physical) characteristics, such as thin lips, flat nose and straight hair, are found in all races.

'Culture' is an imprecise term in research but a useful concept for defining the non-physical influences on individuals that determine their behaviour, attitudes and ways of life. It is often confused with race both in common parlance and in professional thinking, mainly because people who are seen as racially different are conceptualized as having different cultures; and the term 'culture' is used to conceal racism. Ethnicity has both racial and cultural connotations, but its main characteristic is that it implies a sense of belonging. Ethnicity may 'emerge' in a society through pressures and alliances arising from racial discrimination, cultural similarity or other forces that induce people to feel a sense of belonging to an 'ethnic' group.

One's identity is considered as something that develops during childhood and adolescence and then remains static. However, in a mental health context where issues of race and culture are being considered, it is far more reasonable to consider identity as variable and context driven. A person may give precedence to one way of seeing themselves in one context but to another in a different context. In other words, any one person has the capacity for a variety of identities.

Racism has a long history in western culture but the ways in which it is manifested has changed over the years and even then varies according to context. Racism should be distinguished from (racial) prejudice. When racism is implemented and practised through the institutions of society, often without people involved even being aware that they are being racist, it is called 'institutional racism'. Economic and political factors feed into racism, and the psychological needs of the people who stand to gain from institutional racism play a part too. Racism has changed in style and manifestation over the past fifty years. Further changes as a result of increasing cultural hybridity of the developed world, attitude-change among its younger population, and demographic and economic changes in the world may contribute towards a new era dawning in the 'race' scene towards the middle of the twenty-first century.

Chapter 2

Traditional Approaches to Mental Health

Traditions, like cultures, are not fixed entities. But as in the case of culture, exploring established customs, ways of thinking and attitudes of mind – all of which are subsumed in the concept of a tradition – is a useful approach to understanding current realities.

Introduction

The global scene in mental health as it exists is not easy to address without discussing terminology, especially the use of the prefix *western*. Clearly, western psychology and psychiatry as a part of western or allopathic medicine originated in Europe and are rightly seen as a part of western culture. But the West, as it is now constituted, no longer owns these subjects. Similarly systems that developed in other traditions are no longer, strictly speaking, merely eastern or Asian or African. But the political reality today is that the western tradition in psychology and psychiatry tends to dominate the world.

Western psychology may be called 'scientific psychology' or 'secular psychology' for reasons that will become obvious in Chapter 3. Yet, it is only one of many systems of knowledge about 'mind'. The western brand competes with indigenous ideas about mind that come from *non-western* traditions in Asia, Africa, and pre-Columbian America, although admittedly these non-western systems are mostly allocated to religion – where perhaps they belong anyway. Also, all over the world, the term 'psychology' is defined in traditional western terms. The psychology taught by academic institutes is the subject derived from the western tradition; Buddhist psychology, Hindu psychology, African psychologies and those from pre-Columbian American sources are merely topics within religious or cultural studies, seldom recognized as true psychology.

The case of psychiatry is different. In effect, there is only one version of a *medical* specialty concerned with disorder of mind as distinct from body, and that is psychiatry – the system developed in the western tradition, the scientific tradition. What has been called 'Tibetan Psychiatry' (Clifford, 1984) described in Chapter 8 is very different culturally and in its practical

28

application. As psychiatry attempts to maintain a scientific approach, its development in this mode is not just located in the West; scientific endeavour and practical applications of science are now located in Asian countries such as Japan and increasingly in China and India; science is now truly universal. Because of this, it is preferable to speak of biomedicine and biomedical psychiatry – or just psychiatry – rather than *western* medicine and *western* psychiatry. Yet, there are active traditions recognizable as culturally different to psychiatry concerning health, including mental health, and ways of thinking about deviations from health – may be as illness, but also as problems of the mind, spiritual experience, possession by spirits and so on; and these traditions are still very active not only in those parts of the world where they originated but also in western locations: For example, systems exotic to western culture and derived from Asian, African and indigenous American traditions are pursued in European and (Euro-) American contexts, sometimes as 'cults' that use some ideas from, for example, Buddhism or Hinduism.

This chapter begins by discussing the traditions of western psychology and psychiatry from a transcultural perspective; goes on to consider some aspects of traditional medical belief systems that are evident throughout the world; presents a section on stigma; and discusses the issue of 'culture-bound' disorders. Finally, after a discussion tracing briefly some general differences between western and other traditions, the chapter ends with a section on emotional expression across cultures. It should be noted that all discussion is limited by the fact that what goes for 'knowledge' is fashioned, and limited, by the language used to explore and discuss concepts and ideas; culture-bound, ethnocentric viewpoints are difficult to avoid but every effort is made to do just that.

Traditions of western psychology and psychiatry

In spite of considerable overlap between them, western psychology deals mainly with 'normal' mind and psychiatry with the 'abnormal'. Both disciplines developed in tandem and were built on foundations that incorporate traditional western ideas about the nature of human beings and their minds, but psychiatry also incorporated a much more defined tendency to encapsulate ideas in terms of illness and health. Today, western psychology claims to be a science by objectifying as much as possible its observations about human beings, albeit in a predetermined model, and presenting them in the form of statistics. Psychiatry maintains its status as a medical specialty by claiming to use scientific methods of study and research, seemingly objective techniques of observation and assessment of people designated as patients, and an open mind about its information base. Two ideologies are evident in both disciplines: (a) An underlying theme that mind and body are in separate compartments as it were for assessment, study and planning of interventions/therapy; and (b) the dedication to classifying people in terms of types or diagnoses.

Mind-body dichotomy and holism

The proposal in the mid-seventeenth century by René Descartes that mind and body belonged to two 'independent and separate realms' (Capra, 1982, p. 45) composed of 'utterly different substances' (Koyré, 1954, p. xliv) set the stage for western thinking about mind leading to western psychology. The Cartesian doctrine states that the body is governed by mechanical laws but the mind – or soul – is free and immortal, so that a person 'lives through two collateral histories' (Ryle, 1990, p. 13). Descartes suggested that the mind – which was initially referred to as soul – should be studied by introspection and the body by methods of natural science (Capra, 1982; Ryle, 1990). But as western psychology developed in the late eighteenth century, it was influenced by studies of the nervous system, especially reports of correlations between mental activity and brain structure, and by various other theories apparently supporting a mechanistic basis for mental activities. Consequently, its approach deviated from the original Cartesian one although still holding on to its basis – the separation of mind and body, both seen as 'objects' for study (Capra, 1982):

> The structuralists studied the mind through introspection and tried to analyse consciousness into its basic elements, while behaviourists concentrated exclusively on the study of behaviour and so were led to ignore or deny the existence of mind altogether...[and]...both modelled themselves after classical physics, incorporating the basic concepts of Newtonian mechanics [formulated in the late seventeenth century] into their theoretical frameworks. (p. 166)

These matters are discussed further in Chapter 3.

The western tradition in psychology and psychiatry is to see the mind as either a mere function of the brain or as an entity independent of the brain but, in some way, related to it. Torda (1980) considers three models – materialistic monism, dualism and holistic monism: The first model sees the mind as a sort of information system using the brain as a machine – something like software uses the hardware in a computer. This model informs pure scientists in psychology, neurology and the neurosciences. The dualism model sees mind as a totally independent entity with properties that are elusive to current methods of investigation but are likely to create consciousness, thinking and all psychological functions. This model fashions the thinking of clinical psychologists and psychiatrists in their day-to-day work and it underlies the assumptions of much common sense in western culture. Holistic monism postulates that the human brain, being limited by the nature of brain receptors, can only become aware of certain forms of communication and consciousness; its perception as external or internal depends on construction of concepts about the environment. Derived from advanced western science, holistic monism is very similar to, if not identical with, the spiritual holism of eastern philosophies and possibly the traditional thinking that underlies many non-western cultures (see Chapter 8 for further discussion).

Holism is a term that is used rather loosely at times. The word itself is derived from the Greek *holos* meaning 'whole'. In the 1960s, the term 'holism' was used in (western) medical circles to indicate empathic care (Kleinman, 1995) and, since the 1980s, it has been 'appropriated by a commercial movement ... that advocated various nonorthodox [to western medicine] interventions' (p. 26). The use of the term 'holism' in this section ignores these deviant tendencies to consider it as a viewpoint opposite of that which sees human beings in a mind-body dichotomy. Lazlo (1972) proposes that holism applied to the medical field in a narrow sense views the human being as a living system whose components are interconnected and interdependent while, in a broad sense, it recognizes the human being as an integral part of larger systems – implying that not only are people in continual interaction with their physical and social environments but they are also constantly acting upon the environment and modifying it. Elaborating the latter viewpoint would mean that holism indicates a non-divided state of being with no sense of any division of the person into different parts in the first place. The emphasis then is on integrated wholeness where units such as body, mind and environment are seen as semantically convenient but misleading concepts which prevent a true understanding of reality. The influence of holism in thinking about health and illness is discussed later.

The approach of western medicine is to understand the working of the body by focusing on subdivisions of the body, that is, different organs and parts of organs, and identifying functions of each part in precise detail; this is the reductionist approach. Illnesses are located in one or more parts, never in the whole *as a whole*. Interventions (therapies) are directed at correcting one or more faults in one or other part. In clinical psychology, a part of western psychology, the psyche is seen in reductionist terms; and cognitions are seen as separate from emotions, motivation from drive, and so on. Freudians talk of the ego and the superego as separate entities and see 'the unconscious' and 'the conscious' as occupying different compartments in the mind. Jungians identify different strata of the mind in the way that anatomists see layers in the brain, although it must be admitted that many of Jung's concepts, drawn from Chinese philosophy, seem to transcend the mechanistic models of traditional psychology. The psyche, like the body, has been broken into parts – thinking parts or cognitions, feeling parts or emotions, and so on. Further, many phenomena are described as being divided into normal and abnormal categories. Sometimes these are merely semantic categories devoid of real meaning even to psychiatrists. For example, psychiatrists are supposed to differentiate 'withdrawal' (a sign of schizophrenia) from 'retardation' (a sign of depression) although the difference is inferred from context rather than observation of the patient (see later under diagnosis).

Diagnosis

The diagnosis of a psychiatric illness represents the analysis by a practitioner of the problems presented by a patient in a particular style and theoretical framework – the medical model that conforms to the traditional scientific paradigm is discussed in Chapter 3. The prelude to diagnoses is an assessment of what are perceived as symptoms and signs (see below), which are themselves evaluations – essentially comparisons of the patient's feelings, behaviour and beliefs set against values implicit in the discipline of psychiatry. The practical importance of diagnosis arises from the practitioner's need to be sufficiently informed in order to prescribe treatment – for it is assumed, in a medical model, that treatment is geared to diagnosis.

The development, in the 1950s, of powerful drugs – so-called psychotropic drugs – affecting behaviour and thinking of human beings led to an increasing popularity of psychopharmacology and a shift towards a biological approach in psychiatry; the tradition in psychiatry today is correctly described as biomedical (Kleinman, 1995). The idea that there are specific drugs for specific diagnosed illnesses is promoted by commercial organizations tied to big business; and this has resulted in strengthening the need for making clear diagnosis, for training psychiatrists in making these diagnoses and promoting the idea of diagnosis as *fact*, rather than what it actually is – a social construction for describing human problems that may or may not be useful (see Chapter 3 for further discussion of illness-construction).

In attempting to be objective and reliable, psychiatry has turned increasingly to diagnoses based on the descriptive approach (Tischler, 1987). The crucial elements here are so-called symptoms, signs and illness deduced from history-taking and judgements made about a patient's 'mental state'. Complaints, recorded as symptoms, are never a verbatim recording of a patient's statements, but are conclusions drawn by the psychiatrist as a result of questioning the patient and other informants in a particular style. 'History' is very different to a patient's narrative which is a person's story given in their own words and style; patient narratives are not favoured by psychiatrists because it is seen as too subjective. As transcultural psychiatrist Kleinman (1995) points out, symptoms, too, are regarded as too subjective to be of use: 'The physician's task, wherever possible, is to replace these biased observations with *objective* data' (p. 32, italics in original) – namely signs of illness usually referred to as being elicited by the physician. These signs form the patient's 'psychopathology' – abnormality of the psyche closely involved with the definition of the illness that it is supposed to signify. This is the medical model of illness; the 'bio' part of a biomedical model comes from the assumption that, whether currently known or not, the cause of illness is biological.

In the case of psychiatry, the so-called observations on which signs of illness are found are assumed to be objective. As two eminent psychiatrists Peter Tyrer and Derek Steinberg (1998) state: 'the examination of the patient's mind is similar in many ways to the examination of the body ... [and this is done] indirectly, by analysing some of the most important products of the mind, primarily thoughts expressed in the form of speech' (p. 28). Thus, judgements made about the mind of a patient are converted by sleight of psychiatric expertise into what is formally called a mental state examination, analogous to a physical examination of a patient. So history and mental state examination provide the basic material – and the justification – for making a diagnosis. Naturally there is scope for bias at every stage of the process leading up to a psychiatric diagnosis. But, most importantly, whatever the diagnosis, it reflects the assumed correctness of values, philosophies of life and beliefs about the human condition that inform what is assumed to be normal, namely, western ideas of mind and the individual, the Cartesian mind-body dichotomy, and much else inherent in the culture of psychiatry (Chapter 3, Table 3.4).

Judgement of pathology; vagaries of diagnosis

Diagnosis depends on judgement of what is normal and abnormal. So, in certain contexts, some beliefs, feelings, conduct or ways of thinking may be deemed pathological in the light of usual psychiatric practice; for example, delusions, hallucinations, depression, elation and behaviours such as jealousy or talk that appears muddled. The theory of psychiatry states that these are signs of illness of (say) depression, hypomania, paranoia, schizophrenia or psychopathic disorder. The context within which the diagnosis is made is the overall culture of psychiatry and the forces that bear down on the whole process.

Unlike in most other branches of medicine, signs and symptoms in psychiatry overlap. For instance, a patient may complain of depression – that is a symptom – and the psychiatrist may observe that (s)he is depressed – a sign deduced from history and mental state examination. The next step is for the psychiatrist to make deductions about the location in the mind of the pathology underlying the depression. It should be noted here that the 'mind' in psychiatric thinking is a combination of intellect, thinking, feeling and emotion, with a firm distinction between cognition (intellect and thinking) and affect (emotion and feeling). And mental functioning is related to these different parts of the mind, rather than the person as a whole. The pathology may be assumed to be a malfunctioning of a particular location – as in the case of depression where the emotions are at fault – or the malfunctioning of the interplay between parts, as in schizophrenia where intellect is split off from emotions. But treatment is not necessarily directed at the pathology itself; it is usually empirical, its effects being measured and analysed in terms of changes in symptoms and signs, that is, what the patient complains of or what the practitioner observes – or thinks (s)he observes.

Just as psychiatry has developed as a historical process, so have its systems of classification and treatment, the standard ones being the International Classification of Diseases (ICD) (WHO, 1993) and the Diagnostic Statistical

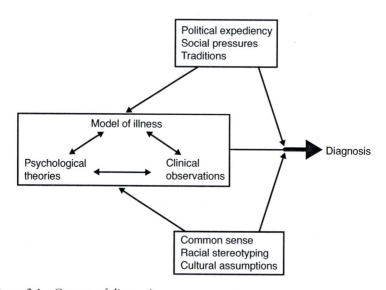

Figure 2.1   Context of diagnosis

Manual (DSM) (APA, 1994); inevitably, the nosology is permeated by ideologies and philosophical concepts from western culture. Thus, in considering diagnosis, two facts should be borne in mind: First, psychiatry is ethnocentric and carries in it the ideologies of western culture including racism; second, the practice of psychiatry, including its ways of diagnosing, is influenced by the social ethos and the political system in which it exists and works (Table 2.1).

Treatment

The medical model of psychiatry separates diagnosis from treatment, although in practice the two processes blend together and influence each other. Also, treatment cannot easily be separated from 'management' or 'care' – terms used within medicine for the ways in which patients are advised, sometimes coerced and generally looked after; the context in which treatment is given – including the ward environment (of inpatients), its rules and regulations, the way staff and patients interact; and adherence to ward routines and occupation during the daytime. In addition, methods of control or discipline including the use of 'seclusion' (solitary confinement) may be seen sometimes as treatment, although usually felt by patients as punishment.

Psychiatric treatment falls into two broad groups – psychological treatment and physical treatment with drugs or ECT (electroconvulsive therapy or electroplexy). The former includes psychotherapy, sometimes called talking therapy, which is generally regarded as a highly specialized form of treatment suitable for selected people only, the criteria for selection being concerned mainly with their 'understanding of problems in psychological terms', motivation for 'insight', and 'capacity to form relationships' (Brown and Pedder, 1979, pp. 181–6). Physical treatment can be given under certain circumstances without the consent of the person receiving it.

Medical belief systems

Although the definition of 'illness' may vary across cultural traditions, concern with departure from health – as illness – is universal (White, 1982). Every culture seems to include a concept of illness (McQueen, 1978); and ways of dealing with illness may be referred to as medical systems, although quite often these cannot be clearly separated from religious or social systems. At a micro level, there are always health beliefs and practices, explanatory models of illness, roles and status of practitioners, and so on; and at a macro level there are socio-economic conditions, political systems, power relationships between and within organizations, allocation of resources and so on (Janzen, 1978). The impact of cultural differences and racist attitudes apply at both levels in somewhat different ways. For example, the value attached to one type of belief or practice in a multicultural and racist society is often determined by its supposed racial connection rather than its cultural relevance or importance; this applies to family and marriage patterns as well as to illness presentations. Thus, the family life of black people in Britain and the USA is often seen as aberrant in terms of sexual behaviour, religion, music styles and eating habits (Brittan and Maynard, 1984). Indigenous beliefs in industrially underdeveloped countries are considered inferior to those derived from western traditions, irrespective of their usefulness in a particular situation or of their efficacy in a particular healing model.

Cultural differences in medical belief systems (that is in ideas about illness) can be examined in different ways. But by this very analysis, inevitably using concepts based on western culture, the significance of non-western ways of conceptualizing illness may be missed. In analysing the concept of illness cross-culturally, Kleinman (1978) distinguishes 'disease' from 'illness'; the former denotes 'a malfunctioning in, or maladaptation of, biological and/ or psychological processes' and the latter the '*experience* of disease (or per-ceived disease) and the societal reaction to disease' (p. 88, italics in original). But Obeyesekere (1985) argues that unlike the case in physical medicine, disease cannot be extracted from illness in the case of mental disease/illness: 'The *conception* of the disease (i.e., illness) *is* the disease. Or to put it differently, there are only illnesses and no diseases' (p. 136, italics in original). Thus, although an illness-disease differentiation is of limited help in under-standing the nature of medical belief systems, Kleinman's (1977) emphasis on the importance of culturally determined explanatory models of illness/ disease is helpful in a situation where psychiatry is applied in non-western cultural settings. From a western standpoint, some models are generally seen as scientific and others as magical; but as Lewis (1986) notes, 'there is fun-damentally a similarity in that both views, ours and theirs, search for some ordering or reason in events' (p. 132). Another common viewpoint is to see western explanatory models as being natural and others as largely supernat-ural in approach. But what is natural or supernatural is determined by the worldview of the culture anyway and is not based on absolute culture-free values. Most cultures blend the natural and the supernatural in determining explanatory models of illness.

In eastern traditions, health is seen as a harmonious balance between vari-ous forces in the person and the social context. In the Chinese way of think-ing, illness is an imbalance of *yin* and *yang*, two complementary poles of life energy, to be corrected by attempts to re-establish balance (Aakster, 1986). The Indian tradition emphasizes the harmony between the person and his/ her group as indicative of health (Kakar, 1984). According to Lambo (1969), the African tradition conceptualizes health as more social than biological, and deviation from health is embedded 'in traditional magico-religious or spiritual explanation of illness' (p. 201). These differences in cultural traditions are only a start. Each overarching culture includes many variations and there are many cultures that may not even be addressed within the Asian-African-Western trio, for example, the vast panoply of cultures in the American continent and those indigenous to Australia.

Across cultures, there is difference not only in the concept of illness but also the ways in which they are perceived – the explanatory models for illness (Kleinman, 1980). In western culture, insanity is set apart as a special type of illness. Although this may apply in many other cultures, too, the understanding of what insanity is and the way in which it is set apart may be very different. Boundaries between health and disease, and between mind and body, are drawn in different ways in different cultural traditions. As a result, for example, the major causes of mental illness (in western terms) may appear to be somato-psychic when classical Ayurvedic theories of Indian medicine are viewed from a western standpoint (Obeyesekere, 1977); and some forms of human distress that are conceptualized in the West as illness may be seen in religious or philosophical terms in the Indian tradition. In Tibetan thinking, based on the Mahayana Buddhist tradition, the most crucial psychological factor involved with insanity is the same as that essential for pursuing enlightenment, namely, the recognition of impermanence (Clifford, 1984). In other words, both insanity and enlightenment have the same basis: 'It all depends on whether or not it is accepted and comprehended and ultimately worked with as the key to liberation. If it is not, it becomes, because the realization is still there unconsciously, the cause of denial, repression and, ultimately, mental illness' (pp. 138–9). Although the western model of illness has developed in a Christian culture, it has no place for Christian concepts such as salvation or damnation, because, in the West, religion and illness are considered to be in separate cultural compartments. This secular approach to illness is not seen in other cultural traditions. In short, the overall worldview within a culture, appertaining to health, religion, psychology and spiritual concerns, determines the meaning within that culture of 'madness', mental illness and mental health. African and Asian concepts of illness, healing and therapy are discussed in Chapter 8.

Stigma and the schizophrenia diagnosis

Stigma denotes a marker – visible or implied – that discredits a person or group of people (Goffman, 1968). But the marker itself carries a baggage of its own, in terms of feelings, attitudes and historical happenings. And it is not just people, or groups of people, who are affected by stigma but stigma may be attached to a diagnoses of illness – and in the mental health field this is called 'psychiatric stigma'. In effect, psychiatric stigma is discrimination against people who are given a psychiatric diagnosis (Fernando, 2003; Sayce, 2000) – usually schizophrenia (Jorm and Griffiths, 2008). And schizophrenia carries images of alienness, fear, dangerousness, deceit (not to be trusted) coming from historical background of its construction (see Fernando, 1998), added to by stereotypes promoted by the media, subconscious fears and prejudices of many people, and so on. And all this comes from a social history of psychiatry, explored in Chapter 3.

The question of how stigma can be counteracted is even more important than the genesis of stigma itself. Essentially, countering stigma means countering the corresponding assumptions underlying it – just telling people not to stigmatize is unlikely to work. In 2000, the Royal College of Psychiatrists embarked on an 'anti-stigma campaign' (Crisp, 2000) by focusing on publicizing (what it saw as) the medical reality of mental illness as treatable. Even while the campaign was under way, some users of psychiatric services in UK objected to it claiming that stigma was being promoted by biological psychiatry and the College should revise its model of diagnosis (Fernando, 2003). In fact, some psychiatrists supported this service-user viewpoint (e.g., Chaplin, 2000; Summerfield, 2001). A study carried out in the 1990s in Germany shows that psychiatric stigma actually increases when people view a mental illness as being caused by brain disease as opposed to psychological causes (Angermeyer and Matschinger, 2005). And, Read *et al.* (2006) reviewing the literature found that biogenetic causal beliefs and diagnostic labelling by the public are positively related to psychiatric stigma: 'Any evidence-based approach to reducing discrimination would seek a range of alternatives to the "mental illness is an illness like any other" approach' (p. 303). The view that biomedical psychiatry promotes stigma tallies with transcultural observations quoted below, but has been challenged by Jorm and Griffiths (2008) on the basis of a study using vignettes. So the question of an inevitable association between biomedical illness model and stigma is an open one.

In analysing the history of psychiatric stigma in western societies, Fabrega (1991) concludes that psychiatric diagnosis may have inherited the discredit attached to incapacity and institutionalization because they enable people to opt out of being productive, but has also become linked to disapproval arising from the dilemma for society when illness is diagnosed without an objective marker, thereby suggesting feigned disability. In other words, he suggests that psychiatric stigma today derives from both 'isolation and alienation promoted by chronic institutionalization' (p. 116) of the mad/insane (today's schizophrenic or psychotic) as well as the blame attached to someone who may be feigning illness. Much earlier, Nancy Waxler (1974), working in Sri

Lanka, reported that psychiatric stigma was almost absent in communities where mental illness was seen as being caused by spirit possession:

> The sick person, himself, is not believed to be responsible for the illness; his body or soul may be possessed but his 'self' remains unchanged. If he follows the appropriate prescriptions, then it is believed that his symptoms will disappear and he will quickly and easily return to normal. There is no stigma attached to mental illness; no one believes that the patient is 'different' and should be treated in a new way after his symptoms have gone. (p. 380)

Today, stigma associated with schizophrenia has spread to the more general 'psychosis' diagnosis. Psychiatric stigma may not be unavoidable in a context where biomedical model of illness predominates but may be extremely difficult to counteract given the way in which the model is interpreted in society today: After all (it could be argued and often assumed) such an illness is a medical condition which we know is associated with dangerousness, violence, confusion and, more than anything else, alienness that renders people afflicted with it as being beyond understanding, irrational and bizarre; that is the way they are. When present-day psychiatrists draw on the Kraepelinian tradition (Kraepelin, 1919) and diagnose schizophrenia, in effect they stigmatize – although admittedly many do not realize it. So the clear message is that to get rid of stigma we need to get rid of the genetic-biomedical model of mental illness (see Chapter 4).

'Culture-bound' syndromes

The concept of culture-bound syndromes has come about through a historical process whereby both psychiatrists and anthropologists have tried to make sense – each using their own particular expertise – of what they found, or thought they found, in non-western cultural settings. The ideology that developed within anthropology was to see a dichotomy between modern/scientific psychiatry and traditional/ethnopsychiatry (Gaines, 1982), the former being authentic and the latter contaminated or distorted by their cultures. And this approach fed into psychiatry where symptom constellations identified in the West were regarded as the standard – for instance, Bebbington (1978) concludes in a survey of depression across cultures that the symptomatology of depression in non-western cultural settings are 'cross-cultural anomalies' (p. 303). In general what happens in developing psychiatric knowledge is that when a symptom constellation identified in a non-western setting cannot be pushed into an illness category within psychiatry, a culture-bound syndrome (CBS) is identified; psychopathology in the West is seen as culturally neutral and so an illness that cannot be bound into a western category becomes culture-bound. In other words, CBS has a distinct racist connotation.

Some writers and practitioners have tried to change the scene. For example, Littlewood and Lipsedge (1987) have argued that a cultural understanding of psychiatric illness is as important in the West as it is in other societies: 'Some general features of those ritual patterns usually classed as "culture-bound syndromes" are applicable to Western neurosis' (p. 289). Others have suggested that anorexia nervosa (Prince, 1983) and premenstrual syndrome (Johnson, 1987) may be CBSs of the West. A major problem in revising *DSM-III* (APA, 1980) was the presence of 'culture-bound disorders' and a vigorous debate arose (Beiser, 1987; Kapur, 1987; Kleinman, 1987; Prince and Tcheng-Laroche, 1987) around an attempt to incorporate them into the DSM system. However, the difficulties were not resolved and *DSM-IV* (APA, 1994) merely lists 'culture-bound syndromes' in an appendix. Similarly, *ICD-10* (WHO, 1993) lists 'culture-specific disorders' in an annex to its criteria for research written by an anthropologist.

Comparison of cultural traditions

All the major cultures have influenced each other historically and continue to do so. Therefore, generalizations and comparisons inevitably oversimplify and do not do justice to the cultural variety – and cultural hybridity – of human society. But some generalizations are required in order to try and understand what 'culture' actually means. So, in spite of the problems in this approach, this section compares the traditions of 'western culture' with those of 'other' cultures – African, Eastern and Native American traditions. The Islamic culture that developed in the geographical area referred to as Middle East is included within eastern culture for the purpose of this chapter. The cultures of indigenous Australians, the Maoris of New Zealand and various other peoples, such as the Polynesians, are not considered here in the interests of brevity. This section is in no way a general comparison but a limited one for the purposes of drawing together some ideas that may help readers to understand the wider topic of mental health, race and culture.

A major problem for this section is that a reliable body of information on the background and traditions of Africa is not available for several reasons (Karenga, 1982): The subject is vast and relatively unresearched; the sources of history in most parts of Africa were 'griots', professional oral historians who held the collective memory of a community or nation – a vulnerable form of record keeping; and European conquest led to the destruction of many documents and evidence of African achievement and to the distortion of history to fit into racist models of African primitiveness. Before the appearance of Cheikh Anta Diop's *African Origin of Civilization* (Diop, 1967), African culture, expounded by western scholars enveloped in an ideology that distorted history, 'cast a fog over cultural understanding of the African people' (Asante and Asante, 1985, p. ix). African studies that attempt to avoid racist assumptions and examine the evidence objectively are a recent phenomenon and not very evident in the English language literature. In other words, the real story of Africa and its culture is incomplete. For similar reasons and since it is difficult to generalize about the thinking traditional to (Native) Americans, either in the past or in the present, this section draws for its 'non-western' examples mainly on traditions from Asia and so tends to discuss East-West differences.

Western Christianity came to influence Africans transported to the Americas through the conversion of African slaves, and to influence Africans in Africa through the influx of missionaries into a continent where societies were being devastated by colonial conquest and internecine conflict. Although the Christian Church was an arm of the slave-owning economy and racist colonialism, the doctrines of the Christian religion were gradually fashioned by Africans to be absorbed into their worldview. A distinctive African American form of Christianity developed as an almost new religion in the USA (Wilmore, 1973), leading to a Black Liberation Theology allied to Black Power (Karenga, 1982). And in South Africa, Black Theology as 'the perception that Jesus belonged historically in a situation of oppression, that he was a member of an oppressed people in an oppressive society, and that he came to set people free' (Stubbs, 1988, p. 234) supported Steve Biko's movement to promote Black Consciousness in the modern African worldview (Biko, 1971).

According to Capra (1982), the spiritual tradition of the East is akin to the approach of modern physics. Writing for a western audience, Graham (1986) states: 'Eastern culture and its institutions are traditionally humanistic in the sense that they are centred around the human potential for transcendence or becoming' (p. 11). But eastern culture is not humanistic in the sense of worshipping the human being as being noble and all-powerful – the sort of thinking that forms the individualistic basis of western culture since the Enlightenment (discussed further in Chapter 3). Religion and psychology are integrated in the traditional philosophies of Hinduism, Buddhism, Zen, Taoism and Islam. In the eastern tradition, rationality is seen as *maya* – illusory and superficial. Chinese philosophy sees reality, whose ultimate essence is called *tao*, as a process of continual flow and change. The second overarching way in which western tradition differs from others, vis-à-vis mental health, is in its clear denial of holism. From this denial flows many differences of practical concern. Some of these are discussed separately but three points may be made here (Table 2.1).

First, holism instills an ideology that enables people to experience external and internal experiences as *one and the same*; experience is both

Table 2.1   Influence of holism on illness experiences

	Cultural tradition	
	Holistic	Non-holistic
External vs internal experiences/Subjective vs objective experiences	Intertwined and interposed within each other	Distinct and separate from each other
Causes of ill health	Experienced as both internal and external *at the same time*	Experienced as either external or internal, one impacting on the other
Experience of health	Sense of harmonious balance between different aspects of self and environment	Sense of subjective well-being distinct from external influences

subjective *and* objective at the same time. The *yin/yang* terminology of Chinese tradition represents such a view. In some ways, this resembles systems theory 'which looks at the world in terms of the interrelatedness and interdependence of all phenomena ... whose properties cannot be reduced to those of its parts' (Capra, 1982, p. 26). This topic is important in contrasting the activity of introspection in western culture with that of its counterpart in the Indian tradition; in the former, definitions of self and identity are contingent upon 'examining, sorting out and scrutinizing' one's own life, while in meditative procedures of 'self-realization', introspection dwells on the self of Indian philosophy 'uncontaminated by time and space' (Kakar, 1984, p. 7). Nobles (1986) notes that 'unlike the mathematical illusion of normality found in the West, normality which would be consistent with African thought is a normal which is equivalent to one's nature' (p. 112).

The second point concerns experience of mental health and ill health. In holistic tradition, an inside-outside division does not occur or, if it does, the inside and outside are so intertwined and interposed that they cannot be usefully separated. So a traditionally western non-holistic approach would promote the attribution of ill health to either an external cause or an internal cause, but not both at the same time. Finally, a holistic tradition promotes a sense of health as a harmonious balance between various forces in the person and the social context as opposed to seeing health as individualized sense of well-being. However, the danger of depicting (e.g., in Table 2.1) sharp divisions between traditions is that of stereotyping. Therefore, holistic/non-holistic dimension implying an East-West division should not be taken too literally; and in particular this should not be connected to racial differences or national differences. For example, there are people with eastern ways of thinking in western countries and vice versa.

Speculations on fusion of traditions

The western worldview, based on control, has within it an assertiveness that has paid off in the achievements of material gain by the West; African and eastern acceptance has promoted a passivity that allowed the West to dominate and exploit both the people and resources of the earth to the point of destruction. But the western worldview has within it a propensity for guilt and fear, promoting ill health that is interpreted as depression. And within the apparent passivity and acceptance of eastern and African cultures there are elements of anger and aggression leading to irrational violence, sometimes seen as illness and dealt with culturally by spiritual and religious movements. However, the rational, justifiable anger of African and Asian people and the understandable guilt of the West – both arising from recent history – are entwined respectively with traditional non-western acceptance and traditional western aggressiveness in the feelings that determine the concept of mental health in their cultures today.

Although the historic past of a people forms the background to their worldview in the present day, a current – and future – worldview must incorporate two dimensions of change that are continuous. First, there is the effect of recent experiences on groups of people identifying in terms of their different backgrounds but yet choosing to live together, interact and integrate. And second, the meeting of people from very different backgrounds that is taking place – especially in recent years – resulting in tensions between cultural, racial and ethnic groups. In such a mixed – contradictory – scenario, it is not clear to what extent and how fusion of cultural traditions vis-à-vis mental health is taking place; the only certainty is that it must be happening. And all this in a context where western, traditional European, culture retains a worldview which incorporates a sense of power and arrogance; while Asian, African and Native American cultures retain the scars of imperial domination and persecution during the era in which genocide, slavery and colonialism flourished, as well as the effects of current economic oppression and indirect political control – neocolonialism. The risk is that power discrepancy may influence the changes that take place in traditional approaches to mental health, on the nature and degree of fusion. These matters are discussed further in Chapters 11 and 12.

Today, there is a distinct shift of power – at least in economic terms – towards Asia away from Europe and possibly the USA. The active stifling of Asian cultures appears to be in the past; and European American groups in the USA appear to be attempting to make amends for the destruction of Native American cultures. The recent election of an African American as president of the USA indicates a move towards a 'more perfect union' – to partially quote the title of a speech by Barack Obama (2008) during his election campaign – in a USA that is multicultural and multiracial. Current interest in Asian cultural forms and New Age religious movements may represent a real cultural shift in what is after all the most powerful western nation in the world today; yet, this may turn out to be merely cult-like fashion confined to a few people and/or adoption of outer trappings of eastern cultural forms rather than the incorporation of their meaning. And, although cultural psychiatry may be making inroads into practical application in non-western countries (see Kleinman, 1988), biomedical psychiatry is distorting the mental health landscape in many low-income, non-western countries (see Chapter 9).

Emotional expression across cultures

In western psychology, the term 'emotion' or 'affect' is usually used to describe intense states of feeling as anxiety, depression, happiness, contentment, and their opposites, as well as milder moods such as feelings of pleasure, displeasure, anger, fear, shame, jealousy, hunger and sexual urge. Emotions are usually conceptualized as internal, subjective experiences, peculiar to the individual and expressed by verbal or non-verbal behaviour – the latter being seen as social signals of subjective experiences used for communication, or as signs of physiological changes that accompany emotion (Argyle, 1975). The general approach in the western tradition today is that 'affect', the state of mind that underlies emotion, is determined by various internal events of both psychological and physiological nature; they are connected with cognitive appraisals, 'action impulses' which either inhibit or express emotion and patterned somatic reactions (Lazarus *et al.*, 1970, 1980).

In his classic book *The Expression of the Emotions in Man and Animals*, Charles Darwin (1872) established a way of thinking about emotions that led to a study of behaviour, called ethology, that emphasized the biological evolution of behaviour, including emotional expression. Ethology sees cultural differences in the expression of emotions as a reflection of evolutionary difference, something resulting from modification of heredity. Inevitably, this approach succumbs to racism since cultural differences of behaviour, including the expression of the emotions, are perceived hierarchically, those of some cultures being seen as superior to those of others (see Konrad Lorenz quoted by Kalikow, 1978).

In the tradition of western psychology, a person's emotions are recognized because they are expressed through behaviour, either verbally by the person concerned describing them in a language that another person understands, or by means of non-verbal communication – for example, body language. Social and cultural influences on the phenomena of affective states and conduct are usually studied in terms of the context in which the affect is felt or expressed, not as having direct influence central to the expression of emotion itself. This approach is too simplistic. In reality, personal, cultural and social meaning may fashion emotional expression; emotions may be suppressed, distorted or exaggerated for psychological, social or cultural reasons; and some feelings, or the way they are expressed, may be designated as 'illness'.

Feelings are often expressed in terms of idioms – complex behaviour patterns including music, poetry, dance and various other art forms – that have become imbued with meaning through usage underscored by symbolic associations. Inevitably, such idioms are determined by habits and traditions arising from culture as well as contextual factors and personal inclinations. Thus the sociocultural dimensions of emotional expression are varied and complex – they are not mere contexts for emotional expression but are primary determinants of affect and integral to their very constitution. Affect cannot be reduced to just biological impulses as in ethology (referred to above). Nichter (1981), an anthropologist, believes that the judgement of a particular idiom of distress as normal or abnormal, adaptive or maladaptive, should not be made until the following have been considered: 'An individual's socio-cultural constraints against and opportunities for expression, alternative modes of expression, personal and cultural meaning and social ramifications of employing modes, and a person's past experience and familiarity with alternative modes' (p. 402).

The importance of communication and rapport between a professional and a help-seeker is fundamental to clinical work of any sort in the mental health field. If both participants in an interaction have similar understanding of the idioms of emotional expression – usually because of similarity of cultural background – communication could be fairly smooth. But if there is a cultural gulf between them, problems arise. Such a gulf can be overcome by knowledge, which can be obtained from the help-seeker – assuming that there are no serious language problems – but this may be blocked if the interaction takes place in a context where the professional is influenced, consciously or unconsciously, by racist value judgements of the person or persons or what is perceived as their cultures. Thus culture plays a major part in the idiomatic expression of distress, while both race and culture are involved in the recognition of the idioms.

Coping with stress

In western psychology, coping with stress is usually perceived in behavioural terms or in relation to an ego psychology model of human functioning (Folkman and Lazarus, 1988). The former, being derived from studies of animal behaviour, emphasizes learned behaviour contributing to survival in the face of dangers that threaten life; in the latter, coping consists of cognitive processes, such as denial, repression and intellectualization. In both, coping is viewed as a response to emotion, felt and/or expressed, and a means of reducing tension – at least unwanted, distressing tension. These concepts of coping ignore the cultural context in which coping occurs and the way coping is perceived and judged in a racist milieu. Culture plays a large part in determining the way in which a particular event of emotional distress is conceptualized in the first place – for example, whether it is seen as illness to be cured or endured, or as a spiritual crisis to be resolved or experienced; the former will call for coping, the latter for understanding. This interrelates with culturally determined concepts of distress, discussed earlier.

The ascription of some desirable and beneficial behaviour or experience as a symptom of illness arises through the inherent confusion in psychiatry itself. For example, depression may well be considered understandable – even helpful – as a way of coping with bereavement but also designated as a symptom of illness treated with antidepressants. Coulter (1979) argues that this type of confusion may be avoided by ensuring that the designation of 'psychological phenomena' as abnormal depends on the (culturally determined) judgement of intentionality and understandability. A coping strategy, by its very nature of being understandable as one, is normal; it should never be seen as a symptom if the judgement is based on culture-sensitive evaluations free of racism. Racist attitudes too may play their part: Voice-hearing may be perceived as a primitive type of coping characteristic of black people, and depression as a strategy of advanced white people; the result is that hallucinatory experiences are seen as undesirable because they are 'primitive' ways of coping and thence slip into being treated as symptoms of illness in spite of being recognized as a coping strategy. Looked at cross-culturally, coping strategies may be confused with psychopathology. Conditions such as depression, anxiety, voice-hearing, guilty preoccupation, passivity feelings, aggression, anger and emotional withdrawal are usually recognized in psychiatry as symptoms of illness; but these may be coping strategies for individuals in particular situations.

Summary

Although we still talk of western psychology or western medicine, including psychiatry, it is important to bear in mind that these subjects are now essentially universal but firmly geared in practice to the paradigms and ways of thinking that derive from western culture. The situation vis-à-vis mental health could have been very different if European nations had not subjugated other people and undermined and part-destroyed their cultures, including medical systems and religions. Just for argument, if (say) the

Ayurvedic medical tradition had been allowed to thrive in British occupied India – or the North American indigenous tradition of healing been promoted, rather than suppressed, during the European colonization of North America – we could envisage that development of ideas about health and illness, including mental health and problems around mental health, would have been on somewhat different lines, driven perhaps by holistic way of thinking, including a spiritual dimension, and so on. But we are where we are and what has happened has happened.

The reality today is that western psychology – scientific psychology/secular psychology – is pursued all over the world, often to the detriment of other psychologies; and biomedical psychiatry, as distinct from indigenous or traditionally non-western systems of medicine, is practised, taught and developed in non-western countries as well as in the West. Concepts of distress, coping, illness and health are all being incorporated into the western system of identifying symptoms of illness and analysing causes of illness constructed within that tradition. Yet, even today, cultural diversity in how illness and health are seen, how distress and coping are handled and the meanings attached to all these – together with racist assumptions connected to all – render the whole system of biomedical psychiatry and western psychology extremely suspect for universal application. That is not to say that another different system can be applied universally. The answer may lie in many different systems contributing to a diversity that respects all traditions – matters explored in Chapters 11 and 12.

Chapter 3

Background and Culture of Psychiatry

Many ideas in current psychiatry can be traced back to Greek roots (Simon, 1978): Methods of dealing with deviancy were foreshadowed when Plato (427–348 BC) proposed in his Laws that atheists, whose lack of faith seemed to arise from ignorance rather than malice, should be placed for five years in a *sophronisterion* (house of sanity). Plato talked of unconscious motivation and the interpretation of dreams; and in *The Republic* he divided the mind into three parts likened to three different kinds of men: the lover of wisdom (*philosophus*) corresponding to the rational, the lover of victory (*philonikos*) to the spirited-affective, and the lover of gain (*philoker-des*) to the appetitive. These ideas led to the concept of mind as being composed of higher and lower parts, the former being rational and aware, the latter being concerned with appetites of the body, somatic sensations and dreaming. Socrates (469–399 BC) saw knowledge as dormant in the soul and talked of unconscious processes. Hippocrates (400 BC) described mania, melancholia and 'phrenitis' – mental confusion – possibly as tendencies rather than illnesses with accounts that stand up well when compared with descriptions of illnesses with similar names in present-day biomedical psychiatry. It is the Hippocratic tradition that continues in the current system of western medicine – or allopathic medicine – of which psychiatry is a part, except that Hippocratic explanations for diseases were based on humoral theories while modern aetiological models attempt to find specific causes for diseases. But Greek ideas did not come to western civilization unchanged – they came via Islamic medicine and Arabic literature.

Mental illness in Islamic medicine

In its heyday between the tenth and thirteenth centuries, the Arabic Empire stretched from central Asia across North Africa to the Atlantic including most of Spain (Saunders, 1965) and the foundations were laid for what later became western science and medicine (Graham, 1967). It was within Islamic medicine that a medical approach to madness was first enunciated and put into practice in hospitals devoted to mental illness – the moristans (Ellenberger, 1974) or māristāns (Dols, 1992). One of the foremost

48

physicians during the twelfth century AD was Maimonides, a Jewish philosopher-physician who was called on to treat dignitaries, including the Caliph. His statue stands in a square in Cordoba, southern Spain. In one of his writings, Maimonides referred to melancholia as 'a disorder that tends towards mania' (p. 140) possibly quoting Ibn Sînâ (see later).

The work of Michael Dols edited after his death by Diana Immisch and published as *Majnûn: The Madman in Medieval Islamic Society* (Dols, 1992) brings together discourses on mental illness in medieval Arabic writings. Although Islamic medicine was continuous with (Greek) Galenic medicine, there was a more defined movement in the former towards medicalizing deviance and something very like symptoms and signs located in the mind were described. Dols (1992) writes:

> Although Galen promoted the humoral theory of disease, he does not appear to have worked out a clearly defined disease entity called 'melancholia', and certainly not one for madness. There was no 'syndrome' – which may be defined as a cluster of symptoms in a predictable sequence – of mental illness based on the predominance or change of a specific humour. (p. 92)

Although melancholia (described below) was the main mental illness mentioned in Islamic medicine, others too were described. Balfour (1876) quotes the work of Nâjâb ud din Unhammad, a mid-eighth-century physician, describing nine classes of mental problems some resembling conditions described in western psychiatry such as obsessive-compulsive disorder (OCD). The best-known medical work in Arabic was by Ibn Sînâ (980–1037 AD) – Avicenna in Greek – where over twenty-five mental illnesses were listed including headache (with thirty subdivisions), phrenitis, skull fracture, loss of memory, mental confusion, loss of imagination, mania, love-sickness, lethargy and of course melancholia (Dols, 1992). As in Galenic medicine, the causes of illness were usually seen as humoral and many of the physical therapies devised were directed at altering these humours in some way.

Dols (1992) finds the relationship between Islamic religion and Galenic medicine in the Medieval Arabic Empire confusing and complex. The Qur'ân says nothing about religious healing and exorcism and 'the image of God as healer, which is central in the Judeo-Christian tradition, is not prominent in the Qur'ân' (p. 212). Yet, 'the belief in demon possession as a cause of madness' is mentioned in the Qur'ân (218). In effect, in Islamic medical practice there was a blending of pre-Islamic folk medicine of the Arabian Bedouin, Galenic concepts such as humours and the overarching principle of 'divine causation' (p. 248). Graham (1967) goes further to write that Islamic medicine encapsulated 'a blissful union of science and religion' (p. 47). It seems that the illness model (for mental illness) was a blending of spiritual and humoral-biological concepts, very different to the biomedical approach of modern (western) psychiatry (see Chapter 2).

Melancholia

Jackson (1986) quotes Ibn Sînā (Avicenna) as defining melancholia as a deviation from the natural state characterized by fear but 'when associated with a tendency to anger, restlessness, and violence it changed its character and was called *mania*' (p. 62, italics in original), thereby describing (what we now know as) the illness 'manic depression' or 'bipolar disorder' about nine hundred years before Kraepelin did so (see later). Melancholia was attributed to an excess of black bile and Ibn Sînā gave instructions for phlebotomy, purges and emetics intended to get rid of black bile; but he also stated that the 'patient [suffering melancholia] should be occupied by listening to story-tellers and singers' (Dols, 1992, p. 83). Manoeuvres to get rid of the offending humour were advised for well-established (chronic) illnesses. Ibn Sînā argued for early intervention for melancholia – 'easy to treat at its outset but difficult to cure when it has taken root' (p. 83), and suggested (for early illness) treatment with medical remedies such as musk and theric; restrictions on diet, for example, avoiding dried meat, or lentils; attention to atmosphere in which the patient lives by, for example, seeking a temperate place that is moist and scented; and finally the need to 'cheer-up' the patient. This combination of medicine, diet and attention to lifestyle is similar to the therapeutic approach recommended in Indian Ayurveda (see Chapter 8).

Mental hospitals

The earliest institutions in the western hemisphere where people suffering from medical illnesses were housed for treatment were in the Arabic Empire – the māristāns, described by Dols (1992). For example a māristān was established in Cairo (Egypt) in AD 683, in Aleppo (Syria) in AD 755, in Baghdad (Iraq) in the late eighth century AD, in Kayseri (Caesarea) in AD 1205–1206 and in Granada (Spain) in AD 1365–1367. The dominant approach in the māristāns was Galenic (Greek) medicine that emphasized somatic (physical) therapies rather than its Persian-Indian counterpart where spiritual ideas were prominent. On the whole, Islam did not favour notions of supernatural healing comparable to that in the Christian tradition and so exorcism was not evident in the māristāns. However, dervishes performing exorcism in Sufi institutions based on the pre-Islamic belief in jinn as a cause of madness is mentioned in the Qur'ān (Dols, 1987, p. 10).

Dols (1992) quotes accounts of māristāns in North Africa as impressive buildings with pools, fountains, flowing water and flower gardens. It seems that great care was taken to decorate the hospital wards to 'cheer the deranged'. And generally there were good conditions such as 'beds with mattresses' and space for patients to wander about. Dols quotes a travelling rabbi, who came across a māristān in Cairo, commenting on special food supplied to patients at the Caliph's expense, but also noting that patients were held 'in iron chains until their reason is restored' (p. 119). There is no doubt that physical restraint was used on mental patients in the māristāns; and visitors had sometimes reported observing beatings. Dispensing of medicines was commonplace; an Arabic text mentions stimulants, sedatives and drugs for 'gladdening of the spirit' (p. 133). Interestingly, it seems that music was used to treat melancholia, reflecting a medico-musical tradition well established in Islamic society at the time going back to David treating Saul with music described in the Old Testament of the Bible. What was strikingly different about the māristāns in the Arabic Empire to the early asylums built in Europe over 500 years later was that the former were not isolated institutions but always in the centre of cities, easily accessible to most people. Clearly, the patients were frequently visited by family and friends and more generally seen as a part of society. As far as we can see these institutions were not used for confinement of people seen as socially undesirable as was the case in European asylums (see Chapter 2). The original māristān building at Aleppo (in Syria) still stands (Maziak, 2006).

End of Arabic Empire

As with all empires, the Arabic Empire was overtaken by events and gradually broke up. As it disintegrated, militant Christendom pushed forward, ultimately driving out the last Muslim ruler in Europe in 1492, when incidentally two other potentially important events took place: The Christian king of Spain expelled European Jews and supported the Catholic Church in persecuting non-believers via the inquisition; and Columbus, sailed from Spain to land in what he thought was India. So, the genocide-slavery-colonialism associated with racism that engulfed three continents for the next five hundred years may be traced to 1492. The Turks carried on the tradition of providing mental hospitals in the Ottoman Empire, that partially replaced the Arabic Empire, into the early twentieth century. The asylum movement of Europe linked to asylum-based model of western psychiatry was exported to the Middle East in the twentieth century as western hegemony was established there.

Beginning of western psychiatry

Unfortunately, little knowledge remains of the details of the Arabic system of care for people designated as being ill with mental conditions. In particular we know nothing about the role played by Islam in treating people diagnosed as mentally ill, although it is reasonable to assume that spirituality played a part in the concept of illness that Islamic medicine was based

Table 3.1   Precursors to science

Sixteenth–seventeenth centuries

Separation of natural philosophy ('science') and theology ('religion')
Descartes' mind-body dualism
Newton's mechanistic physics

Eighteenth-century 'Enlightenment'

Science replaces religion as source of knowledge
Observation and analysis replaces deductive reasoning
Individuality emphasized
Freedom of thought encouraged
Racism re-enforced

on. Arabic work was translated into Latin and became available in Europe and so, undoubtedly, ideas from Islamic medicine may have come through. Indeed the Hippocratic-Galenic ideas inspired the *Treatise on Melancholia* by Timothy Bright (1586) and Robert Burton's *The Anatomy of Melancholia* (Burton, 1806) published in 1621. But the sort of approach to madness – and thence to mental health in general – that led to the birth of western psychiatry described in the next few paragraphs (see Table 3.1) was very different to the situation that apparently flourished under Islamic rule in the Arabic Empire (Dols, 1992; Graham, 1967).

Precursors to science

Murphy (1938) traces the beginnings of western psychology to the revival of learning in Europe in the Renaissance leading to the Enlightenment in the eighteenth century. Descartes was influential in the seventeenth century utilizing the notion of 'animal spirits' within nerves, going on to postulate the fundamental difference between animals and human beings – 'animals were machines; their bodies controlled by physical laws' while humans were mechanically controlled but with an additional spirit or mind (p. 10). The Cartesian doctrine set in the seventeenth century is described by Ryle (1990) as the 'dogma of the Ghost in the Machine…that there exist both bodies and minds; that there occur physical processes and mental processes; that there are mechanical causes of corporeal movements and mental causes of cor-poreal movements' (p. 23). Later that century, Newtonian physics came on the scene. The natural world became a mechanical system to be manipulated and exploited; living organisms were seen as machines constructed from separate parts, each part being broken into further divisions. Finally, there emerged the view of mind as an objective 'thing' to be studied by objectified methods. Scientists, 'encouraged by their success in treating living organisms as machines, tend to believe that they are *nothing but* machines' (Capra, 1982, p. 47, italics in original). As a result of all this, the theory that underpinned the birth of western psychology and psychiatry – and still does so – is the Cartesian-Newtonian model of human functioning; it is this that drives the diagnostic approach and the illness model of mental health (Chapter 2). But it was not until the flowering of science in the Enlightenment of the eighteenth century that these two disciplines really took off.

Two points should be noted at this stage: In sixteenth and seventeenth century Europe, the term 'science' was not in use but the discourse we now identify as science was included within natural philosophy, and discussion of religion was within 'theology' (Outram, 2005). The discourses within what we now know as science and religion started to draw apart from the sixteenth century onwards – a separation that reached a peak in the Enlightenment of the eighteenth century.

Enlightenment values

The age of 'the Enlightenment' during the eighteenth century is also called the 'Age of Reason' (Barzun, 2000; Smith, 2008). In medicine, old methods of superstition were abandoned as science took over on foundations of rational thinking based on observation and analysis laid by Isaac Newton, rather than the deductive reasoning of seventeenth century (Smith, 2008). And, Cartesian dualism remained a fundamental tenet of medical discourse. Science began to replace religion as the main source of knowledge about the human condition – so much so that 'at the beginning of the century the most widely purchased books were theological; [but] by the end of the century they were fiction or popular science' (Outram, 2005, p. 107). Consequently, ideas that had been allied to religion, such as spirituality, were excluded from both psychiatry and western psychology as these disciplines developed 'scientific' approaches. So the model for mental states – the pathological ones indicating illness – was devoid of spiritual considerations.

The eighteenth century saw a blossoming of European arts and science and a philosophical discourse around ideas of individuality and freedom, including freedom of thought, leading finally to individual human rights – sometimes incorrectly and arrogantly referred to as 'European values'. The age of the Enlightenment was sometimes described as the 'age of the autonomous individual' (Roger, 1994, p. 72). Yet, what is sometimes forgotten or ignored is that Enlightenment values of freedom and justice came on stream at a time when the Atlantic slave trade was at its peak (Morrison, 1993; Patterson, 1982). In fact, the values articulated by major Enlightenment figures were riddled with racism (as discussed in Chapter 1).

The scientific paradigm

A scientific approach is implemented within what Kuhn (1962) calls a 'paradigm', meaning a system of beliefs and assumptions that determines fact-gathering within the science – 'the rules of the game' that are often implicit, rather than being clearly stated, more like shared beliefs (pp. 40–5). And the paradigm determines 'what constitutes useful and respectable data, what form theories [within the discipline] should take, what sort of language [the] scientists should use, how they go about their business' and so on (Ingleby, 1980, p. 25).

The main features of the paradigm within which western psychology and psychiatry developed is depicted in Table 3.2: (a) Positivism, the belief that reality is rooted only in what can be observed and knowledge limited to events and to empirically verifiable connections to events; this means ignoring everything prohibited by the existing 'reality' – 'that is everything that does not exist, but would under other conditions, be historically possible' (Martín-Baró, 1994, p. 21); (b) causality yielding a mechanical cause and effect model, implying that nothing is truly random and nothing beyond understanding (i.e., supernatural); (c) objectivism, where feelings become things 'out there' to be studied as objects, and moral judgements are not valid; and (d) rationality, where the final arbiter of truth is reason and all

Table 3.2   Scientific paradigm

Beliefs

Positivism
Reality is rooted only in what can be observed

Causality
Nothing occurs randomly
Natural causes for all events and effects

Objectivism
Feelings, thoughts etc. regarded as objects

Rationality
Reason superior to emotion
All assertions verifiable by logical proof

Approaches

Mechanistic
Newtonian physics as opposed to modern physics

Reductionist
Sum of the parts equals to whole

Logical reasoning
Intellectual exercise

assertions verifiable by logical reasoning. The methods of study promoted by scientific thinking were (a) the mechanistic approach of Newtonian physics; (b) reducing complex systems into its parts; and (c) intellectual, logical reasoning as opposed to any other type of understanding, such as intuition. It should be noted that modern science (the 'new physics') promotes a very different paradigm with Einstein's theory of relativity, Heisenberg's uncertainty principle, and chaos theory suggesting the importance of unpredictability (see Davies and Gribben, 1991).

Later influences

In the latter part of the nineteenth century, psychology in the western tradition became increasingly biological under the influence of Darwinism (Murphy, 1938): Francis Galton was foremost in applying 'the principles of variation, selection, and adaptation, to the study of human individuals and races' (p. 123). Hereditary factors were soon quoted for nearly every individual or group variation or difference, seen against a background of evolutionary advantage and survival of the fittest. Meanwhile psychiatry was seeing mental illnesses as physical entities. And with psychology espousing eugenics, mental illness was attributed to inborn defects that could not be corrected, tying in with Morel's concept of degeneration of the mid-nineteenth century (see below) and the developing science of genetics. By the 1920s, mental illness was firmly seen as a genetic problem, the (then) recently named 'schizophrenia' being the epitomy of genetic illness. By the middle of the twentieth century all mental disorders were firmly set as inborn conditions, which *ipso facto* (at that time) were not amenable to treatment.

Post-war scene in psychiatry

The medical viewpoint with a one-illness-one-cause approach based on a genetic medical-illness model dominated psychiatry in Europe until the Second World War (1939–45). In the early 1950s, there was a slight swing to empiricism – defining each illness in terms of observed phenomena, away from looking for a single cause towards the idea of multifactorial aetiology, especially for so-callled minor illnesses, neuroses. For example, Eysenck (1952) advocated that disorders should be classified on the basis of points on three dimensions, psychoticism, neuroticism and extraversion-introversion. Psychiatrists holding on to the concept of specific disorders found in-between diagnoses, like 'schizo-affective disorders' and 'borderline syndromes', appearing in their vocabulary. Attempts to preserve the one-diagnosis model when illnesses were not clear-cut have given rise to a hierarchy of importance in classification. Thus, for example, organic disorders, schizophrenia, manic depression, neurotic depression and anxiety states formed a hierarchy in which the diagnosis higher up on the list took precedence over the ones lower down (Wing, 1978).

In the 1960s there was a short period of optimism of 'cure' with the advent of seemingly effective drugs for mental illness. The idea of absolute genetic causation was threatened and a shift occurred into illness being seen as biomedical with merely genetic tendencies. But by the 1990s, when it became clear that the hope of cure by psychotropic medication was non-existent and the best to be hoped from drug therapy was symptom-control, the genetic part of the model returned. Today, although there is some doubt being expressed in psychiatric circles on the value of looking for putative biological mechanisms and genetic causes for mental illnesses (see Kingdom and Young, 2007), the general assumption within standard psychiatric practice is (to quote a response to the Kingdom and Young paper) that 'current clinical practice rests on a consensus that...[mental disorders] ... are primary biological diseases with strong genetic components and psychosocial factors that contribute to the disease process' (Pattanayak and Pattanayak, 2008). There is a lesson to be drawn from the fact that the last quotation is from two psychiatrists practising in India; the illness model originally developed in a western scientific paradigm is now being applied universally (see Chapter 7). With the power of the pharmaceutical industry behind it, twenty-first century psychiatry is dominated by a narrow biomedical model of illness to be treated (usually with the aim of symptom-control) by drugs or ECT with social and psychological interventions as adjuncts to drug therapy. Movements such as 'cultural psychiatry' or 'transcultural psychiatry' or even a 'critical psychiatry' exist but are marginal to the mainstream or merely terms used to sell the mainstream biomedical model to increasingly sceptical users of mental health services in the West. There is further discussion of post-war changes later when the place of psychiatry in British mental-heath service provision post-asylum is discussed.

Illness models compared

The illness model that dominates today in western psychology and psychiatry is the secular (non-spiritual) genetic-biomedical one where 'medical' implies a one-cause-one-illness approach with causation being entirely natural (rather than supernatural). This illness model differs from that in medieval Islamic medicine of a blending of spiritual with humoral-biological concepts (see above) and from that in Greek medicine where the humours are seen as less biological and not genetic. The illness model in the Ayurvedic tradition (considered in Chapter 8) is different from all three models considered here, being holistic and allowing a spiritual dimension within causation of all illness. An approximate comparison of the four illness models are given in Table 3.3.

Table 3.3   Illness models compared

Model	Location	Causation
Western medicine	Mind *or* body Individual	Genetic-biomedical Natural events
Islamic medicine	Mind *and* body Individual	Humoral-biological Blended with spirituality
Greek medicine	Mind *and* body Individual	Humoral Natural events
Ayurvedic medicine	Mind-body-spirit Holistic	Humoral-imbalance Spiritual influence

Western asylum movement and community care

Asylums that were founded in Europe during the fifteenth century were largely under religious (Christian), rather than medical, jurisdiction. However, it was in the early nineteenth century that the asylum movement really took off. Scull (1984) argues that 'the development of a capitalistic market system' resulted in a segregative response to madness leading to the building of large asylums in Britain; and similar movements occurred all over Europe and North America. The building of asylums for lunatics separated off the insane from the wider category of troublesome people and groups of people emerged as '"experts" in the control of various forms of deviance...[lending] an aura of objectivity to the process of rigidification of the various subcategories of deviance' (1984, p. 30). Psychiatry was given a base in society and psychiatrists given considerable power over their charges.

Each institution tended to develop its own classification. The first English textbook on psychiatry – *A Manual of Psychological Medicine* by John Bucknill and Daniel Hack Tuke – appeared in 1858. In 1885, the Congress of Mental Medicine in Antwerp appointed a committee to develop a uniform classification but without much success in having it accepted generally. Then, in the 1890s, Kraepelin (in Germany) described dementia praecox and manic depression in the sixth edition of his book *Psychiatrie: Lehrbuch fur Studirende und Artze* (Kraepelin, 1899). The former, which was renamed 'schizophrenia' in 1911 by Bleuler (1950), was underpinned by the concept of degeneration popularized by Morel (1852) – a matter described in detail elsewhere (Fernando, 1998). In the 1890s, Janet and Charcot in France popularized 'hysteria' as an illness; and in the 1920s, Freud developed the notion of hysteria as linked with anxiety. The concept of melancholia developed into that of depression after Meyer (1905) spoke against the use of the older term; depression was given a new impetus by Freud (1917) when he linked it to guilt, and the diagnosis of depression has soared in popularity ever since the 1960s when antidepressant medication was popularized.

Psychiatry in the USA developed in tandem with its European counterpart but was less hospital centred than it was in Europe, especially England, until the Second World War (Lewis, 1974). The first institution to care for the 'mentally ill' was a hospital, Pennsylvania Hospital in Philadelphia, which started to admit mentally disordered patients in 1752 and kept them in cells in different parts of the hospital. One of the first institutions specifically for the mentally disordered was the Bloomingdale Asylum in New York City that opened in 1821, although this, too, was linked to the New York Hospital. In the early part of the twentieth century, Southard 'developed the psychopathic hospital idea and also brought into the foreground the train-ing of social workers in psychiatry' (Lewis, 1974, p. 36). The influence of Freud was more strongly felt in psychiatric circles in the USA than it was in Europe, thus promoting the development of psychotherapy in that country and a psychoanalytic approach in psychiatric practice generally.

Practice in European asylums

Although the asylums established in the nineteenth century were mainly for custodial care, 'treatment' had to be given since the inmates were deemed 'ill'. Concepts of morality vied with those of active illness, usually on the model applied to infectious diseases. Both moral treatment and physical treatment went hand in hand, but the former 'threatened the status and very existence of physicians within asylums: if cures could be affected by nonmedical means, then the administrators of physic were reduced to mere custodians of the insane' (Cooter, 1981, p. 76). Gradually, moral therapy dropped away as a 'medical' approach began to dominate the scene towards the end of the nineteenth century. And the power of medical psychiatry as a social force developed rapidly in spite of rivalries between different groups of practitioners (Busfield, 1986). In England, the Association of Medical Officers of Asylums and Hospitals for the Insane was established in 1841, although even earlier, in 1811, the first chair of psychological medi-cine was established in Leipzig, Germany (Hunter and MacAlpine, 1963). The American Psychiatric Association – originally called the Association of Medical Superintendents of American Institutions for the Insane – was established in 1844 (Mora, 1961).

By the early twentieth century psychiatry was fully accepted as a medical discipline with the right to control and take decision on behalf of people given diagnoses. Psychiatrists had become the custodians of those people that society excluded from its mainstream as well as the 'alienists' who decided who was acceptable and who was alien to society. As the power and status of psychiatry were recognized, its practitioners were given legal functions with legally enforceable powers attached and psychiatry became an explicit part of the structure of social control in western societies (exported of course across the globe). Psychiatry is now seen by society as having the final word on the presence or absence of mental illness, but more importantly, society still looks to psychiatrists to carry out their traditional 'alienist' function by diagnosing not just illness but forms of behaviour – and the potential for behaviour – that are unacceptable to society. Thus psychiatrists are seen as experts in the prediction of dangerous behaviour, although the validity of doing so is questionable (Estroff and Zimmer, 1994; Steadman, 1983).

Post-war changes in service provision

In the 1950s and 1960s, British mental hospitals developed 'therapeutic community' approaches for inpatient care – for example, at Claybury Hospital near London (Shoenberg, 1972) and Dingleton Hospital in Scotland (Jones, 1968) – and crisis intervention was developed – for example, at Napsbury Hospital in St Albans (Scott, 1960) – by staff from asylums going into people's homes to consult together with patients and their families. Also, a service model, written up as the so-called Camberwell service model (Wing and Haley, 1972), promoted a view of people who develop 'mental illness' as suffering an acute illness followed by social handicap – acute treatment in hospital to be followed by rehabilitation, then resettlement with long-term supports for supposedly residual handicaps. This type of 'social psychiatry' accepted social factors as contributing to illness rather than causing illness which remained firmly genetic-biological in nature – very different to seeing illness as being socially constructed as described by Scheff (1966). Finally, the emptying of mental hospitals, de-institutionalization (Scull, 1984), started in the 1970s and accelerated in the 1980s and 1990s when the era of community care came into being. Drug therapy had little to do with de-institutionalization (Eisenberg, 2000; Scull, 1984), although it may have helped later, especially in persuading doctors that it was safe to allow patients to live in the community. One major advantage of community care is that a variety of professional staff are involved with people designated as mentally ill; this means that users of the services are open to a variety of influences and that the medical approach of treating their 'illness' does not always dominate their lives.

Today, in the first decade of the twenty-first century, whatever the location in which psychiatrists see patients, biomedical psychiatry continues to view mental health problems that are diagnosable as predominantly medical illnesses where the first line of treatment is drug therapy – but some diagnoses are seen as more 'medical' than others; conditions designated as psychosis, schizophrenia, manic depression (also called bipolar disorder or mood disorders) are definitely viewed as almost entirely genetic-biological while

Table 3.4   Culture of psychiatry

Cartesian mind-body dichotomy
Newtonian mechanistic view of life
Materialistic concept of mind
Reductionist approach to the individual
Problems constructed as illness
Natural causation of illness
Illness implies biomedical change

others, such as anxiety states, OCD, less so. The current tendency in Britain is to organize services as either generic community mental health teams or functionally specialized teams providing 'functional' interventions such as 'crisis intervention', 'home treatment', 'assertive outreach' and rehabilitation – or a mixture of approaches. However, something that is often not publicized is the emphasis on forensic psychiatry often hidden from public gaze with increasing numbers of people being held in virtual custody with little in the way of 'treatment' – in other words an exacerbation of the social control aspect of mental health services. Recent changes in mental health law in England and Wales (see Inyama, 2009) has strengthened this socio-political shift. In British practice, while community care encourages non-medical models of care to play a part and the new discourses in mental health described in Chapter 5 to be implemented, the narrow medical model of interventionist 'therapies' aimed at control – or no therapy at all just control – is being re-enforced in the forensic field, possibly covering over social issues of poverty, homelessness and racism (see Chapter 4).

Summary

The culture of psychiatry derived from historical processes, ideologies of the Enlightenment and the scientific paradigm are characterized by the items shown in Table 3.4. This biomedical psychiatry has obvious problems in terms of universal applicability but its links with western medicine and western power seem to be ensuring its spread through a form of imperialism (Chapter 7). The people of the world will be better served if some sort of amalgam between western psychology and psychiatry, on the one hand, and, on the other, non-western systems of psychology and healing comes about – matters discussed in Chapters 11 and 12.

Chapter 4

Racism in Psychiatry

When the basis of psychiatry was being laid down in the mid-nineteenth century, psychiatrists and psychologists, like others around them, had very definite ideas on which races were civilized and which were not. A paper published at the time in the *Journal of Mental Science*, which later became the *British Journal of Psychiatry*, by a former physician superintendent of Norfolk County Asylum (England) who was working in Turkey referred to that land as 'a country which forms the link between civilization and barbarism' (Foote, 1858, p. 444); in the same journal, another eminent British psychiatrist, Daniel H. Tuke (1858), denoted Eskimos, Chinese, Egyptians and American blacks as 'uncivilized' people, contrasting them with Europeans and American whites referred to as 'civilized' people, but with a grudging reference to China as 'in some respects decidedly civilized' (1858, p. 108). The description of Africans as 'child-like savages' by Arrah B. Evarts (1913, p. 393), a physician at the Government Hospital for the Insane in Washington, DC (USA), was typical of opinion among psychiatrists in the USA during the early twentieth century.

In the nineteenth century, Darwin's theory of evolution (1871) was used as a model for theories of human psychological development, and races were held to exist at different stages of development on a biological ladder of human evolution – so-called Social Darwinism. An important proponent of this phylogenetic concept of race, or 'evolutionary racism', Herbert Spencer, who incidentally coined the term 'survival of the fittest' (Fryer, 1984), suggested that 'to understand the minds of "primitive" races, "civilized" races should look at the minds of their own children' (pp. 179–80); and that social practices, such as 'monogamy had been developed only by the higher races' (Thomas and Sillen, 1972, p. 6). Nineteenth-century anthropologists contributed to the consensus by confining their work to people they called 'savages' encountered by European explorers and colonialists (Porter, 2004). Nineteenth-century sociologists 'assumed that when they were studying human society they were studying innate racial characteristics at the same time; white skin and "Anglo-Saxon" civilization were seen as the culmination of the evolutionary process' (Fryer, 1984, p. 179). Francis Galton (1869), a cousin of Charles Darwin and the founder of eugenics, claimed that the 'Negro race' included a large number 'of those whom we should call half-witted' (p. 339). The main thrust of the pseudo-science of eugenics was to identify 'inferior' races; and eminent people, such as Karl Pearson (1901), saw the extermination of such races as an inevitable part of the evolutionary process. The view that black people had inferior brains and/or defective personalities were commonplace in the nineteenth century and early part of the twentieth (see later); and these ideas were taken on board very easily and naturally by psychiatry and western psychology. Although overt racism has been less obvious since the Second World War, racism persists in the present in the common sense of traditional European thinking. Thus in British society today, pairs of words such as 'culture' and 'race', 'primitive' and 'underdeveloped', 'advanced' and 'western', 'alien' and 'inferior', and 'immigrant' and 'black' are often confounded or used purposefully to obscure racist contentions. Further, racial images are raised in references to 'muggers', 'inner-city decay', 'alien cultures', and most recently in the UK, 'terrorists'.

Mind and mental illness

Three distinct views about the mind of non-western peoples, usually identified in racial terms, were discernible during the development of psychiatry. In the mid-eighteenth century, Rousseau's concept of the 'Noble Savage' proposed the view that 'savages' who lacked the civilizing influence of western culture were free of mental disorder; later, in the late eighteenth and nineteenth centuries, Daniel Tuke (1858) and Maudsley (1867, 1879) in England, Esquirol (cited by Jarvis, 1852) in France and Rush (cited by Rosen, 1968) in the USA voiced similar views, expressed most firmly by J. C. Prichard (1835) in his *Treatise on Insanity*: 'In savage countries, I mean among such tribes as the negroes of Africa and the native Americans, insanity is stated by all…to be extremely rare' (p. 349). Lewis (1965) pointed out that a second, somewhat different, stance was also evident in Europe about that time, namely, the view that non-Europeans were mentally degenerate because they lacked western culture. A third viewpoint was voiced in the USA by psychiatrists arguing for the retention of slavery: Epidemiological studies based on the Sixth USA Census of 1840 (Anon., 1851) were used to justify a claim that the black person was relatively free of madness in a state of slavery, 'but becomes prey to mental disturbance when he is set free' (Thomas and Sillen, 1972, p. 16). The underlying supposition was that inherent mental inferiority of the African justified slavery. However, Benjamin Rush, the father of American psychiatry, refuted such arguments and maintained that the mental capacity of black people could not be evaluated while they were slaves because slavery affected their minds adversely (Plummer, 1970).

Although the 'Noble Savage' viewpoint idealized non-European culture in some ways and the 'degenerate primitive' attitude vilified it, both approaches sprang from the same source – a racist perception of culture which supposed that European culture alone, associated with white races, was 'civilized' and that cultures of black people were 'primitive' and inherently degenerate. American views determined by a warped perception of the lives of black Americans – or more correctly, determined by a need to justify slavery – had no room for cultural considerations at all; in fact an assumption that black Americans lacked a culture was implicit in the way these ideas developed. Almost into the twentieth century, Babcock (1895), a psychiatrist from South Carolina, was to use pro-slavery arguments to develop the theme that Africans were inherently incapable of coping with civilized life. In a paper, 'The Colored Insane', Babcock juxtaposed the idea that mental disease was 'almost unknown among savage tribes of Africa' with the alleged observations in the USA on the 'increase of insanity [among African Americans] since emancipation'; he quoted causes for this increase as the deleterious effect of freedom on 'sluggish and uncultivated brains' and 'the removal [during emancipation] of all healthy restraints', and forecast 'a constant accumulation of [black] lunatics' in the years to come (p. 423).

The underlying theoretical question addressed in the discussions about 'civilization' and mental disorder noted above was akin to the current discussion about the universality of schizophrenia – reviewed by Richard Warner (1985) and Fuller Torrey (1987). As then, the matter is currently confused by racism. Most cross-cultural studies in the first forty years of this century designated or perceived – and reported – non-western cultures as primitive cultures. Demerath (1942), reviewing a spate of such studies, observed that some of the non-western societies that had been studied 'were not truly primitive, but on the contrary were either traditionally literate, or had been exposed to Euro-American culture' (p. 705) thereby suggesting that not *all* non-Europeans were primitive since some had languages of their own or had become civilized by contact with Europeans. A review by Benedict and Jacks (1954) of studies on Maoris of New Zealand, indigenous Fijians, Hawaiians of the USA and people of so-called Negro Africa, was entitled *Mental Illness in Primitive Societies* – a review which, according to Torrey (1973), was largely responsible for the acceptance by mainstream psychiatry of the universality of schizophrenia as an illness.

From the mid-nineteenth century onwards, racist ideas were evident in many scientific theories. For example, the seminal paper by John Langdon Down (1866) claimed to have found physical characteristics of Malays, Ethiopians, Natives of America and Mongols, among so-called idiots and imbeciles in hospitals in South London, concluding that a 'very large number of congenital idiots are typical Mongols' (p. 16). German psychiatrist, Kraepelin (1913), claimed that people of Java seldom became depressed and that when they were depressed they rarely felt sinful. Kraepelin (1920) perceived the differences in terms of genetic and physical influences rather than cultural ones – a reflection, not only of the biological orientation in German psychiatry at the time, but also of the acceptance of racial explanations for cultural difference. In fact, Kraepelin (1921) saw the Javanese as 'a *psychically underdeveloped* population...[akin to]...*immature* European youth', and looked to ways of racial-cultural comparison as a method of scientific study (p. 171, italics in original).

Psychological and intellectual differences

The nineteenth-century anthropological and medical view that the brains of black people were inferior to those of white people was supported by dubious research. For example, even as late as early in the twentieth century Robert Bean (1906) claimed that in studying 103 brains from American Negroes and 49 white Americans he found that '[The] Negro is more objective and the Caucasian more subjective. The Negro has lower mental faculties (smell, sight, handcraftmanship, body-sense, melody) well developed, the Caucasian the higher (self-control, willpower, ethical and aesthetic senses and reason)' (p. 412). Significantly, reports that did not support the ethos of white superiority, such as the report that brains of Eskimos were larger than those of the average white person (Connolly, 1950), were ignored.

A racist ideology is evident in the development of modern psychology from the nineteenth century onwards. Francis Galton (1865) claimed that European 'civilized races' alone possessed the 'instinct of continuous steady labour' while non-European 'savages' showed an innate 'wild untameable restlessness' (p. 157). A classic text on adolescence written by Stanley Hall, the founder of the *American Journal of Psychology* published in 1904, had a chapter on 'Adolescent Races' in which the supposed psychological characteristics of Indians, Africans and North American 'Aborigines' were likened to those of immature children who 'live a life of feeling, emotion and impulse' (Hall, 1904, p. 80). The author of a standard textbook on social psychology, McDougall (1921), formulated the concept that different races produced different 'group minds'; Nordics showed a propensity for scientific work, Mediterraneans for architecture and oratory and, Negroes, an 'instinct for submission' (p. 119).

In *Totem and Taboo*, Freud (1913) saw similarities between 'the mental lives of savages and [European] neurotics' (title page); and he wrote of the 'great world-dominating nations of white race on whom the leadership of the human species has fallen' (Freud, 1915, p. 276). Freud merely reflected prevalent ideas of his time and it was Carl Jung who fancied himself as a specialist on black people since he had actually visited Asia and Africa. In 1939, Jung (1964) wrote that India was a 'dream-like world' where 'people carry on an apparently meaningless life...a gigantic monotony of endlessly repeated life' (pp. 516–7). On visiting the USA, Jung (1930) felt dissatisfied at being unable to 'size them up' – referring to the white population; he could not, at first, understand 'how the Americans descending from European stock have arrived at their striking peculiarities'. He focused on 'the Negro' as the cause. In postulating a psychological danger to white people of living in close proximity to blacks, Jung deduced the theory of 'racial infection': 'The inferior man exercises a tremendous pull upon civilized beings who are forced to live with him, because he fascinates the inferior layers of our psyche, which has lived through untold ages of similar conditions' (pp. 195–6).

After analysing Jung's writings, British psychotherapist Dalal (1988) concludes that Jung 'feared the black man...His error was in assuming that because the black symbolized the primitive to himself, therefore they were primitive' (p. 13). In a similar way, stereotypes in society could link up with personal fears and anxieties of modern-day therapists unless they take precautions to avoid this happening: 'Analysts [and other therapists], no less than their patients, imbibe the world view that is endemic to the society that they grow up in' (Dalal, 2002, p. 74).

The study of intelligence is another field with a long history of racism. Army data on cognitive test results gathered during the 1914–18 war led to a discussion of the reasons for racial differences in scores on intelligence tests (IQs) done in the USA; a 'racist IQ movement' that envisaged genetic inferiority of blacks in comparison to whites (Thomas and Sillen, 1972) developed, but died down after the horrors perpetrated by the Nazis in the name of race. But Arthur Jensen (1969), professor of educational psychology at the University of California, revived the argument with a paper in the *Harvard Educational Review* proposing that differences between blacks and whites on scores on IQ tests were genetically determined. Further, he postulated two categories of mental ability – abstract reasoning ability characteristic of white people and rote learning among blacks. Eysenck (1971, 1973) supported Jensen's views while he was professor of psychology at the Institute of Psychiatry (London), but other British psychologists (Kamin, 1974; Stott, 1983) opposed them as scientifically invalid. The racist tradition in studies of intelligence carried into the 1990s in books such as *The Bell Curve* (Herrnstein and Murray, 1994) and numerous publications by Rushton in the 1990s quoted by Howitt (1991) and Richards (1997). And to cap it all, in October 2007, James Watson, renowned scientist and Nobel Laureate, claimed in an interview to the *Sunday Times* newspaper published in London that black people were less intelligent than white people (Nugent, 2007).

Post-war psychiatry and psychology

A British colonial psychiatrist who achieved the distinction of producing a monograph for WHO, *The African Mind in Health and Disease*, was

J. C. Carothers. His first paper (Carothers, 1947) was an analysis of Africans admitted to a mental hospital in Kenya between 1939 and 1943. He proposed several explanations for the 'peculiarities' he observed: He deduced that 'the rarity of insanity in primitive life is due to the absence of problems in the social, sexual and economic spheres...[and that] ... the African may be less heavily loaded with deleterious genes than the European...[because]...nat-ural selection might be expected to eliminate the genes concerned more rapidly in a primitive community' (Carothers, 1947, pp. 586–7). After com-menting upon the lack of pressure on Africans because they (allegedly) had no long-term 'aims' in life, he deduced the reason for the apparent lack of depression among Africans: 'Perhaps the most striking difference between the European and African cultures is that the former demands self-reliance, personal responsibility, and initiative, whereas there is no place in the latter for such an attitude' (Carothers, 1947, p. 592).

Four years later, Carothers (1951) took his 'studies' further in order to devise tests for the selection of (what he called) 'reliable Africans' for work in medical laboratories (p. 25). He made some preliminary general observa-tions on (what he called) 'the neuro-physiological basis of African thinking and character': there was 'a striking resemblance between African thinking and that of leucotomized Europeans' (p. 12) – something he attributed to normal Africans under-using their frontal lobes.

Apart from the publications by Carothers, overt expression of racism has been rare in post-war psychiatric and psychological literature. But a theory that has been propagated over several years and even now in psychiatric textbooks is concerned with the 'differentiation of emotions'. The original study (Leff, 1973) from the Institute of Psychiatry in London used data collected for the International Pilot Study of Schizophrenia (IPSS) (WHO, 1973, 1975) on measures of anxiety and depression made by psychiatrists, supplemented by data on black Americans and white Americans from the USA-UK study (Cooper *et al.*, 1972). The conclusion arrived at by Leff (1973) was that '[people from] developed countries show a greater differ-entiation of emotional states than [do people from] developing countries' (p. 305), except for African Americans who resemble the latter. The racial undertones in Leff's initial presentations became more overt when he later presented his theory as representing an evolutionary process (Leff, 1981).

A basic fault in Leff's theory, when viewed in a global, multicultural con-text, is noted by O'Nell (1989): Leff derives his data from ethnocentric methods of assessment, mainly the psychiatric tool devised in Britain called the 'present state examination' (PSE) (Wing *et al.*, 1974); he uses culturally constructed concepts of emotional expression *cross-culturally*; and he takes a 'paternalistic and judgmental view of non-Western idioms for emotional distress' (O'Nell, 1989, p. 54). Lutz (1985) points out that the ability to differentiate emotions seems to centre on western concepts: 'Leff takes it as given that the goal of all peoples should be to distinguish depression as conceptualized by the British psychiatric community' (p. 90). Bebbington (1978), who, like Leff, was at the British Institute of Psychiatry at the time, concludes a review of the 'epidemiology of depressive disorder' by arguing for 'a provisional syndromal definition of depression as used by a consensus of Western psychiatrists against which cross-cultural anomalies can be tested', claiming that the World Health Organization supports this. In other words, the 'depression' of non-western peoples is hailed as an 'anomaly', and their emotional states as 'anomalies' (p. 303). It is not necessarily the racial prejudices of individual research workers but the pervasive influence of a racist ideology within which they carry out their work that is expressed in these theories and ideas. But what goes for depression goes also for other diagnoses.

Racism in diagnosis

The social construction of mental illness was shown up dramatically in the political abuses of psychiatry in the Soviet Union (Bloch and Reddaway, 1984) and the decision of the American Psychiatric Association in 1973 that homosexuality had ceased to be an 'illness' (Bayer, 1981). In both instances, political forces determined the nature of what constituted illness. Similarly, racist considerations are evident in the construction of two diagnostic categories reported in the USA at the time of slavery and described by Cartwright (1851) as peculiar to black people.

Dysaesthesia Aethiopis was described as a disease affecting both mind and body, with 'insensibility' of the skin and 'hebetude' of mind. Cartwright reckoned it to be commoner 'among free slaves living in clusters by themselves than among slaves in our plantations, and attacks only such slaves as live like free negroes in regard to diet, drinks, exercise, etc.', but stating his disinterest in treating the 'disease' among 'free negroes'. The symptoms were clear-cut:

> they break, waste, and destroy everything they handle – abuse horses and cattle, – tear, burn, or rend their clothing, and paying no attention to the rights of property, they steal from other's to replace what they have destroyed....They raise disturbances with their overseers and fellow servants without cause or motive, and seem to be insensible to pain when subject to punishment. (p. 321)

Cartwright argued against 'punishment' since 'the unfortunate individual...neither feels pain of any consequence, or shows any unusual resentment'; but proposed the application of oil to the skin 'all over...and to slap the oil in with a broad leather strap, and then put the patient to some hard kind of work in the open air' (pp. 322–3).

The second disease described by Cartwright was more straightforward – *Drapetomania* or the disease 'that induces the negro to run away from service'. After attributing the condition to 'treating them as equal' or frightening them by cruelty, Cartwright advocated a mixture of 'care, kindness, attention and humanity', with punishment 'if any one or more of them, at any time, are inclined to raise their heads to a level with their master or overseer...until they fall into that submissive state which was intended for them to occupy' (pp. 319–20).

The influence of ideological and political forces in determining diagnosis, and sometimes treatment, is not usually as obvious as it is in the four examples given above, namely, the illness contained in dissenting politically in the Soviet Union, the de-medicalization of homosexuality in the USA, the illness induced by freedom given to black slaves and the disease of running away that affected black slaves. The influence of racism in the social construction of commonly diagnosed categories of mental disorder is not always easy to discern. Political, social and ideological pressures current in society always impinge on the diagnostic process by influencing questions of intelligibility, common sense, clinical opinion, pragmatism and tradition. And racism acts through these pressures.

Psychiatric diagnoses carry their own special images which may connect up with other images derived from (say) common sense. Thus, alienness is linked to schizophrenia (as a diagnosis) and to racial inferiority (as a human type). The result may be an overdiagnosis of schizophrenia among black people who are seen as both 'alien' and 'inferior'. Similarly, if psychiatry is called upon to 'diagnose' dangerousness, common-sense images of dangerous people are taken on – and black people seen as excessively dangerous. In some situations, pragmatic considerations may promote the denial of illness if political influences encourage some types of behaviour to be ignored or punished. Racist images of the 'lazy black' may lead to the ignoring of self-neglect as indicative of illness among black people; the idea that blacks should not smoke cannabis, but do so, enters into the construction of the disease of 'cannabis psychosis' – a British diagnosis that was given in the 1980s almost exclusively to blacks (McGovern and Cope, 1987). In a context in Britain where public images, fostered by the media and police, associate race with drug abuse and attribute the anger of black youth to their use of cannabis, value judgements attached to drug abuse and the need to 'pathologize' the anger of black people seem to come together in this diagnosis. Diagnoses specific to groups of people identified racially may carry racism within them, when they are derived in a racist context. Racism implicated in so-called culture-bound syndromes is discussed in Chapter 2.

Depression is a diagnosis with social implications; Brown and Harris (1978) referred to it as occupying a 'pivotal position in the explanation of what is wrong with our society' (1978, p. 3). The history of its diagnosis reflects wider issues. The following comment by the clinical director of Georgia State Sanatorium (Green, 1914) about the apparent rarity of depression among blacks in the southern states of USA in the early part of the twentieth century is typical of the general views among psychiatrists at the time:

> It appears that the negro mind does not dwell upon unpleasant subjects; he is irresponsible, unthinking, easily aroused to happiness, and his unhappiness is transitory, disappearing as a child's when other interests attract his attention. ... Depression is rarely encountered even under circumstances in which a white person would be overwhelmed by it. (p. 703)

Carothers (1953) claimed that depression was rare among Africans in Africa because they lacked 'a sense of responsibility' (p. 148). Raymond Prince (1968), reviewing twenty-eight reports of depression among Africans between 1895 and 1964, found that a distinct change occurred in the diagnosis of depression among Africans around 1957 when Ghana became independent. He concluded that 'observing psychiatrists were being influenced in what they were able to diagnose by the prevailing climate of opinion at the time' (p. 186). In other words, the diagnosis of depression was biased by what we would now call institutional racism. It should be noted at this point, that depression is now frequently diagnosed among Africans in Africa – possibly as a consequence of the marketing of antidepressants.

In addition to the (racist) pressures arising from the context in which diagnoses are made, the diagnostic process is affected by racism at various points – during the recognition and evaluation of symptoms or psychopathology; in their assessment for the purpose of illness recognition; and in making the decision on the propriety of designating illness. For example, the failure to acknowledge racism as a real threat to black people may result in the designation of anger and fear as 'paranoia'; and the dismissal of culturally determined ways of emotional expression by a black person as an 'inferior' mode of expression may negate the value of 'symptoms' that are identified. Also, the context of the diagnostic interview itself may be significant: For example, in transactions between a black patient and a white professional, the former may be unwilling to divulge information because of the racist misperceptions (held by the latter) of his/her family life and culture, while the white professional may have very little knowledge of, or 'feeling' for, black lifestyles and attitudes. Indeed, the rapport between the participants of an interracial psychiatric interview may be totally disjointed in a racist context.

Post-war social and cultural studies

Although sociology had shown little interest in issues around racism in the early part of the twentieth century, social science studies after the Second

World War appeared to recognize the importance of doing so. A renowned study that focused on the effects of discrimination and social conditions on the personalities of black people was the book *The Mark of Oppression* by Kardiner and Ovesey (1951). The book was based on a psychodynamic assessment of twenty-five case records of black people considered against a background of the history of African Americans in American society. The authors argued that the original African culture of black people in America had been 'smashed, be it by design or accident' (p. 39); African Americans were seen as people living in a sort of cultural vacuum, their family life as disorganized and the dominance of African American women as disturbing family cohesion. The authors concluded that racial discrimination had resulted in a low self-esteem and self-hatred within the black personality, partly dealt with by being 'projected' as aggression and anxiety. 'There is not one personality trait of the Negro the source of which cannot be traced to his difficult living conditions. There are no exceptions to this rule....The final result is a wretched internal life' (p. 81).

A report by Moynihan (1965), which informed American social policy and also influenced the thinking of psychologists and sociologists, argued that the experience and deprivations of slavery had resulted in a matriarchal structure in African American families that is out of keeping with American society. The arguments themselves were based on a naive view of human development where negative experiences were assumed to lead to personality defects. Judgements about such matters as family cohesion or the role of women were deductions made from a white perspective assuming that white families and white people were the norm. A major failure of such approaches was not to recognize that oppression might uplift as well as depress self-worth and may promote as well as destroy communal cohesion. A sociological approach that transfers the focus of emphasis from the oppression – racist oppression in this case – to the oppressed inevitably has the effect of pathologizing and stigmatizing the oppressed.

American ideas about black families were transferred across the Atlantic to be represented in British research as negative images about African Caribbean and Asian families. The former were seen as having a family life that was weak and unstable, with lack of a sense of paternal responsibility towards children; and the latter as strong 'but the very strength of Asian culture...[was seen as] ... a source of both actual and potential weaknesses' (Lawrence, 1982, p. 118). The American 'Moynihan Report' (Moynihan, 1965) called the black American family 'a tangle of pathology'; in the UK, a Select Committee on Race Relations (1977) reported a connection between the problems of African Caribbean British families and family life in the Caribbean which was seen as unsuited to British society.

Fortunately, the decade beginning in the 1980s saw a shift away from the racist notions of the earlier years. This change resulted not from academic studies using scientific methods but from black people themselves striving for equality by political action – for example, in challenging police brutality and psychiatric racism – supplemented by writings of black and Asian authors on both sides of the Atlantic, such as (to mention a few) Stuart Hall (in Hall *et al.*, 1978), Paul Gilroy (1993), homi bhabha (1994), Edward Said (1994), bell hooks (1994) and Cornel West (1994). A review of their work and other relevant literature is beyond the scope of this section. The main lessons for the mental health field that come through are about the positive results of the struggles of black people during the many years of slavery; the richness and variety of black and Asian cultures that have developed in the UK and USA; the interaction and melding together of cultures; the changing nature of racism; the forging of new identities and ethnicities; and the struggles against racism. Unfortunately, mainstream psychiatry and psychology have so far failed on the whole to take on board the insights available in the progressive thinking that flooded the British and American scene at the end of the twentieth century.

Addressing racism in UK mental health services

In the late 1980s, the Mental Health Act Commission (MHAC), a government inspectorate, took up issues of race and culture at an official level through its reports (MHAC, 1987, 1991, 1993, 1995, 1997). Ground work done within some statutory organizations such as the Central Council for Education and Training of Social Workers (CCETSW) was significant at the time too (see Dominelli, 1988). The Transcultural Psychiatry Society (TCPS) highlighted racial injustices within British psychiatry and psychology in conferences held around the country (Fernando, 1988, 2003). Public consciousness was raised; government began to take notice; several health authorities appointed development workers in an effort to explore what needed to be done; some projects aimed at meeting needs of specific groups were developed within the National Health Service (NHS); and most importantly, black and Asian people began to get together to develop services for their own people outside the statutory mental health sector, often with government support (see Fernando, 2005a; Keating, 2002).

In the early 1990s, the government introduced ethnic monitoring of admissions to psychiatric institutes but its implementation was half-hearted. A government document, *Dialogue for Change* (Mental Health Task Force, 1994) noted the need for action to redress injustices in the mental health system affecting black and Asian people, but nothing much was done. Meanwhile, the ethnic scene in the workforce of statutory health services had changed considerably from that in the early 1980s. Black and Asian people were a visible presence in many levels of the health professions and management – although still relatively poorly represented in its higher echelons. In this context, the interest in race issues lapsed in the mid-1990s possibly because there was a feeling at governmental levels that having a fair number of black and Asian professionals in positions of influence represented 'change'. Yet, an official report into deaths of black people at Broadmoor Hospital (SHSA, 1993) highlighted racism as a major factor in the events leading to the deaths, recommending 'further research into the diagnosis of schizophrenia in Afro-Caribbeans...[and the monitoring of] patterns of diagnosis among minority ethnic groups in the special hospital system' (p. 52). The hospital authorities rejected the report and the Royal College of Psychiatrists failed to take up the challenge.

The advent of a Labour government in Britain in June 1997 raised the hopes of many people for positive action in redressing various injustices – not least issues around racism. Following the Macpherson report (Home Department, 1999) (see Chapter 1), many public bodies, including the Department of Health, instituted audits of institutional racism. A government commissioned report, '*Inside Outside*' (NIMHE, 2003), called for radical changes in the statutory services (the 'inside') together with work with BME communities and the voluntary sector (the 'outside'). Here, two issues that had never been directly pinpointed in an official report before then were highlighted: First, current mental health services being underpinned by models of illness, therapy and care are rooted in narrow western thinking – in other words are ethnocentric; and second, services had been designed with 'white people' alone in mind reflecting attitudes towards 'others' that are essentially racist – at least not designed to address racism.

The stage was set to work out an implementation plan for *Inside Outside* but instead, the Department of Health brought out a new document *Delivering Race Equality* ('DRE') (Department of Health, 2003) drawn up in a university department without any consultation with BME people. Although having 'race' in its title, the approach proposed was mainly to do with 'culture' (see Chapter 1 for definitions). The emphasis on changing statutory services was changed into one on collecting information; instead of 'community development' (as in *Inside Outside*) there appeared 'community engagement' and plans were outlined for more research projects. Meanwhile another inquiry concluded that institutional racism was to blame for some of the events leading to a violent death of a black patient (David Bennett) in a mental hospital (Norfolk, Suffolk and Cambridgeshire SHA, 2003). And a new version of DRE (Department of Health, 2005) came out repeating much of the earlier plan but adding a commitment to 'whole systems change' and a scheme to pilot changes in the statutory sector. During 2006 it seemed evident that DRE was hitting trouble (Fernando, 2006) and in early December 2006 the main author of DRE resigned his lead position, confirming an impression gaining ground at the time of writing (June 2009) that little change is likely to ensue in the statutory sector as a result of DRE.

Summary

What happens at the coal face of everyday psychiatric practice is characterized by: (a) The failure by most professionals in the mental health field, whatever their ethnicity, to allow for racial bias in practice and institutional racism in the delivery of services; (b) institutional practices, such as mental health assessments and risk assessments that are inherently institutionally racist being put through in a colour-blind fashion that does not allow for bias; (c) social pressures that apply differentially to people from BME communities not being picked up so that, for example, justified anger arising from racism in society is not taken into the equation when mental health assessments are made; (d) the sense of alienation felt by many people from BME communities being interpreted as a sign of illness – often seen as *their problem,* rather than a problem for society as a whole.

The net result of the problems outlined above is that a disease model (reflected in symptoms of illness) or criminal model (requiring control) – or both – is seen as the most appropriate response to many BME people presenting to the services, or brought into the service compulsorily. Institutional racism lies at the heart of a pattern in British society whereby there are three interconnected happenings: (a) disproportionate numbers of black men being compulsorily detained and diagnosed as 'schizophrenic' by the mental health system; (b) disproportionate numbers of black youngsters being subject to stop and search, arrest and then being charged, leading to magistrates and judges sending them to prison; (c) disproportionate numbers of black children being excluded from school. All this adds up to failures in three social systems, mental health, criminal justice and education, reflecting institutional racism in society as a whole (see Fernando, 2009).

Chapter 5

Changing Discourse in Mental Health

'Change' has been a popular cry in the political arenas of both the UK and USA since the mid-2008. However, there is doubt as to whether it is backed up by substance or even the political will. The pressure on psychiatry and style of mental health care in UK to change comes mainly from service users – or as they were called in the 1990s, survivors of the psychiatric system. But it also comes from sections of the general public, especially BME people – or more specifically black people, namely people from African and African Caribbean ethnicities, for the reasons evident in many of the chapters in this book, especially Chapter 7. Western psychology too catches some of the criticism but mainly at an academic level (see e.g., Parker *et al.*, 1995 and Parker, 2007).

This chapter discusses recent discourses that have achieved prominence in the mental health field – recovery, spirituality, values, well-being and resilience. Many of the ideas contained in these discourses seem to address problems located in psychiatry and a dissonance between lay people's lived experience – although not necessarily BME people – and the ethos concerning mental health promoted by this discipline.

Pressures on psychiatry

In a context of pressure to change, psychiatrists appear divided on what constitutes their territory and are ambivalent about using the power that they still possess in influencing national policies and, more importantly, delivery of services at grass roots. The *British Journal of Psychiatry* in its July 2008 issue had (a) an editorial claiming that 2008 is 'psychiatry's 200th birthday' because it seems a German first introduced the term 'psychiatry'– the ending 'iatry' being from the Greek meaning *iatros,* physician – to emphasize its place as a 'core medical discipline and not a philosophical or theological one' (Marneros, 2008, p. 1); and (b) an article titled 'Wake-up call for British Psychiatry' signed by thirty-seven well-known psychiatrists arguing that 'British psychiatry faces an identity crisis' because of the downgrading of 'diagnostic assessment with formulation of aetiology, diagnosis and prognosis followed by specific treatments aimed at recovery' (Craddock *et al.*, 2008, p. 6).

Many books on general themes calling for change in psychiatric practice look to replacing the 'medical approach' with the 'psychosocial' – for example, in *Mental Health at the Crossroads* by Shulamit Ramon and Janet Williams (editors) (2005) and *Social Perspectives in Mental Health* by Jerry Tew (editor) (2005). Problems with the diagnosis of 'schizophrenia' have been repeatedly highlighted for over two decades (Bentall, 1990; Boyle, 1990; Fernando, 1988), reiterated recently (Bentall, 2003; Boyle, 2002; Fernando, 2003) and a Campaign to Abolish the Schizophrenia Label ('CASL') has been launched (see BBC News, 2008). The need for radical changes in the statutory services, implying change in psychiatric theory and practice, was most recently voiced in an official report *'Inside Outside'* (NIMHE, 2003) referred to in Chapter 4.

In responding to pressures for change in psychiatric practice, the Royal College of Psychiatrists (2008) published *Fair Deal,* a document outlining eight priority areas for specific campaigns: 'Funding, access to services, inpatient services, recovery and rehabilitation, discrimination and stigma, engagement with service users and carers, availability of psychological therapies and linking physical and mental health' (p. 5). Although far from showing much appreciation of the extent of criticism of psychiatric practice itself, the document is a welcome change from the extreme conservatism that the College has shown in the past.

Recovery

The model being promoted currently (June, 2009) in the UK as 'recovery' was imported from the USA via New Zealand. It came out of service-user movements, sometimes called survivor or consumer movements outside the UK, and represents a significant move for people who used to be called 'patients' from focusing on survival of the psychiatric system to actually being full human beings (Sayce and Perkins, 2000). Recovery subsumes the pursuit of personal goals of hope, making sense of experiences, understanding and empowerment (Repper and Perkins, 2003) – a sort of journey to regaining a sense of purpose and self after a major life disruption (Kloos, 2005). Rachel Perkins (2005), a service user and professional, believes that hope is central to the recovery approach: 'It is not possible to rebuild your life if you do not believe that a better future is possible or if everywhere you turn you are debarred from doing the things that give your life meaning and value' (p. 119).

Unfortunately, this new imaginative approach has come up against a meaning of recovery that is well established in the medical literature, although it had got somewhat lost in psychiatry. In fact, 'recovery' has been integral to the medical model of illness from time immemorial, the aim of medical treatment being either rapid 'cure' or the promotion of recovery, meaning a gradual return to some sort of 'normality' (Pearsall and Trumble, 1995), usually through control of symptoms and rehabilitation. So, in effect, currently there are two definitions of recovery in the public discourse on mental health (Schrank and Slade, 2007) – the psychiatric one of the long-term goal of remission of symptoms (Andreasen *et al.*, 2005) or the pursuit of personal goals as described above, irrespective of the illness label.

Recovery as a medical concept

The theme chosen for the Annual Meeting of the Royal College of Psychiatrists in 2007 was 'recovery'; many sessions at the meeting had the word in its title although few actually addressed the approach as put forward by service users. A recent book with a variety of chapters on psychiatric rehabilitation (Roberts *et al.*, 2006) published by Gaskell, an imprint of the Royal College of Psychiatrists, is actually titled *Enabling Recovery* and subtitled *The Principles and Practice of Rehabilitation*. Although admittedly some of the chapters by service users express the ideas from the recovery approach devised by service users, others give serious cause for concern – for example, when early intervention (Power *et al.*, 2006) and medication management (Sweeting, 2006) are presented as necessary parts of the recovery approach being promoted by the book.

Recovery, race and culture

So far, the recovery approach has not been exposed to transcultural examination or to evaluation in a context of power politics and institutional racism in mental health systems – at least not in a British context. The closest to such an examination was work done by Social Perspectives Network (SPN) in conducting focus groups of BME service users to talk about recovery and then holding a study day on the topic (SPN, 2007).

   In a multicultural context of British society with a mental health system that is dominated by biomedical psychiatry, a danger of not considering cultural diversity is that the recovery journey (as put forward by service users) may mimic the reductionist approach of western medicine – so-called scientific thought. What could easily happen is that recovery gets divided into recovery of different, separate aspects of a person; ignores issues of social pressures that arise from limitations for progress in society at large; and fails to address problems of occupation and employment, especially those that result from racial, ethnic and cultural prejudice and social exclusion as racialized 'other'.

   The focus so far in the recovery approach has been on personal journeys, and on emphasizing individuality as the centre of the human condition – very much a part of western culture that gave rise to western psychology and bio-medical psychiatry (see Chapter 3). This emphasis does not connect with people from non-western cultural backgrounds where communality, rather than indi-viduality, may be emphasized. In the world of twenty-first-century Britain, the reality for many black service users is being stuck in the system with heavy diagnoses and 'sectioning' (compulsory detention) as dangerous people; their journey from darkness into light (as the recovery approach envisages), if it ever takes place, entails circumventing or overcoming many barriers of a social and political nature where family, religion and community are important. It is not just a limited *personal* journey that they have to make in becoming real people again. The journey for them is as much *social* as personal. A danger, too, in an individualized approach to recovery is that it may feed into the psychiatric model of 'recovery' from a personal illness usually through some intervention or therapy, rather than a model of finding a way through complicated and dif-ficult life situations that involve social systems and relationships.

Finally there is the issue of racism. For black people and others who are involved in a struggle against racism, not just in the mental health system but in many other aspects of life – judicial, educational and employment – the social journey has strong *political* dimensions. And black people can only take their political/social/personal journeys if allowed to do so by society at large or, more likely, if they manage to seize their own freedom from society at large. The barriers are real ones: mental health law in England and Wales has recently been tightened against them (see Inyama, 2009); attitudes in society often block their progress; and most professionals, black and white, connive in denying the impact of racism in the mental health system as shown in an article by the National Director of Mental Health in England, Louis Appleby (2008). In such a context, recovery seems far too mild a word to encompass a black person's journey towards a respectable and ful-filling life. Discussions at a workshop facilitated by Kinouani *et al.* (2007) at the SPN study-day referred to earlier indicate that black Caribbean service users have reservations about using the word 'recovery' because of what they perceive as implicit biological and Eurocentric assumptions; and they envisage various problems with the recovery approach, such as its failure to foster cultural pride and address the racism that they suffer from. Unless it is changed substantially, the recovery discourse may well exclude many BME people caught up in mental health services.

Future of the recovery approach

The publication, *A Common Purpose: Recovery in Future Mental Health Services* (CSIP, RCPsych, SCIE, 2007) gives official UK backing to the recov-ery approach but has distorted some important aspects of the approach put forward by service users, especially in connection with the use of medication.

According to May (2008), the report avoids putting service user's views at the heart of the approach and repeatedly defends established medical treatments. Clearly, the Royal College of Psychiatrists got their way in preparing the document. Kalathil (2007), who kept notes on a workshop at a study-day conducted by SPN, reports that Jerry Tew, an academic and former social worker, believes that recovery is being 'appropriated by mental health professionals and re-articulated in the form of models that many people feel disempower service users' (p. 39).

The apparent tussle over the interpretation of 'recovery' between the service-user movement and the psychiatric establishment in the UK should be seen in the context of a subtle power struggle that appears to be taking in the British mental health scene; on the one hand there is the professional systemic power of the medical establishment, allied to economic interest of capital mainly via the pharmaceutical industry and, on the other the voice of service users allied to sociological critiques of the medical model and libertarians. People complaining of racism and cultural problems in delivery of services appear as a third dimension in this struggle; it is often difficult to determine where exactly they are placed – they are largely excluded from official debates on recovery. The word 'recovery' may be one of the battle-grounds for this power struggle, although still at a level of discourse rather than its practical effect on service provision. The indication at present (June 2009) is that the medical establishment is winning as far as the recovery model is concerned. This view is strengthened by the fact that the report by the Healthcare Commission (HCC, 2008) on inpatient psychiatric services – where the emphasis is nearly always on medication – is actually titled *The Pathway to Recovery.*

Spirituality

One of the main criticisms from a cultural viewpoint made by service users is that biomedical psychiatry and western psychology lack a sense of spirituality. Chapter 3 shows how western psychology and psychiatry developed within a paradigm that had no place for spirituality – and that is the situation currently. In the classic book *Zen Buddhism and Psychoanalysis*, Erich Fromm (Fromm *et al.*, 1960) proposes that psychoanalysis emerged in the late nineteenth and early twentieth centuries as an attempt in European thinking to find a solution to what Fromm calls 'Western man's spiritual crisis' (1960, p. 80) – a crisis attributed by Fromm to Europe's 'abandonment of theistic ideas in the nineteenth century' with 'a big plunge into objectivity' (p. 79). Cultures in Asia and Africa did not undergo this change and, although undoubtedly influenced later by western ideas, they appear to have maintained a spiritual dimension to their thinking in many ways until the present. Perhaps, Asian, African and pre-Columbian cultural traditions (see Chapter 2) still carry spirituality as central to human experience – and this 'spirituality' is different to belief or cognition or emotional state.

A Spirituality and Mental Health Project was started by the National Institute for Mental Health in England (NIMHE) in 2003 (NIMHE/MMF, 2003). Peter Gilbert (2007), who led the project at NIMHE, sees the central features of spirituality itself as meaning, value, transcendence, connecting, and becoming; and suggests that 'to gain a sense of wholeness' (which he seems to see as the crux of spirituality) individuals 'need to relate to themselves, other people, the practical world around them, and a sense of the Other, which may for many people be God or gods' (p. 25). On the whole, much of the recent writing on spirituality and health, for example, by Cornah (2006), Gilbert (2007) and Nicholls (2007) does not consider practical issues of application in mental health service provision, nor does it connect with broader cultural dimensions of spirituality in UK today.

The desire to include spirituality in mental health service provision is understandable. However, going down the road of clear-cut definition, with training programmes and action plans for its incorporation into, for example, psychotherapy or nursing practice, could easily lead to a sort of packaging of spirituality that loses its sense; this may well make it into a saleable product for a consumerist society but at the risk of losing its meaning. The danger in other words is of commodification. 'There is no view from nowhere – no Archimedian point outside of history – from which one could determine a fixed and universal meaning for the term "spirituality"' (Carrette and King, 2005, p. 3).

The negative consequences of commodification are evident, for example, in the USA where 'prosperity religions' are a thriving business pandering to New Age enthusiasts (Carrette and King, 2005). Even in India where spirituality still has a deep and sustainable meaning for many people, commodification driven by market forces has led to problems: The police in the state of Kerala have been investigating numerous 'godmen', backed up by business syndicates, donning 'spirituality' to exploit uneducated rural people (Mathew, 2008).

Culture

The search for knowledge, the seeking after an understanding of the human condition, the yearning for knowing the 'truth', all this characterizes human societies the world over. But ways in which societies and individuals have gone about this search are diverse – representing the diversity of cultures themselves.

The majority of people who suffer from mental health problems through-out the world, unless they come into contact with western-trained psych-iatrists or psychologists, are treated by so-called folk healers or other indigenous practitioners. These people are guided by traditional wisdom that sees illness as a disorder of the whole person who is not divided into body and mind and is in close relation to the cosmos and the deities (Capra, 1982). And in many traditions across the world, spirituality is woven into everyday life and is very much a part of what is understood as mental health (see Chapter 8). The best cross-cultural approach to understanding spiritu-ality is to try and comprehend how people – ordinary people – seem to work spirituality into their lives.

In the worldview of many first nations (Natives) of North America, every-thing has a *spirit* or energy. One's own spirit connects with the 'unseen' world inhabited by spirits (or 'energies'); so, breaking of taboos results in 'being out of balance' with the spirits and restitution of balance comes from appeasing the spirits through medicine or magic (Freke and Wa'Nee'Che, 1996, pp. 68–70). In developing a similar theme, the 'I and I' principle of the Rastafarians 'expresses the oneness between two persons' (Cashmore, 1979, p. 135), the personal and the 'other' being (as it were) *the same*, connected spiritually – the expression perhaps of a community spirit that comes from belonging to a faith community. This may relate to what Du Bois (1970) called 'spiritual striving' as a cultural ideal of black (African) Americans – not an impediment but often a strength.

In the Vedantic (Hindu) tradition of the Indian subcontinent, there is 'no dualism of the natural and the supernatural...the spiritual is an emergent of the natural and is rooted in it' (Radhakrishnan, 1980, p. 88). In eastern Sri Lanka, Hindu goddess cults represented by oracles empowered through possession by spirits are known to provide spiritual healing for people traumatized by war (Lawrence, 2000). In Theravada Buddhism, spiritual life is about cultivation of serenity and moving from ignorance to wisdom where one comes to understand impermanence, suffering and the realiza-tion of 'self' as illusion (Pande, 1995). Although essentially an atheist or agnostic religion, in practice, Buddhism is associated with a rich cosmol-ogy that includes a world of non-material beings (spirits); and many gods and demons, like humans, inhabit the cosmos, granting favours, punishing, acquiring merit and interacting with each other and with humans through intermediaries (Gombrich and Obeyesekere, 1988).

What we can conclude from exploring spirituality and mental health across cultures is that certain themes crop up in many traditions. First the importance of a sense of connectedness – to one another (community spirit), to a land or environment (an ecological spirit), to the cosmos or (what some religions call) 'God' or a pantheon of gods, demons and such-like. Second, spirituality is not a solitary, self-centred, *selfish* feeling but one harboured in religion and community. Third, although spirituality is not necessarily the same as adherence to an organized religion with a specific dogma interpreted by a hierarchy, 'being religious' and 'being spiritual' are similar and may well be identical sometimes. Fourth, in some cultural traditions, contact with the spirit world or 'spirits' as non-physical beings with human characteristics is important – resembling aspects of western psychological theories of 'forces' exerted by unseen entities such as the 'ego' or 'id'. Clearly, when particular entities are identified as 'spirits' they have a profound meaning to both individuals and communities, and communication with these spirits (e.g., during séances or possession states) is bound up with the sense of connectedness that characterizes spirituality in a wider sense.

Conclusions

The major question from considering cultural diversity in relation to spirituality is whether – and if so how – spirituality may influence, or better still permeate, western psychology and psychiatry. What seems clear is that the significance of spirituality in any society comes from its religion-culture-community base. Western psychology excluded spirituality a long time ago and so did psychiatry (Chapter 3). Bringing it back as a sort of add-on – and this may well be the aim of the NIMHE project – is likely to be at best a marketing ploy that may bring people into the psychiatric fold but at the cost of disillusionment, at least in the case of people from non-western cultural background; at worst, adding spirituality on to the current biomedical model of psychiatry will debase the meaning of spirituality as understood in most – perhaps all – cultures. However, that is not to say that there is a great deal to gain for most people from an improved sense of being human *spiritually*, from exploring spirituality for themselves, perhaps each according to their own backgrounds and inclinations. However, if western psychology were to shift fundamentally, especially in broadening its base to become informed by a variety of cultures, and, to some extent at least, undergo a paradigm shift, it could well become a *spiritual* psychology and promote a psychiatry that is very different to the present-day discipline.

Values

The discourse on values in mental health practice developed from academic writing in philosophy and bioethics (see e.g., Fulford, *et al.*, 2002). A values-based approach to mental health care was taken up in England and Wales by NIMHE when it launched a 'Values Project Group' with ministerial announcement in 2001; the net result was the NIMHE's principles for values-based practice (VBP) (Table 5.1) and training on what is claimed to be a new

Table 5.1   NIMHE principles for values-based practice

1. Recognition – NIMHE recognizes the role of values alongside evidence in all areas of mental health policy and practice.
2. Raising awareness – NIMHE is committed to raising awareness of the values involved in different contexts, the role/s they play and their impact on practice in mental health.
3. Respect – NIMHE respects diversity of values and will support ways of working with such diversity that makes the principle of service-user centrality a unifying focus for practice. This means that the values of each individual service user/client and their communities must be the starting point and key determinant for all actions by professionals.

Respect for diversity of values encompasses a number of specific policies and principles concerned with equality of citizenship. In particular, it is anti-discriminatory because discrimination in all its forms is intolerant of diversity. Thus, respect for diversity of values has the consequence that it is unacceptable (and unlawful in some instances) to discriminate on grounds such as gender, sexual orientation, class, age, abilities, religion, race, culture or language.

Source: Adapted from Woodbridge and Fulford, 2004.

Table 5.2   Ten essential shared capabilities

Working in partnership
Respecting diversity
Practising ethically
Challenging inequality
Promoting recovery
Identifying people's needs and strengths
Providing service-user centred care
Making difference
Promoting safety and positive risk taking
Personal development and learning

Source: NIMHE, SCMH, NHSU, 2004.

approach (Woodbridge and Fulford, 2004). Apart from emphasizing the principles of recognition of values, raising awareness of values and respect for diversity, the NIMHE Framework mentions user-centredness, recovery orientation and multidisciplinary work as aspects of its framework which it claims to be associated with attitudes that are 'dynamic, reflective, balanced and relational' (Fulford *et al.*, 2006, p. 524). NIMHE, with other organizations, used values-based thinking to develop the 'Ten Essential Shared Capabilities' (NIMHE, SCMH and NHSU, 2004), aiming to set the standard for competencies that training should develop in the mental health workforce (Table 5.2).

Clearly, there is little to criticize in the Ten Essential Shared Capabilities if this is what values-based practice is all about. The questions are whether the systems that are in place within mental health, especially biomedical psychiatry, will be affected to any extent by these 'capabilities' and whether the workforce can in fact deliver on the competencies in the current setup.

Race and culture

Cultural diversity of values held by people is a topic too complex to address here; suffice to say that value systems that affect people may be considered at various points on a continuum: From those that form the fundamental philosophies of life and the universe at one end to, at the other, values that determine day-to-day decisions that people take. It is noteworthy that the academic discourse out of which ideas about values in mental health work arose was entirely in a western cultural context. For instance, there is no input from Indian or African philosophies about life or mental health. Ethics too is seen in a west European context, largely that arising from ideas of the Enlightenment (Chapter 3). For example, the concept of human rights that permeates European thinking is largely determined by its Enlightenment emphasis on the individual, rather than community; and of course racism does not enter very much into the equation since, if anything, it was re-enforced during the Enlightenment (Chapter 3).

Certain values come down through traditions to underpin the way mental health is seen and services are organized; and these values determine what is held to be normal or abnormal in thinking, believing and feeling – the base on which western psychology and biomedical psychiatry are built upon. So when the society that western psychology and psychiatry finds itself confronting today in UK is multicultural, in being composed of people from many different cultural and religious backgrounds, clash of values is inevitable both at a fundamental level – for example, about the importance of individuality, self-esteem, the supernatural and spirituality – and at a level of day-to-day values, for example, about sexual mores, food taboos and gender differences. A values-based approach taught from a point of view of western ethics is very likely to be blind to the cultural diversity of British society, not to speak of the dimension of racism that western ethics is unlikely to address anyway. In other words, values thinking that comes from a mainly European cultural setting may not address much of what is important for people from other cultural backgrounds, although admittedly there are commonalities across cultures; but sets of values such as the ten essential shared capabilities though welcome should be merely a start to a much longer and broader – and perhaps very difficult – discussion, the discussion about racism in particular.

Future of values-based practice

The book by Fulford *et al.* (2006) includes a training manual for VBP. Clearly, what is envisaged is a fundamental reappraisal of the psychiatric system not unlike some of the suggestions evident in this book – except that race and culture are unlikely to be addressed. The problems and limitations of the VBP approach may arise from its strategy of dealing with particular parts of the psychiatric system in isolation. Fulford *et al.* (2006) suggest that practice must be both evidence based and values based and they urge the need to address 'patient's values' in coming to a diagnosis: 'If values operative in psychiatry are diverse – that is, they vary from person to person, from culture to culture, and from time to time – and values come into diagnosis, then it is clear that coming to an understanding of the values of individual patients should be part of the process of diagnostic assessment'. While admitting that this is easier said than done and that there are fundamental issues such as the lack of validity of psychiatric diagnoses that are in common use, there is little indication on how a values-based approach could affect current practice at all; the authors fall back on 'this is an area in which research is urgently needed' while suggesting approaches such as 'good communication, balance of evaluative perspectives, a culture (and gender) de-centred approach' (pp. 597–8).

It was argued in Chapter 2, in discussing the way diagnoses are arrived at in the psychiatric system, that the prelude to making a diagnosis is an 'evaluation' – a process of setting what is 'observed' about a patient against values set down within psychiatry about feelings, behaviour and beliefs. Values embedded in the psychiatric system cannot easily be shifted without abandoning the system altogether. Hence, any changes in the values reflected in diagnosis that may be made as a result of VBP could not be any more than marginal to the diagnostic system that is part and parcel of psychiatry. Therefore, VBP cannot possibly shift psychiatry towards being multicultural and certainly cannot address racism. In any case, given the power wielded by the diagnostic system of biomedical psychiatry, the likelihood of VBP getting beyond the level of discourse is remote.

Well-being

The discourse on well-being in connection with mental health comes from several sources: From the field of mental health promotion (HEA, 1997) often carried out under the aegis of community health (Watt and Rodmell, 1993) and/or that of psychosocial care (Ramon, 2005); from community psychology (Buunk and Gibbons, 1994; Diener, 1984; Nelson and Prilleltensky, 2005); and from development studies (see Chambers 1992, 1997). In fact in all instances it has emerged from a dissatisfaction with medical dominance of the mental health discourse and service provision and a search for ways of studying and evaluating people's lives from their own perspectives rather than imposed models of health and illness – in other words, to understand people's needs in the mental sphere bottom-up, starting with people themselves, rather than theories about them.

Well-being has been used in the past decade as an approach to accessing the meaning attributed to mental health. The well-being approach is justified on the grounds that it is very different to assessments of mental health by so-called experts who base their knowledge on academic discourse, theories of 'mind', social constructions of 'pathology' and 'normality', and so on. It is claimed that well-being (a) is based on standards and values chosen by people themselves; (b) reflects success or failure in achieving norms and values that people themselves seek; and (c) includes components 'dependent on pleasure and the fulfillment of basic human needs, but also includes people's ethical and evaluative judgments of their lives' (Diener and Suh, 2000, p. 4). At a personal level, well-being – sometimes called 'subjective well-being' (SWB) (Diener, 1984, 2000) – is a positive state of affairs brought about by satisfaction of personal, relational and collective needs (Prilleltensky *et al.*, 2001). When community perceptions of well-being are accessed in community psychology and development studies, these individual components are added to by 'the synergy created by all of them [i.e., personal, relational and collective needs] together' (Nelson and Prilleltensky, 2005, p. 56).

A group of research methods used in development studies in Asia were brought together by Robert Chambers as 'Participatory Rural Appraisal' (PRA) and 'Rapid Rural Appraisal' (RRA) discussed in his classic book *Whose Reality Counts? Putting the First Last* (Chambers, 1997). On well-being Chambers (1997) writes:

> *The objective of development is well-being for all.* Well-being can be described as the experience of good quality of life. Well-being and its opposite ill-being differ from wealth and poverty. Well-being and ill-being are words with equivalents in many languages. Unlike wealth, well-being is open to the whole range of human experience, social, mental and spiritual as well as material. (pp. 9–10, italics in original)

Well-being as defined by people themselves is one of the central constructs in PRA research that takes as its starting point the personal realities of individuals, investigated by participatory methods that are community based. Approaching well-being from a social science perspective connects with well-being initially seen from a psychological perspective (see above) to feed into a concept that may prove useful as an adjunct to the concept of mental health or even as an alternative to it: For example, well-being has been successfully used in a study using PRA methodology in Sri Lanka

(Weerackody and Fernando, 2008, 2009); in that study, well-being was used to access a holistic approach to mental health seen as 'denoting material advancement, social aspirations, sense of security, and health seen as physical, mental and moral dimensions ... [covering both] subjective feelings and external circumstances' experienced as a 'whole' – 'holistically' – and not as separate 'factors' (Weerackody and Fernando, 2008, p. 55). The authors have gone on from that study to propose a model for developing community mental health in Sri Lanka (Weerackody and Fernando, 2009).

Culture and race

One of the problems in using well-being as a concept for research leading to service provision arises from differences in how well-being is conceptualized in different cultural settings and social contexts. Black people when compared with white people living in a racist society may have very different ideas about what is important for well-being. Similarly, poor people may differ from rich people in how they view well-being. It has been found that people from collectivist cultures tend to base their judgements of well-being on mainly external factors (such as roles and obligations to family and society) rather than individual inner experience, while those from individualistic societies tend to look to personal emotions, that is private inner experience, rather than external factors (Suh, 2000). Also there are issues arising from socioculturally determined ways in which well-being may be conceptualized. Differences in well-being may well relate to what people value and this may vary in relation to importance given to material prosperity, spiritual development and family connections (see Diener and Oishi, 2000) – and moreover social background may play a part in this too. So well-being should not be seen as an ostensibly objective measure comparing societies or even individuals, although it could be a good guide to a sort of consensus view of how people in a community view their quality of life.

Future of well-being discourse

A publication for the Scottish Executive states: 'The definition of mental health as a "positive sense of well-being" challenges the idea that mental health is the opposite of mental illness' (Myers *et al.*, 2005, p. 18). In the UK, well-being is often used in conjunction with mental health as 'mental health and wellbeing', for example, in a report issued by the NIMHE (2005), *Making It Possible: Improving Mental Health and Well-Being*. In this document, the term well-being is used to emphasize a personal responsibility on people themselves to look after their own mental health by lifestyle changes, diet and so on; 'mental health' itself is seen in a traditional psychiatric sense of absence of mental illness while 'well-being' covers everything else. Another official document authored by Lane (2007) for Care Services Improvement Partnership (CSIP) takes the same approach about 'mental health and well-being' of black and minority ethnic elders. In other words, the discourse on well-being in Britain is not very far from traditional ways of seeing mental health and illness.

But the well-being discourse is more advanced in other places, and may be getting close to being equated to mental health, in situations where the traditional western concept (of mental health) is obviously problematic for communities trying to develop their own services. Well-being may turn out to supersede mental health as a concept with universal relevance; it certainly has the advantage in being successfully used in development studies in third world countries (see above) and, together with the word 'ill-being' 'are words with equivalents in many languages' (Chambers, 1997, p. 9). So the message from community psychology and development studies is that the term 'well-being' shifts the notion of mental heath from avoidance of designating inherent illness to one that sees human experience holistically; from prevention of illness to promotion of health. Well-being as a discourse appears to offer a way forward in addressing race and culture in mental health so long as the meaning given to it in community psychology and development studies is maintained.

Resilience

The approach implicit in the western medical model (Chapter 2) that informs biomedical psychiatry is overwhelmingly deficit-focused. Initially, deficits were sought in individuals who were attributed with (psychological) 'pathology' in their psyches resulting from genetic predisposition, their personalities and cognitive styles; then attributions were broadened to include life styles, relationships and families. For example, in the 1970s, the fashion to blame dysfunctional families and social systems for causing mental pathology was evident in movements such as the so-called anti-psychiatry movement (see Laing, 1967; Laing and Esterson, 1964); now (June 2009) well into the twenty-first century and influenced strongly by the power of the pharmaceutical industry, blame is placed firmly on brain chemistry as well as genetic predisposition.

The conventional wisdom today is that trauma, adverse experiences, some noxious influences and so on – or all of these 'factors' acting together – damage people who are vulnerable because of their genetic predisposition, giving rise to emotional problems sooner or later. And that the effects of these factors are manifested via disturbance of brain chemistry. The concept of personal resilience challenges this approach fundamentally by stating that when faced with adversity, trauma, and so on, most people bounce back 'strengthened and more resourceful' (Walsh, 2006, p. 4). In fact, the term resilience originally referred to the propensity of a substance to spring back to its original state from being compressed (Pearsall and Trumble, 1995). The concept resembles recovery (see earlier) but is more forthright in the statement it makes about people. Although it is still very marginal to discourse in the British mental health scene, it may achieve greater prominence in association with recovery; a recent publication discussing the theoretical connections between social capital, inequality and health postulates that resilience – seen in this publication as basically physiological – is a crucial element in the capacity of individuals to recover from stress (Friedli, 2008). However, the concept of resilience and related ideas like 'personal strength' are fairly prominent in mental health discourse in discussion on trauma when people are exposed to armed conflict and disaster (see section on 'trauma therapy' in Chapter 6 and the section on 'resilience in the face of trauma and exile' in Chapter 10).

Initially resilience was seen as something inherited – a rugged individuality – but it has moved into being seen as arising from interaction, supported by strong relationships (see Rutter, 1999). Froma Walsh (2006) takes this even further to link resilience to family and community:

> A family resilience framework fundamentally alters traditional deficit-based perspectives. Instead of focusing on how families have failed, we direct our attention to how they can succeed. Rather than giving up on troubled families and salvaging individual survivors, we can draw out the best in families, building on key processes to encourage both individual and family growth. (Walsh, 2006, p. 4)

However, the reality should be noted that families, marriages and communities today may be defined in diverse ways, not necessarily traditional ones. So it is not just individual personality traits that make up resilience but, more importantly, ways in which families as interacting groups of individuals connect together, and adapt and relate to other families; in short the ways in which communities function. So for example, belief systems play a part in giving meaning to what happens to people and why; religious rituals may be important in dealing with the unexpected and the unknowable; and community links are crucial in sharing the experiences of loss and bereavement. Resilience is embedded within systems – within the individual, the culture and the society. It is not something that can be dissected out and packaged, not a therapy that can be standardized and delivered.

Summary

The themes discussed as changing discourse in mental health are exciting in themselves. Even if the movements being voiced turn out to be mere buzz words or passing fashions, the very fact that these new ideas are being voiced – and seemingly supported in high places – can shift thinking in subtle ways. The major question for practitioners and service users is whether – and if so how – the changing discourse in mental health discussed in this chapter can get translated into practical change; and that means changing psychiatric practice and clinical psychology, the disciplines that underpin professional practice in mental services. In the UK today, there is very little in the way of top-down direction to professionals on how to implement – or even whether they should implement – new ways of working represented by new discourse. For discourse to affect public policy that changes practice at grass roots one has to look to influencing professional training and getting legal backing through legislation. And, unless the changes become embedded in the system of mental health services – especially in psychiatric practice – it will remain as mere talk.

It could be said from the start that legal backing is not there today in the UK for the changes represented by the new ideas voiced through the discourses considered in this chapter. In fact, changes in mental health legislation in England and Wales implemented in November 2008 (Department of Health, 2007) have re-enforced medicalization of social problems, allowed mental disorder to be diagnosed in much broader terms (compared with current practice), shifted the emphasis from voluntary seeking of help to compulsion, and promoted the linkage of danger with 'mental illness' both in the public mind and professional practice (see Fernando and Keating 2009b; Inyama, 2009). These changes have set a framework that is strongly antipathetic to the sort of changes envisaged by the discourses referred to in this chapter. So any hope that they may affect mental health practice rests on changes in professional training alone. But here the lack of legal reasons for practitioners to take on change is a drawback, especially since many professionals today feel over-cautious about veering from the straight and narrow traditional ways of doing things because of the 'blame culture' they work in. However, if training is sufficiently robust and pressures – and resources – allow, there is hope that the discourses discussed here, in spite of the limitations discussed above, may well make a difference.

Of the themes discussed in this chapter, recovery is the discourse that has caught on most strongly in the UK. But, it seems to be facing the threat of being absorbed into mainstream psychiatry in a form that fits in well into its traditional ways of working in a genetic-biomedical model. It is a pity that a different word was not chosen to express the recovery approach formulated by service users. Perhaps 'liberation' may have expressed this approach more clearly and 'liberation' may well have resonated with BME people who feel oppressed by a variety of forces, such as racism and social exclusion, apart from stigma and the system of psychiatry. Hopefully, the recovery discourse will be combined with liberation as it progresses. Spirituality is clearly the most interesting – and potentially the most fundamental as far as psychiatry is concerned – of the new discourses covered in this chapter. Although there are serious doubts about the feasibility of spirituality as an add-on to western psychology and psychiatry, the wider implications of intensifying the spirituality discourse could well have important positive effects in addressing the current drawbacks of psychiatry seen from a race and culture perspective. But, the cultural dimension of spirituality needs to be addressed (Fernando, 2007) if spirituality is to have any real meaning in a multicultural society.

A values-based approach seems on the surface an attractive proposition; but, as with spirituality, it is not easy to see how 'values' can be incorporated into systems such as western psychology and psychiatry that are strongly set in their ways of functioning with embedded values which seem to even incorporate such antisocial elements as racism. But unlike the case of spirituality, VBP, with training schemes attached, seems to have a strong academic lobby and (perhaps) resources attached. So the question is whether VBP can address some of the problems that people face when they come into contact with psychiatry and western psychology. An encouraging sign is that the proponents of VBP (to judge by published material) seem to favour radical changes to psychiatry. Indeed, if a values-based psychiatry really does reconstruct the disciplines that underpin mental health – or help to do so – confronting the forces of conservatism entrenched within the professions of western psychology and biomedical psychiatry, values-based discourse may turn out to be a constructive start to the reformation of the mental health system. But at present that seems a long shot.

The discourse of well-being has entered the mental health field rather tentatively and does not seem to have really developed very far yet in the UK, although its use in community psychology and development studies augers well for the future. However, from a race and culture perspective, this is the discourse that offers a simple alternative approach to mental health that can rescue it from the 'illness' rut that it seems to have got into. Well-being is a concept that is integral to mental health and is promoted by WHO, at least for non-western developing countries (see Chapter 9). If used in a more determined manner, the concept of well-being has the potential to promote a service-user perspective as well as a community bottom-up perspective within mental health services – and hopefully shift thinking in psychiatry itself. Resilience is not talked about much in British mental health circles but is coming to the fore in other parts of the world, especially those affected by calamities and armed conflict. It is crucial to the discourse that should be applied in work done to help refugees who reach the UK and the USA and obtain permission to stay as refugees (see Chapter 10).

So what about the future of the discourses themselves? The outlook in the UK is not good. Official mental health policies in the UK do *appear* to endorse the changing discourse discussed in this chapter, but the agendas that are not stated openly do not inspire confidence. The ease with which the UK Government seems to succumb to public prejudice and into supporting the 'brain disease' idea of mental illness linked to violence and danger does not bode well for major shifts in mental health being pushed through by government – at least not in the short term. At a more general level, human rights are being undermined (see Kennedy, 2004). In the light of all this, there are serious doubts about the extent to which the new discourses referred to here (recovery, spirituality, values, well-being and resilience) will make a fundamental difference to the way psychiatry functions. Also, in all these discourses the cultural dimension has been minimally addressed so far, while it is difficult to see that racism in mental health services and within psychiatry itself will be countered in any significant way by the new ideas expounded in them. But while the changing discourse exists there are grounds for hope of change.

Chapter 6

Trauma and Post-traumatic Stress; Suffering and Violence

'Trauma', meaning psychogenic trauma or mental trauma when used in a mental health context, has become a key word in western psychology through which both academic discourse and clinical work approach the human experience of events involving violence and their aftermath. Originally, trauma was purely about physical wounds but 'was extended, *via analogy*, to include cognitive-emotional states that cause psychological and existential pain and suffering' (Young, 1997, p. 246, italics in original). But in many ways, the concept of trauma has been widened 'to cover a vast array of situations of extremity and equally varied individual and collective responses' (Kirmayer *et al.*, 2007a, p. 1). It has even been used to highlight current racism in the USA against African Americans by calling its impact on their minds passed down the generations as amounting to an illness of 'post traumatic slave syndrome' (DeGruy Leary, 2005, title page).

The current importance attached to trauma in psychiatric discourse and service provision can be traced to the emergence of Post Traumatic Stress Disorder (PTSD) as an illness in the 1980s with its inclusion in the Diagnostic and Statistical Manual (DSM) (APA, 1980), *DSM-III*, and the subsequent blossoming of therapies for trauma. But the discourse on trauma within psychiatry has moved on in the past ten years, especially in the face of many conflicts around the world; as it happened, most of the conflicts have occurred in regions with non-western cultural traditions and the narrow individualized 'illness' approach of PTSD was found not to encompass the complex array of influences and corollaries around the experience of violence and war (see discussions of this topic by Bracken, 2002; Bracken *et al.*, 1995; Boyden and Gibbs, 1996; Galappatti, 2003; Hart *et al.*, 2007; Salih and Samarasinghe, 2006; Summerfield, 1999). Many of the critiques of PTSD as a diagnosis point to its tendency to reduce to a medical problem located in the individual what is in reality a complex array of social, personal and psychological problems that people exposed to conflict face; and the problems with this diagnosis are even more evident when it is given to refugees in developed western countries because it results in obscuring problems they face after migration such as hostility from host populations in the place they flee to (see Chapter 10). Also, the discourse derived from associating refugee mental health with PTSD sets refugee mental health in a paradigm that is exclusively negative, of refugee *pathology* rather than one that addresses refugee health from a point of view of their suffering and their resilience – their 'social competence or other types of functional adequacy despite losses and stressors' (Muecke, 1992, p. 520).

A different approach to the issues that have given rise to the trauma discourse comes from a social and cultural perspective, focusing on the context in which the (alleged) 'trauma' occurs, namely violence and suffering experienced by individuals and communities. Suffering has always been a part of the human condition and the striving to escape from it is one of the basic struggles that human beings have been involved in from the dawn of civilization – struggles expressed in a variety of ways. Violent political conflicts as well as natural disasters in many parts of the world have been a major cause of suffering during the past twenty years. Suffering associated with violence – from groups of people or even states, violence from individuals, and structural violence through poverty, discrimination and oppression – in most instances are attributable to persons: they are man-made. In the case of natural disasters, however, the causes of suffering – the attributions associated with the suffering – are not clearly identifiable.

Recently, there has been an interest in traumatic experiences during childhood of people who, as adults, are diagnosed as 'psychotic' or experience so-called psychosis-like mental states. The November 2005 issue of *Acta Psychiatrica Scandinavica*, the foremost Nordic psychiatric journal, carries several articles exploring the links between self-reported childhood trauma, usually physical abuse, and adult schizophrenia (e.g., Bak *et al.*, 2005). And a recent review (Krabbendam, 2008) claims 'there is little doubt that the frequency of self-reported developmental trauma is increased in individuals with psychotic disorder' (p. 1405). Further, there are reports claiming that vulnerability to depression in adults may result from childhood trauma from physical abuse (Harkness and Monroe, 2002). This chapter does not enter into the topic of the association between childhood trauma and adult mental illness. It is limited to exploring the discourse on trauma and traumatic memory in a context of suffering as a result of conflict and violence, often politically driven, and/or a result of natural disaster.

Trauma as medical pathology

The idea of traumatic memory and the notion of stress during combat in war have been around in psychiatric thinking for many years, usually seen as causing neurotic illness. But something changed in the 1970–1980s. According to Young (1995), the result of reports in news media of 'suicides, antisocial acts and bizarre behaviors committed by Vietnam war Veterans...[in the 1970s]...the "crazy Vietnam vet" – angry, violent and emotionally unstable – had become an American archetype' (p. 108). In this context, there developed a view among mental health professionals that these war veterans were *victims* of the war and deserved to be diagnosed as suffering an authentic service-connected illness; and then followed a campaign to claim trauma as a cause of 'illness' finally leading to PTSD being included in *DSM III*. Numerous therapies then developed specifically for illnesses caused by 'trauma', designed in one way or other to counteract its prolonged effects. But PTSD is very different to most other illnesses constructed within psychiatry. In elaborating the peculiar nature of PTSD, Young (1995) points to (a) the fundamental nature of its structure designating 'traumatic memory'; (b) its connections historically with earlier psychiatric concepts of shell-shock and hysteria; and (c) its emergence through the socio-political forces set off by the American war in Vietnam. In practical terms, the model of PTSD is of a central pathology involving traumatic memory surrounded by depression and anxiety. So, PTSD was from the beginning treated with both pharmacological and psychological therapies – the former consisting mainly of antidepressants and anxiolytics, and the latter of behaviour therapy, cognitive therapy and psychodynamic (psychoanalytic) therapies aimed at enabling patients to develop skills for controlling devalued emotional states associated with PTSD and (in the case of psychodynamic therapy) concentrating on the content of the traumatic memory itself.

Trauma therapy

A result of trauma being identified as 'pathology' has led to the concept of therapy to counteract trauma – or the memory of trauma. Various forms of formal psychotherapy focused on psychological malfunctioning attributed to trauma are described, including psychoanalytic approaches (MacCann and Pearlman, 1990), behavioural approaches involving exposure and/ or cognitive behavioural therapy, and eye movement desensitization and reprocessing (EMDR) (Foa and Cahill, 2006; Rothbaum *et al.*, 2000). Also, less formal trauma therapy is being popularized, often referred to loosely as counselling, debriefing or single psychological interventions (Dyregrov, 1989; Mitchell, 1983) and offered to people involved in various situations that are assumed to induce trauma – such as train or road accidents (Hobbs and Adshead, 1996). Although the efficacy of debriefing has long been questioned as not being evidence based (Bisson and Deahl, 1994), its use seems to continue.

The notion that long-term deleterious effects of trauma are inevitable and invariable in the case of people exposed to violent conflicts has informed much of the mental health work carried out among refugees and asylum seekers in the Europe and North America. But this approach has been criticized by advocates of the need for mental health services for refugees to take a broad perspective – for example, Watters and Ingleby (2004) and Birman and Tran (2008). Many areas of conflict and places where disasters have struck during the past twenty years have been in low- and middle-income countries which depend at times of humanitarian crises on help from high-income, mainly western nations (see Chapter 9 for definitions of low, middle and high-income countries).

Interventions in developing countries

The problems arising from the uncritical application of trauma therapies in non-western settings were commented upon after wars in the Balkans following the disintegration of the former Yugoslavia – for example, by de Jong *et al.* (2003) and Stubbs (2005); and these problems achieved greater publicity after the Indian Ocean tsunami in December 2004 when many interventions in communities affected by the tsunami were labelled 'psychosocial'. In the case of Sri Lanka: 'Psychosocial intervention swiftly attained the status of a priority...alongside provision of shelter,...adequate water and sanitation facilities for displaced persons' (Galappatti, 2005, p. 65). Wickramage (2006) describes some of the emergency psychosocial interventions that were practised as a 'carnival': For example, how in 'a once-only psychosocial workshop with children and young people of the affected communities (predominantly Muslim)' participants were asked to join in drama and music as a means of 'psychosocial release'; and people affected by the disaster who were identified by therapists as 'withdrawn' or 'solitary' being induced to vocalize traumatic experiences (pp. 168–9).

Cultural issues

There is a great deal of controversy and uncertainty about the effectiveness of many of the therapies developed within western psychology and biomedical psychiatry as treatments for PTSD (Bisson and Andrew, 2007). It has been argued that failure of individualized therapies for trauma to demonstrate effectiveness may reflect the diversity of problems gathered together under the rubrics of trauma and PTSD (Kirmayer *et al.*, 2007b). In addition, the likelihood is that in non-western settings individualized therapy may not be just ineffective but, because it is in conflict with cultural norms, they may undermine natural systems of self-help and recovery in the communities themselves. In other words, the concept 'trauma' may well be inappropriately applied; its application may disregard the reality of life events experienced by people and communities in terms of the connections these events have with a variety of social, cultural, psychological and political corollaries each of which may be felt and interpreted differently depending on the background of each individual, family and community. The individualized approach that underpins western psychotherapy may well miss most or all of these.

A matter that is underemphasized in standard western textbooks on therapies for 'trauma', and even the guidance issued by WHO, is the importance of acknowledging and promoting ways of dealing with the effects of conflict and violence that are in tune with the social and cultural mores of the communities concerned. For example, a way of dealing with inner conflict or social stress available in the Buddhist tradition is to 'withdraw one's attention from the external world and meditate. Another is to evade the harsh realities of daily life in ecstatic emotion, the love of god' (Gombrich and Obeyesekere, 1988, p. 15). Kakar (1984) points out that in the Hindu tradition, identification with gods and goddesses promotes the experience of inner states of consciousness – perhaps a form of therapy in the western idiom – that enables people to accept suffering. Patricia Lawrence (2000, 2003), an anthropologist, describes how, in the face of the suffering resulting from political violence in eastern Sri Lanka, traumatized people obtain protection and healing from Hindu goddess cults and local oracles – mainly people who have been empowered through possession.

Changing scene

It is noteworthy that the limited knowledge base of current models of trauma in western psychology is now being recognized (Rousseau and Measham, 2007). In the psychiatric field, there is interest in the varied responses to potentially traumatic events (Shalev and Ursano, 2003) and the importance of resilience both of individuals and communities (Konner, 2007). Recent articles in medical psychiatric publications have argued for 'cultural sensitivity' in devising programmes for psychosocial interventions for war-affected people preferably delivered by locally based personnel (de Jong and Kleber, 2003); and the importance of general support being available together with any specific interventions (Ajdukovic and Ajdukovic, 2003). Innovative ways of working in non-western settings affected by conflict have been reported, for example, in Bosnia (de Jong and Kleber, 2003), Cambodia (van de Put and Eisenbruch, 2004) and Angola (Wessels and Monteiro, 2004). More importantly, medical literature is beginning to pay attention to the need for social reconstruction and community healing (Ajdukovic and Ajdukovic, 2003; Ayalon, 1998) and the fostering of resilience, coping and recovery (Ørner and Schnyder, 2003a); and early intervention with specific individualized therapies is being questioned and cautioned against in the present state of knowledge: 'The era of confident assertions about routine prescriptions for post-incident care has come to an end. In its place has dawned a realization that survivors' needs are probably as diverse as they are changeable. Even the notion of a narrow range of protocol prescriptions being sufficient to respond to all eventualities seems ill advised' (Ørner and Schnyder, 2003b, p. 41).

Officials of the WHO (van Ommeren *et al.*, 2005) suggest that good practice in providing mental health care in developing countries after acute emergencies should look to a public health model, veering towards a psychosocial approach rather than psychiatric model of specific individualized therapy. First, during and immediately after the emergency there should be social interventions to provide for physical needs, access to general health care and management of communicable diseases. But during the post-emergency period, WHO sees a role for mental health specialists to train community staff to conduct outreach work, such as organizing self-help support groups brainstorming for effective ways of coping, collaboration with traditional sources of help and promoting community support. 'The development of a multitude of specialized trauma-focused services should be avoided unless mental health care is available in general health care and other community settings (the school system, for example)' (p. 73). WHO suggests that any trauma-focused work that is considered at a later stage should be integrated into general mental health care. Since then, an agency established by WHO called Inter-Agency Standing Committee (IASC, 2007) has issued detailed advice on how best mental health care may be organized within the totality of humanitarian aid delivered after natural disasters or violent conflict.

Conclusions

Trauma therapy has a vast investment in terms of time, effort and resources and it borders on being an industry in its own right – and one that is poorly regulated. For example, EMDR has an international institute and numerous websites offering therapy for numerous ailments – at a price. Trauma therapy, as a business, sells its products worldwide and all too often finds markets that are easy to penetrate in low-income countries experiencing conflict and disaster. Schedules, handbooks and training courses in the field of trauma therapy are numerous – for example, *Children and Disaster: Teaching Recovery Techniques* (Smith *et al.*, 1999). Yet, there is little evidence that these therapies work and even less evidence that they are suitable in their current form for communities in non-western cultural settings. However, it should be recognized that some of the people practising trauma therapy may provide benefit of an unintended nature, merely by the fact that they reach out to people in trouble who have few sources of human contact and sympathy. So it would be foolish to dismiss these practitioners *as people* altogether, although the methods that they use may be inappropriate or even harmful. The trauma treatment manual by Schmookler (1996), for example, seems to provide a framework for befriending people who have been through terrifying experiences in a sensible and sensitive fashion. But what is crucial in determining the approach to helping individuals affected by violence and conflict to recover is their cultural background, including religion, and the natural means of support and stress-relief that people are used to seeking. It is essential, therefore, to consult closely with communities in planning help for people affected by conflict – the so-called traumatized.

Social suffering and violence

The discourse on trauma within a medical model may be suspect but the suffering in the face of violence and disaster is real enough in the wider socio-political world that human beings live. Social suffering is a term which brings together 'human problems that have their origins and con-sequences in the devastating injuries that social force can inflict on human experience ... [and] ... simultaneously involve health, welfare, legal, moral and religious issues' (Kleinman *et al.*, 1997, p. ix). Moreover, designating suffering as 'social' emphasizes the linkages between personal (individual) problems and those of society and community.

Unlike the situation in the days of colonialism and slavery, today, the suf-fering of people living in low- and middle-income countries is big news. In commenting upon a photograph that won a Pulitzer Prize for the *New York Times* in 1993, of a vulture perching near a little girl in the Sudan who had collapsed from hunger, Arthur and Joan Kleinman (1997) write: 'Suffering is presented as if it existed free of local people and local worlds. ... That assump-tion almost invariably leads to the development of regional or national pol-icies that are imposed on local worlds. When those localities end up resisting or not complying with policies and programs that are meant to assist them, such acts are then labeled irrational or self-destructive. The local world is deemed incompetent, or worse'. The Kleinmans go on to suggest that when people manage to flee from places where they experience violence, their 'memories (their intimately interior images) of violation are made over into *trauma stories* ... [which] ... then become the currency ... to achieve the status of political refugee' (pp. 7–10, italics in original). And professionals rewrite social suffering in medical terms sometimes as the quintessential PTSD.

The effect of political violence on Columbian communities is described by Buitrago Cuéllar (2004) as the 'deterioration of the social fabric', that is, the breakup of communities, arising from widespread distrust impeding communication among people when, for instance, meeting each other is dangerous or 'leadership activities are persecuted' (p. 235). Somasunderam and Sivayokan (2005), working in Jaffna, northern Sri Lanka, describe how (what they call) 'collective trauma' results in a variety of 'responses ... [being] accepted as a normal part of life' (p. 80). Therefore, recovery from social suffering is part and parcel of social and community restoration.

The remedies for social suffering that can be traced back to events in history are difficult to fathom pragmatically. Looked at politically, whole groups of nations suffer from the aftermath of colonialism; people who identify as, or are perceived as, being of African descent, especially if they are African Americans or African Caribbeans, suffer from the legacies of slavery. It is possible that a clear apology from the descendents of the oppressors – or those who have inherited the benefits thereof – is necessary for recovery. But perhaps the answers are more economic than just saying 'sorry'. In July 2008, the American House of Representatives in the USA passed a resolution apologizing for the 'injustice, cruelty, brutality and inhumanity of slavery and Jim Crow' – Jim Crow refers to the denial of civic rights to African Americans between 1870 and 1965 in some southern States of USA. But there are no signs that the US government will address the question of reparations (CNN News, 2008, p. 1). The British are yet to even say sorry for slavery.

It is assumed today that reconciliation between different groups in society that may have been on opposing sides of a conflict is part of the remedy for social suffering that occurred during violent conflict. Post-apartheid South Africa attempted to effect a sort of 'closure' to the apartheid era through its Truth and Reconciliation Commission (TRC, 2001) by public exposure of the 'truth' based on admissions of guilt associated with apology – a model of confession and forgiveness. But Nigerian writer, Nobel Laureate Wole Soyinka (1999) challenges the notion of simple forgiveness as a strategy of social healing: While acknowledging the need for some degree of pragmatism for the transformation of society or building new societies based on quality, Soyinka argues that justice must accompany the quest for truth. Nineteenth-century French philosopher Ernest Renan (1990 [1882]) suggested that 'forgetting is a crucial factor in building a nation' (p. 11). The same may be said of rebuilding communities after prolonged political violence or civil war. The question is how to promote this. After the Biafran secessionist war of the 1960s, when there were atrocities on all sides, the Nigerian Government disallowed public debate, blame or celebration about the war. People had to just leave the past in the past and get on with 'being able to work together, to live as neighbours as and when necessary' (Last, 2000, p. 316). If healing – if that is the right word – took place, it would have been in private around religious and community institutes (Last, 2000). In fact, this seems to be the political approach generally in other places too – for instance, in Ireland.

Perhaps there is no secular way of promoting reconciliation. Spencer (2000), an anthropologist from Edinburgh, worked in Sri Lanka during the

1980s at the height of the war there between the government and a militant group demanding an ethnic state for Tamils – a war which ended in May 2009. Spencer observed that 'symbolic resolution' after the war may come from within the country's own religious traditions; in other words that the role of the state is limited – perhaps to enabling forgetting to take place by redressing political and economic disparities that gave rise to the demand for a separate state in the first place.

Summary

It would seem that the theoretical discourse on trauma and its practical applications in terms of help for people suffering as a result of exposure to conflict, natural disasters and accidents are in some disarray if not chaos. Looked at from an individualistic point of view, the PTSD approach of expecting either symptoms of illness or a sort of absolute resilience that ensures continuing health is, to say the least, naive (Rousseau and Measham, 2007). 'Instead, the effect of psychic trauma may be to transform the person, who is also continuing on a developmental trajectory' (p. 280); therefore, 'rather than understanding trauma as solely producing psychopathology, it is more helpful in clinical practice to conceptualize the traumatic experience as a process that triggers a transformation or metamorphosis that evokes both strengths and vulnerabilities' (2007, pp. 290–1). But, from a social-cultural standpoint, a catastrophic (traumatic) event that has physical-psychological concomitants felt at an individual level constitutes *at the same time* 'a narrative theme in explanations of individual and social suffering' (Kirmayer *et al.*, 2007a, p. 1). And from this 'narrative effect' ripples of change – both positive and negative – would spread out in various directions, into changing a person's sense of identity, into the loyalties and values they may adhere to or not, into deconstruction or reconstruction of religious beliefs, and into their community life. If trauma is looked at from a communal, rather than individualistic, angle, a traumatic event has diverse strands that may well have long-term effects on community cohesion/disruption, kinship ties and antagonisms, and the way people relate to each other both as individuals and as communities.

In practical terms of service provision in situations where violence or disaster has occurred, or is a continuing problem, several points may be made: First, the assumption in most trauma therapy approaches that disclosure – talking about the events – is helpful is not established. The same is true for many other assumptions, such as the value given to establishing trust, seeking meaning in the (traumatic) experiences and establishing social bonds. In the present state of knowledge and information, there is need for extreme caution in instituting individualistic therapies of any sort. As a result of the critique of a predominantly biomedical or psycho-medical approach to the consequences of disaster and war – as epitomized in the promotion of PTSD and the popularization of trauma therapy and mixture of interventions subsumed under the umbrella term 'psychosocial support' – WHO has pursued consultations on developing universally applicable guidance for practitioners on how to respond to humanitarian crises (Silove, 2005; van Ommeren *et al.*, 2005). In this 'emerging consensus' (van Ommeren *et al.*, 2005) WHO argues against 'separating *psychosocial* care services from *mental health* care services'; and that, faced with an emergency, there is no need for responsible authorities to choose between 'setting-up vertical (separate) trauma mental health programmes, setting-up vertical psychosocial care programmes outside existing systems, or ignoring mental health care altogether' (pp. 71–2, italics in original). Instead, WHO suggests strategies – largely based on common sense – to be followed during and immediately after an acute emergency caused by violent conflict or disaster; this is basically a public health approach underpinned by social and cultural understanding of what mental health means in the particular context of conflict or disaster.

In attempting to define an overall framework for provision of longer-term programmes in areas of disaster and violent conflict, Miller and Rasco (2004) bring together under one umbrella – calling them 'ecological interventions' (p. 4) – many different forms of intervention and help within a mixture of community psychology and public health models: The approaches described in their book range from empowering women through group sessions (Tribe and The Family Rehabilitation Centre Staff, 2004) to promoting indigenous support systems and religious healing (van de Put and Eisenbruch, 2004). The two main characteristics of the services described are that they are pragmatic and innovative, depending on local need and context, rather than being carefully pre-planned or linked to predetermined models. It is claimed that this 'ecological' approach can respond to what is seen as necessary on the ground and culturally acceptable to the people receiving the services. However, hard data on outcome, or even perceived usefulness, of service provision in the field of psychosocial and mental health care for people affected by violent conflict and disaster are seriously deficient. Further there is very little information on what the users of the services think of the efficacy of the varied services provided by humanitarian and other organizations in the many areas of conflict that are predominantly located in places where most people come from non-western cultural backgrounds.

A piece of work is currently (June 2009) being pursued in Sri Lanka, as part of a four-nation mental health program on Trauma and Global Health (TGH), the main thrust of which is to build capacity for mental health promotion in four low- and middle-income countries affected by conflict and disaster. The initial part of the programme in Sri Lanka has been to gather information through community consultation about perspectives

Part II

Practice and Innovation

Chapter 7

Application of Psychiatry: Bias and Imperialism

The application of biomedical psychiatry in multicultural societies and across the world raises several issues around validity. Also, the importance of racial bias in the practice of psychiatry in multiracial settings is often ignored except when obvious – as it was in the case of South Africa in the days of apartheid (Jewkes, 1984; WHO, 1977). This chapter attempts to explore these problems.

The Euro-American scene: Racial bias

In Britain, racist practice is not publicly or openly encouraged by local or central government, but there is little doubt that it exists – usually as institutional racism (Home Department, 1999). Racism within psychiatry derives from the traditions of the discipline, its history, its ways of assessing and diagnosing, the nature of the criteria it uses for designating treatment, its organization, its involvement with the powers of the state and with western power internationally (and the racist dimension to the exercise of power), and its struggle to be accepted as a scientific discipline. Racism in the provision of psychiatric services derives from the manner in which institutions are constructed and fashioned and the failure by most organizations to confront the fact of inherent and historically determined racism.

Clinical evaluation

The practice of psychiatry at an individual level depends, in the final analysis, on the process of clinical evaluation – a process that precedes diagnosis (see Chapter 2) and has the remit of setting what is thought of as observed against what is thought of as known. This is primarily based on information obtained from a person ('patient') as history, an estimation of their basic personality and judgements made as to their mental state. This process, discussed in Chapter 2, incorporates several points where bias could creep in.

The psychiatrist influences the content of what is obtained as 'history' and 'personality' in two interrelated ways within the overall, variable limitations of communication. First, the type and extent of information given by the patient and others are fashioned by the perceptions of the psychiatrist about the people providing the information and preconceptions about the patient. For example, a black Asian patient, aware of the negative value attached to Asian marriage customs, is unlikely to tell a white doctor or social worker much about his/her marriage. This may be interpreted as secretiveness or deviousness of the patient, not as a quality of the doctor or social worker. Second, the picking and choosing that occurs during history-taking – the emphasis given to one item of information as opposed to another or the meaning attached to an incident – is dependent on the beliefs, value judgements, understanding and knowledge of the psychiatrist. For example, a psychiatrist who is a part of an establishment that does not appreciate the extent of racial discrimination in employment is likely to take down a history of persistent unemployment of a black person without qualification, that is having the same significance for both black and white patients. Since white psychiatrists lack personal experience of predominantly black areas, such as Harlem (New York), Tower Hamlets (London) or St Paul's (Bristol, England), they are likely to be unaware of the pressures impinging on black people who live there and hence misinterpret their lifestyles and behaviour – misinterpretations which often reinforce any racist prejudices they may harbour.

The mental state examination is of crucial importance in determining the diagnosis given to a patient – probably the major determinant (Gauron and Dickinson, 1966). The validity of deductions made in this process is suspect (Grounds, 1987) at the best of times when there is absolute rapport and full understanding between the participants at the interview; but in a multicultural setting, and especially when barriers arising from racist preconceptions are rife, the possibility of making valid deductions from questions asked at an interview is highly questionable. The meanings attached to experiences and perceptions, the concept of illness, and the overall significance of the interview situation (during which 'the mental state' is deduced) are but some of the parameters along which variation occurs when cultural differences are present between the participants of an interaction. And racism adds to this problem in ways best illustrated by quoting, in much shortened form, a case given elsewhere (Fernando, 1988):

> A black person on remand in prison was diagnosed by the prison doctor as suffering from a chronic schizophrenic illness with an acute exacerbation. He was said to have mainly negative symptoms of withdrawal, social deterioration, and emotional blunting, and to lack insight, to be unwilling to have treatment informally and to be near-mute. When I met him in prison he told me his story with feeling and precision. Soon after I left, it seems, he relapsed into the earlier state. (pp. 112–3)

The mental state of the patient referred to above was accurately described in the tradition of psychiatry and the diagnosis was reasonably reliable, since it was just on the one occasion that he behaved in a way different from that of a 'schizophrenic' patient. *In psychiatric terms he had schizophrenia.* It was the application of a standard biomedical model to that man's particular situation that was at fault; it was the meaning given to his 'schizophrenia' that was misleading. And the whole process added up to a racist system.

Issues in diagnosis

The psychiatric diagnostic process, critically described in Chapter 2, allows the discipline of psychiatry to function in a way that fails to allow for the biases that come into assessments – biases endemic in the culture in which psychiatry has grown and in which psychiatry functions.

Early reports of a relatively high rate of black inpatients being diagnosed as 'psychotic' in the USA during the latter part of the nineteenth century and the first half of the twentieth (Babcock, 1895; Wilson and Lantz, 1957) were criticized by Pasamanick (1963) on methodological grounds; he concluded from studies in Baltimore that, while the non-white rates for psychosis were higher than those for whites in state hospitals, the white rates were higher in Veterans Administration hospitals and private institutions. Moreover, he calculated that, for non-institutional patients, the white rate for psychosis was higher than the non-white rate. Also, Pasamanick observed that, between 1920 and 1955, there was a change in the style of diagnosis of black people in the USA; the diagnosis of schizophrenia increased while that of manic depression decreased. Indeed, American studies in the 1950s and 1960s (Jaco, 1960; Simon, 1965) reported a lower rate of affective illness diagnosed among blacks compared with whites and, corresponding to this, reports published in the 1970s quoted a higher rate of schizophrenia among blacks compared with whites – for example, nearly double in the case of male admissions to state and county hospitals in 1969 (NIMH, 1971) and 60 per cent higher among referrals to a private psychiatric inpatient service of a university hospital in Brooklyn (Steinberg *et al.*, 1977). Further, when a distinction was established in diagnosis between 'process schizophrenia' and 'reactive schizophrenia' (the former having a relatively high genetic component), blacks, particularly males, were disproportionately given the diagnosis of process schizophrenia, irrespective of socio-economic status (Allon, 1971). At the same time, American psychiatrists noted difficulties encountered by white psychiatrists in comprehending, and therefore properly evaluating feelings and behaviour of black people because of mutual mistrust and hostility between racial groups (St Clair, 1951).

The overdiagnosis of schizophrenia in the USA may not be confined to African Americans but may well apply also to Native and Hispanic Americans. A hospital survey of inpatients reports a diagnosis of schizophrenia being given at a significantly higher rate to patients from 'Indian reserves' compared with 'non-Indian' patients in Saskatchewan (Roy *et al.*, 1970) and a community survey reports a relatively high 'prevalence rate' of all major psychoses among the Eskimos (Inuit) of the Canadian Arctic (Sampath, 1974). Hispanic Americans seem to be underrepresented as patients attending both public and private psychiatric services (Karno, 1966) and are thought to suffer mainly from major psychiatric disorders (Adams *et al.*, 1984). A study of outpatients of an inner-city municipal hospital in New York diagnosed as suffering from bipolar illness (manic depression) found that previous 'misdiagnosis' as 'schizophrenic' was significantly greater for both Hispanics and blacks when compared with whites (Mukherjee *et al.*, 1983).

Several studies of British inpatients in the 1960s and 1970s (Bagley, 1971; Cochrane, 1977) revealed that the diagnosis of schizophrenia was given more frequently to people from many immigrant groups when compared with native-born people, especially people originating in Africa, Asia and the Caribbean (Carpenter and Brockington, 1980; Dean *et al.*, 1981) – all 'black' in racial terms. A survey of inpatients compulsorily detained in a hospital in Birmingham (England) showed that about two-thirds of (black) West Indian patients, as opposed to one-third of the whites, were diagnosed as 'schizophrenic' (McGovern and Cope, 1987); and a study in Nottingham (Harrison *et al.*, 1988) showed that (black) African Caribbean people were 10 to 12 times more likely to be so diagnosed. Later studies of people referred to psychiatric services in London, Nottingham and Bristol (Bhugra *et al.*, 1997; Fearon *et al.*, 2006; Harrison *et al.*, 1997; King *et al.*, 1994) confirmed similar degrees of excessive diagnosis.

So far, there is no clear message from ethnic studies of diagnostic patterns in European countries (apart from UK) as there seems to be in the UK. But it should be noted that these countries have poor ethnic statistics for researchers to work with. A study in The Hague (the Netherlands) (Selten *et al.*, 2001) found that the relative risk to a foreign-born person of getting a schizophrenia diagnosis on first contact with a physician is between 3.1 times (for Surinamese) and 4.7 times (for Moroccans), when compared with native Dutch people. In a study of official diagnoses given to inpatients across Sweden in the 1990s (Hern *et al.*, 2004), the relative risk of getting a schizophrenia diagnosis in the case of 'second-generation immigrants' (Swedish-born people of foreign parentage) when compared with native Swedish was 2.5 when place of birth (of parents) was Finland, 2.1 when it was Eastern Europe and 2.5 when it was outside Europe.

Although Australia and New Zealand are well-established 'white' nations which have minorities that are culturally non-western and racially non-white, there is very little information on ethnic differences in diagnostic patterns vis-à-vis schizophrenia. One problem is that the methodology of the official survey of mental health in New Zealand (Oakley Browne *et al.*, 2006) precludes the use of research instruments that incorporate DSM diagnoses because they are considered 'too blunt to allow any meaningful interpretation of cultural norms or to accommodate Mâori understanding of mental incapacity' (Baxter *et al.*, 2006, p. 145).

The 2003 statistics published by the New Zealand Health Research Council (Gaines *et al.*, 2003) reports that diagnostic profiles in national records show that the diagnoses schizophrenia, paranoia and acute psychotic disorders were given in acute inpatient episodes to about two-thirds of Mâori and Pacific Island people compared with only 39 per cent in the case of Europeans; this contrasts with the population breakdown of Mâoris constituting 14.7 per cent, Pacific Islanders 6.4 per cent and Europeans (Pakeha) 71.53 per cent (Kumar and Oakley Browne, 2008). In specialist psychiatric services, Mâori were more likely to be diagnosed as suffering schizophrenia (Tapsell and Mellsop, 2007). According to Masters (1997), Te Puni Kōkiri (1993) reports that first admission rates indicate that Mâori are diagnosed with schizophrenia twice as often as non-Mâori and raises issues about cultural alienation among Mâori and the accuracy of diagnoses given to them.

Researchers in New York (Simon *et al.*, 1973), comparing diagnoses given by hospital psychiatrists and research psychiatrists using a structured interview, conclude that the excessive diagnosis of schizophrenia among black people is a reflection of US hospital psychiatrists' diagnostic habits. But others such as Adebimpe *et al.* (1982) claim that symptom profiles for diagnosed schizophrenia differ across racial groups for cultural reasons. Another American team (Bromberg and Simon, 1968) suggests that African Americans may present with (what they call) 'protest psychosis' – essentially an expression of anger with repudiation of white people and their social structures. A British study in the late 1970s (Littlewood and Lipsedge, 1981) suggested that atypical syndromes among black patients may be misdiagnosed as schizophrenia. But studies carried out in the 1990s discount misdiagnosis claiming that strict criteria are observed for making the diagnosis; for instance, Harrison *et al.* (1988) and King *et al.* (1994) argue that, by using the interview schedule called the PSE (Wing *et al.*, 1974) misdiagnosis is avoided. It should be noted that the context in which a diagnosis is made has a major implication for its authenticity and appropriateness, and the process for making a diagnosis is wide open to bias. So, a diagnosis may be accurate in terms of following a set process, such as PSE, but yet inappropriate – not fit for the purpose of encapsulating the type and nature of the problems experienced by the person given the diagnosis. To put it more succinctly, diagnosis may be accurate but if the influence of racism in distorting its objectivity is not addressed, the diagnosis itself becomes inappropriate and even misleading.

Diagnostic bias arising from racism is poorly researched. However, Loring and Powell (1988) did investigate this issue in a carefully controlled study of the diagnostic approaches of 290 American psychiatrists. In that study, psychiatrists were asked certain questions after being provided with written case histories, using exactly similar information about clients except for details of gender and race. Black clients, compared with white clients, were given a diagnosis of schizophrenia more frequently by both black and white clinicians – although this was done to a lesser extent by the former; and clinicians ascribed feelings of violence, suspiciousness and dangerousness to black clients even though the case studies (apart from racial designation) were the same as those for the white clients. It has been noted in Britain, too, that black people in psychiatric hospitals are being seen as dangerous without adequate objective reasons for doing so (Harrison *et al.*, 1984); and the fact that black patients are overrepresented among compulsorily detained patients in British hospitals is well documented (Audini and Lelliott, 2002; Davies *et al.*, 1996; Ineichen *et al.*, 1984; McGovern and Cope, 1987; Morgan *et al.*, 2005; Owens *et al.*, 1991). The American researchers Loring and Powell (1988) draw the conclusion from their research that whites and blacks are 'diagnosed differentially even if they exhibit the same behaviour', and point out that 'these differences will be reflected and legitimized in official statistics on psychopathology' (p. 19); the same is likely to happen in the UK. And so, through the power of myths, self-fulfilling prophecies and genuine but inappropriate diagnoses, the racist tendency to designate black people as schizophrenic is perpetuated.

Issues in treatment and management

Littlewood and Cross (1980) found in Hackney, London, that stereotyped attitudes led to 'assumptions that (a) ECT is suitable for non-depressive reactions in black patients, (b) black patients require more ECT and (c) intramuscular medication is more efficacious in black patients' (p. 200). Also, Shaikh (1985) observed in Leicester 'an excess of electroconvulsive therapy use among Asians who received the diagnosis of schizophrenia as compared to indigenous patients with this diagnosis'. A study in Newham, east London, strongly suggested that black men born in the West Indies, compared with British-born white men, were more likely to be given long-acting (depot) injections of tranquillizers (Glover and Malcolm, 1988).

A retrospective study of over 100 male patients diagnosed as schizophrenic admitted to a teaching hospital unit in Illinois, USA, revealed that, although black patients were similar to white patients on illness ratings, chronicity, marital status, employment level and age, the former spent less time in hospital, obtained less privileges while there, were given more emergency medication, were less likely to receive recreation therapy and occupational therapy, and were more likely to have been placed in seclusion (Flaherty and Meagher, 1980). The authors postulated that 'the stereotype of the black male made the staff feel and act as if blacks were more dangerous, prompting more restrictive measures' (p. 681). In a different study (Lawson *et al.*, 1984), researchers in California found that, although ward physicians and nursing staff believed that their black patients, compared with white patients, were more violent, when a graduated behaviour count of violent behaviour was carried out, blacks were significantly *less* violent.

There is no doubt that seclusion is overused for black patients because of racist stereotyping: a detailed study of seclusion in a university hospital in Pittsburgh (USA) found just three factors, all independent of each other, to be associated with the increased use of seclusion, namely, chronicity of illness, legal status (of being 'committed'), and the fact of being black (Soloff and Turner, 1981). In the UK, Bolton (1984) found that in a south London hospital, of patients recognized as uncooperative but not aggressive, West Indians, Indians and Africans (i.e., black people) were more likely to be sent to locked wards when compared with white English patients, irrespective of diagnosis. A recent one-day census of patients across the UK found that black Caribbean patients were 29 per cent more likely than average to be subjected to a form of physical restraint permitted in British hospitals called 'control and restraint' (CSIP, NIMHE and HCC, 2005). In subsequent censuses, the measurement of 'control and restraint' was dropped in favour of so-called hands-on restraint; in the 2008 census, some non-white ethnic groups were found to have higher than average hands-on restraint rates (CSIP, NIMHE and HCC, 2008).

A high dropout rate from psychotherapy was reported many years ago in the case of black patients in the USA – for example, by Rosenthal and Frank (1958). A major study of nearly 600 outpatients attending a state hospital in California found significant differences in the treatment of ethnic minorities, mainly African and Hispanic Americans, when compared with that of white Americans (Yamamoto *et al.*, 1968): the former were less often taken on for psychotherapy, more often given minimal support or drug therapy, and much more likely to end treatment, either by self-discharge or discharge by therapist. In a complementary study (Yamamoto *et al.*, 1967), the researchers showed clearly that the differences were largely related to what they called 'ethnocentricity' of the therapist, which may be described more aptly as racism. A similar situation probably exists in the UK too (Campling, 1989), although it is inadequately researched.

Although racism resulting in the differential use of specific forms of therapy, such as psychotherapy, and repressive forms of management/treatment, such as seclusion, causes most concern, racial bias in treatment goes much further. Indeed, the perception of the ward atmosphere as a whole, which should be therapeutic, is often very different for black people, compared with whites, in most British and American hospitals – where most of the senior staff are white – because they have a racist 'feel' about them. This situation is difficult to pinpoint or research, but a study of the perceptions of inpatients in a Veterans Administration Hospital in Illinois shows that blacks, compared with whites, have a significantly negative perception of ward environment as restricting their spontaneity and exercise of responsibility (Flaherty *et al.*, 1981). The high black dropout rates from treatment reported in the USA and the frequently reported tendency for black people to abscond from psychiatric facilities in Britain (personal communications from various people) are very likely to represent the effects of racism institutionalized in psychiatry.

Discriminatory practices arising from racism may present in quite subtle ways. For example, a patient in hospital may be judged to be in need of control because the reasons for his/her anger is not understood; and repressive action or controlling treatment such as seclusion or tranquillizers at a high dosage may be perceived (by staff) as being required. On the other hand, if the anger is recognized as emanating from psychological or social problems, psychotherapy or 'sociotherapy' (ways of influencing behaviour by manipulating the environment) may be seen as the patient's need. If the cause of a person's depression is appreciated by the psychiatrist, psychological treatment may be used, while if it is not, ECT or antidepressant medication may be considered.

The global scene: Psychiatric imperialism

As Euro-American influence and political domination spread into Asian and African countries, psychiatry has followed suit for several reasons. First, psychiatry accompanied western medicine which was seen as superior to other – non-scientific – approaches. And with underdevelopment – and sometimes active suppression – of indigenous systems of medicine and healing as part of the colonial/imperial approach, western medicine outshone them across the globe. The fact that psychiatry itself has not been shown to be applicable cross-culturally or to be free of both racial and cultural bias has become obscured by its overt attachment to medicine, the prestige of the latter rubbing off on to psychiatry. Second, psychiatry, being presented and accepted as a part of scientific medicine, is assumed to be a scientific discipline with objective diagnoses and treatments that are free of cultural bias. As such, psychiatry is seen as being applicable to all people in all conditions, irrespective of culture, race and social system, although this is clearly not so. Third, the content of psychiatry is not questioned because of its 'western' aura – it is taken on trust since something western is perceived as being superior to something non-western. Finally, psychiatry is pushed on to non-western societies by economic and political forces allied to western power. The promotion of drugs manufactured in the West goes hand in hand with biomedical psychiatry; 'centres of excellence' usually based in the West and, more recently, their copies in Asia and Africa maintain their dominance as the fonts of all knowledge.

The type of psychiatry promoted in Asia and Africa has been set during the past 200 years by whatever is done in western countries – the standard of what is modern. So when institutional care and psychoanalysis were popular in the West, these models were exported to Asia and Africa; and more recently when community care and cognitive behaviour therapy (CBT) became popular in the West, these are the models being imposed in Asia and Africa. One of the practical consequences of this psychiatric imperialism has been the underdevelopment of medical approaches to mental health and illness indigenous to Asian and African cultural traditions and the suppression of indigenous ways of dealing with human suffering, family problems and social disturbance. These issues are explored further in Chapter 8.

The mental hospitals in countries which were occupied and colonized by Britain and France are little different from those in Europe. Those that still exist continue to be staffed by professionals trained in (western) biomedical psychiatry alone. While there is recent pressure for community-care models to be promoted (see WHO Regional Office for South-East Asia, 2008), the governments concerned often think they have little choice except to seek advice from western 'experts' from (western) centres of excellence (usually via WHO) who generally promote systems they are familiar with but often unsuited to local conditions (see Chapter 9). Inevitably, (western) pharmaceutical companies get in on the act – sometimes under the aegis of 'aid'; and bolstering all this are the research projects backed by prestigious centres in the West which promote biomedical psychiatry and all that goes with it.

Imperialism through research

Scientific research is a powerful force in the promotion of psychiatry across the globe. The biggest and best-known international research project that claims to be 'cross-cultural' is the International Pilot Study of Schizophrenia (WHO, 1973, 1979), commonly called the IPSS. The main aim of the study was defined as 'to tackle certain methodological problems and to answer questions about the nature and distribution of schizophrenia'; other expressed aims were to establish differences in 'form and content' of schizophrenia which could be 'cultural' in origin and to compare the course and outcome of the 'disease' (WHO, 1979, p. 2). Three basic instruments were selected for use – the 'Present State Examination' (PSE), the psychiatric history schedule (PH) and the social description schedule (SD). The PSE (Wing *et al.*, 1974) has been described by one of its inventors, John Wing (1978), as 'a special technique of interviewing patients...which is simply a standardized form of psychiatric diagnostic interview ordinarily used in Western Europe, based on a detailed glossary of differential definitions of symptoms' (p. 103).

The basic assumptions underlying the IPSS were concerned with the meaning of schizophrenia: it was assumed to be an objective entity rather than a 'hypothesis' or a mere diagnostic formulation, and, moreover, an entity that is 'present' in objective form all over the world with a universally similar, if not identical, meaning irrespective of culture. The validity of schizophrenia as a universally applicable concept or illness was not questioned and not researched; and the tentative attempts to examine predictive and content validity were unconvincing. The design of the research method used in the IPSS specifically excluded cultural variables from its protocol (Favazza, 1985). The IPSS was largely successful in publicizing the PSE as a tool for identifying biomedical construct schizophrenia and justifying its acceptance across the world as something 'scientific' and 'objective'.

Like the IPSS, later studies conducted by the WHO – the Collaborative Study on the Assessment and Reduction of Psychiatric Disability (Jablensky *et al.*, 1980) and the Determinants of Outcome of Severe Mental Disorders (Sartorius *et al.*, 1986; WHO, 1986) – take as their starting point assumptions about the universal validity of western diagnostic formulations. The justification for so doing, when the universal validity – or the usefulness – of these illness models, especially schizophrenia, has not been shown must derive from the tradition of western imperialism. Another field in which WHO actively promotes western models of illness is that of 'depression' – for instance, in the series of clinical, epidemiological and therapeutic investigations on depression described by Sartorius *et al.* (1980).

Incidentally, the follow-up studies of the IPSS are striking: The cohorts of patients in industrially less developed – on the whole, non-western – countries who had been identified as 'schizophrenic' showed greater improvement compared with their counterparts in the industrially developed western countries, in both two- and five-year follow-up studies (Sartorius *et al.*, 1986; WHO, 1979), although the latter had more thorough psychiatric treatment and aftercare compared with the former. And this result was maintained in a 13–17-year follow-up conducted in 1997 (Hopper and Wanderling, 2000; Sartorius *et al.*, 1996). The obvious conclusions from the IPSS – *if* the diagnostic construct schizophrenia is valid (a most doubtful proposition that is unproved) – are that: (a) People diagnosed as 'schizophrenic' in non-western countries do better without treatment formulated in the West; or (b) diagnosing 'schizophrenia' as an illness has no predictive validity in terms of outcome with treatment. But in reality the IPSS had a major fundamental fault (Kleinman, 1977) – 'category fallacy', the fallacy of imposing a category derived in the West on to the study of mental disorder in other cultures.

The deleterious effects of imposing western illness models across the globe is not just applicable to the use of specific diagnoses, such as schizophrenia and depression, cross-culturally; a general change that is occurring with the spread of psychiatry into the non-western vulnerable developing world is that personal distress, normally dealt with in religious modes or as problems within family and social systems, is being forced into illness modes to be treated by manufactured drugs or psychotherapies developed in an alien culture. This is the imperialism of psychiatry – an imperialism that is less obvious than the military domination by Europeans in the nineteenth century and its economic counterpart of the twentieth, but no less powerful and as destructive to the vast majority of people in the world. In the past, it resulted in the imposition of the 'lunatic asylum' as a way of dealing with 'madness'; in the future, it will no doubt result in the imposition of other, equally alien, systems of 'care' derived in the West for 'psychiatric cases' defined on western terms. That is, unless something is done about the relentless 'westernization of the world' (Harrison, 1979) currently taking place, carrying psychiatry with it.

Is depression as pathology universal?

The concept of depression as an illness came out of the tradition of 'melancholia' as illness which goes back to the times of Hippocrates (Jones, 1823). But the validity of the current understanding of depression as an illness that is universally recognizable is very dubious. Reviews of cross-cultural research based on looking for a western model of depression as illness, such as that by Singer (1975), produce the inevitable conclusion that a core illness of depression is universally recognizable; but it is not just this core illness that is diagnosed as depression in psychiatric circles. H. B. M. Murphy (1973), the father of transcultural psychiatry, postulates that the primary psychological pathology was a 'sense of failure of the "We" relationship', and, when this is viewed in a context of the (culturally determined) degree to which 'self' is differentiated from 'non-self' (p. 712), the sense of failure may be experienced as being towards 'self' – as guilt – or towards others, as shame. Three feeling states emerge from Murphy's ideas: First, a sense of isolation or alienation because of (sense of) loss of group membership; second, (sense of) failure towards others felt as shame; and third, failure towards self felt as guilt.

Marsella (1978), taking onboard the reports that 'depression' in non-European cultures is characterized by somatic symptoms rather than psychic ones, argues that if depression is essentially an experience, a psychologically experienced depression is different from one associated with somatic experience, so depression as illness should be regarded as a disorder of the western (cultural) world alone. But anthropologist Obeyesekere (1985), exploring the meaning of depression in different cultural settings, postulates that 'a painful series of affects pertaining to sorrow' may be universally identifiable, but it is illogical to assume that a constellation of symptoms reflecting this situation is a universal illness just because it has been designated as such in western culture. The affects that are designated as illness of depression in the West are seen in the Sinhala-Buddhist culture (of Sri Lanka) and in some cultures of West Africa as arising out of life conditions and inseparable 'from their involvement in an existential issue (such as the nature of life)'. Even though these affects are relatively free floating – and so rightly attributed to illness – in western societies, in African and Asian cultures, and possibly many others, they are 'anchored to an ideology' and dealt with culturally without recourse to an illness model (p. 135). Table 7.1 illustrates the different explanations for depression at present available from the literature in transcultural psychiatry.

A political lesson from considering depression across cultures concerns the effects of imposing the depression category across cultures. Obeyesekere (1985) suggests that a biomedical psychiatrist may well assume the presence of severe depressive illness if a devout Buddhist articulates a 'depressive affect' (according to a western formulation) expressed as a sense of hopelessness generalized into 'an ontological problem or existence, defined in its Buddhist sense as "suffering"' (p. 139). In other words, what amount to religious beliefs in one cultural tradition become symptoms of illness in another. The danger is that if a person for whom the psychiatric tradition is inappropriate – for example, a devout Buddhist – is caught up in the psychiatric system, they could well be treated with either physical treatment – antidepressant medication or ECT – or CBT, which is currently seen as the treatment of choice for 'mild and moderate depression' and the correct treatment for 'severe depression' if combined with antidepressant medication (NICE, 2007). Either of the physical therapies may well be harmful in such an instance. The question of possible damage resulting from CBT

Table 7.1 Explanations of depression across cultures

Processes	References
Sense of failure or loss in context of differentiating 'self' and 'other': Loss of group membership = Isolation/alienation Failure towards others = Shame Failure towards oneself = Guilt	Murphy, 1973
Depression occurs in cultures that 'psychologize' experience	Marsella, 1978
Depression is an illness in cultures where 'depressive affects' are free-floating and not tied to religion	Obeyesekere, 1985

is more complicated; the procedure involves educating the person who is identified as suffering symptoms of depression to recognize thinking styles that are associated with the symptoms, and then working with the person in re-evaluating the alleged dysfunctional beliefs in order to cope with them or change them (Scott and Beck, 2008). According to Fennell (2009) writing in the most up to date textbook on psychiatry edited by Gelder *et al.* (2009), these beliefs may well be 'about the self (e.g., "I am useless"), the world (e.g., "My situation is intolerable"), and the future (e.g., "Nothing will ever change")' (2009, p. 1304). Such belief-change seems to come very close to undermining someone's philosophy of life or religious convictions.

Colour-blind, culture-blind psychiatry

The tendency to deny the importance of race and culture in psychiatric practice – the colour-blind, culture-blind approach – is problematic for several reasons: If colour-blind, the observer's own racial bias is likely to be denied or ignored and therefore not taken into account. And, even if the observer allows for bias at a personal level, the effects of racism in society at large are often ignored. The person being observed is invalidated by being seen as a person without a colour – and colour represents race, an important determinant of self-perception as well as of social opportunities open to people, their rights and their life experiences in a racist society. A colour-blind approach is therefore a denial, both of individual perceptions in a racist society, and, more importantly, the fact that race matters because of the way most societies function. The effect of a culture-blind observation, that is one that sees an individual without perceiving their culture, is somewhat different: First, the person observed is out of context; (s)he is not a part of a society or a group with, for example, allegiances and hostilities towards other people, influenced by other people and dependent on a wide circle of people for what (s)he is. Second, any difference from other people that the person may show is likely to be perceived as an individual difference to be judged in terms of its deviance from a generalized norm, rather than one determined by upbringing or experience reflecting a cultural norm. Thus the colour-blind, culture-blind approach in psychiatric practice falls into a trap of denying social realities of race and culture.

Culture-blindness interacts with colour-blindness, when, for example, a 'symptom', such as retardation (slowness), is being considered in an Asian person. The 'observation' fails to note that the person concerned may consider a passive demeanour to be a correct posture in an interaction with a professional; alternatively or simultaneously, the person may be intimidated by the racism in society that gives black people an inferior position in comparison with whites. The possibility that the apparent 'retardation' is 'cultural' rather than pathological will be distorted by the (likely) belief that Asian behaviour is 'primitive' and so should be seen as socially pathological anyway. Similarly, identification of excitement, disinhibition, paranoia, aggressiveness and 'hearing voices' as symptoms would be carried out in a context where cultural and racial stereotypes are allowed to exert their influence by a psychiatry that is blind to the influence of culture and race in the process of diagnosis.

Conclusions arrived at in a culture-blind and colour-blind way are reinforced by being acceptable to the general common sense of society, often fitting into political and social 'norms' which may include the need for minority groups to be exploited, integrated or rejected. Two illustrations are given below, one drawn from American cross-cultural clinical research and the other from British clinical experience of the author.

Illustration 1

A study of refugees from Laos settled in Minnesota (USA) is reported by Westermeyer (1989) as confirming that 'the prevalence and incidence of paranoid disorders among refugees are high compared to other groups' (p. 47).

> The Hmong people who were selected for this study were given both self-ratings and psychiatrist ratings for 'paranoid symptoms', as well as scores on a 'Hmong culture scale' and an 'American acculturation scale'. The researchers found 'considerable stability' over time in the level of 'paranoid symptoms' on the self-rating scale but a low correlation between this and the psychiatrist rating of paranoia. In line with usual psychiatric practice, the latter were seen as 'objective' ratings, implying that these are correct, while the self-perception of the Hmong, their 'subjective ratings', were given a lower status as 'subjective'. The researcher reported that Hmong people 'with more subjective (but not objective) paranoid symptoms retained more traditional affiliations and behaviors' (1989: 53); and that low acculturation (to American ways of life) correlated positively with two of the three 'objective' measures of paranoia that were used.

The culture-blind, race-blind approach is shown by the following facts: The items selected for identifying paranoid tendencies/symptoms were 'imposed' on the Hmong, disregarding their origins in western questionnaires and the different meanings they may carry in the Hmong cultural context; the meaning of paranoia in a setting where an influx of Asians may have aroused hostility (because of racism) was ignored; the attitudes of psychiatrists towards the Hmong and racial stereotyping (racism) inherent in the process employed by them in making their ratings were not considered; and finally, the feelings engendered in the Hmong people by being interviewed were largely disregarded. Although presented as an academic study, its conclusions were clearly political, reflecting American expectations and cultural arrogance. In fact, the research findings were used to argue that 'acculturation might reduce paranoid symptoms [among the Hmong]' and that 'welfare dependency may contribute to paranoid symptoms by facilitating unemployment with its subsequent isolation from United States society' (Westermeyer, 1989, p. 58).

Illustration 2

This is a case study of a man of West Indian origin who was seen by the author in the Accident and Emergency Department of a general hospital near London:

> An African-Caribbean man in his late twenties was brought to hospital by four policemen under section 136 of the Mental Health Act (HMSO, 1983) which entitles the police to apprehend a person in a public place who may be suffering from mental illness. The police alleged that he was dangerous and that he had a history of psychiatric illness. They insisted on staying with him in the Accident and Emergency Department. The staff, including doctors and nurses, reckoned that he was in need of further observation in hospital but too dangerous to be kept in a general hospital. Their assessment was based on three bits of psychiatric information obtained in the usual professional manner. First, there was the police report that he had talked to strangers in the street in an abusive manner; secondly, it was observed that he would not speak to anyone in the Accident and Emergency Department, that his reactions – and hence his 'affect' – were not in keeping with the situation and that his behaviour and speech indicated 'grandiose delusions'; and finally, everyone agreed that he 'looked' dangerous. When the consultant, a black doctor, was called, he decided to interview the man on his own. The staff expressed alarm at this and stayed nearby. It turned out that he was an artist who could not get a job; he had been looking for a friend, but not knowing the exact address was looking at houses along a street trying to recognize the friend's house. He had tried to talk to people but was brushed off and became angry. Then the police were called and he was brought to hospital. He remained angry, claiming that he had often been tricked into hospitalization in this way.

This man was dealt with impartially in the best traditions of psychiatry; the consultant who was called was not even told that he was black. His level of dangerousness was assessed objectively on the basis of information and the likelihood of mental illness based on his history and an examination of his mental state. His race and culture – in this case of artistic eccentricity – seemed not to cloud the psychiatric assessment; but clearly the assessment that he was dangerous – and a lot more besides – was determined by racial stereotypes of black people. His inability to gain employment and his general low status in society, probably determined by racism, were rationalized into an illness because his race and culture were ignored.

The culture-blind and colour-blind approach in psychiatric practice is sometimes claimed as a liberal stance because the person being judged seems to be considered as an individual irrespective of cultural and racial background. This is a serious fallacy arising from the notion that being 'blind' to something nullifies its effects or significance. Justice cannot be done in any judgement – and psychiatric observations and diagnoses are judgements (see Chapter 2) – unless a person is seen in context which includes his/her culture and, more importantly, the racism that is prevalent both at individual and institutional levels in British society. To ignore culture in psychiatric practice is a mistake; to ignore race is racist.

Summary

In its confrontation with people seen as 'different', whether they live as majorities outside Europe and North America or as ethnic/racial minorities within the European world, psychiatry fails to recognize the validity of cultural experiences of this 'other'. Further, current psychiatry is failing to meet the challenges of a changing world, where many societies are increasingly multiracial in composition and self-conscious about being multicultural. In the context of multiracial and multicultural populations of the UK and the USA, a major problem for people who are designated 'black' is the excessive diagnosis ascribed to them of schizophrenia – essentially a statement of the inability of the system to provide some means of understanding them as people.

The introduction of psychiatry into societies where cultural traditions are very different from those in the West results in the suppression of indigenous, culturally consonant, ways of dealing with emotional problems and 'madness'. Clearly, psychiatry should not be applied indiscriminately in the style that it is formulated and practised at present; neither its form nor its content is suitable for global application. However, against this, it is necessary to point to certain traditions in western medicine that have rubbed off on to the discipline and the way it is practised – at least in many western settings – traditions that could be usefully copied elsewhere.

The humanitarian tradition of medicine represented in psychiatry was probably instrumental in bringing about improvements in the living conditions of people admitted to asylums; and it was the designation of madness as an illness coupled with the medical tradition to study illness that resulted in serious attempts being made to alleviate problems of people thought of as being insane. Since medical illness absolves the individual afflicted by 'illness' of responsibility – or partial responsibility – from their actions, the intervention of psychiatry has protected countless numbers of people from suffering punishment that may have done no good to anyone.

Most importantly, the medical tradition behoves physicians to consider the interests of their patients once disease is diagnosed; and the intervention of psychiatrists has often been crucial in ensuring support for people in trouble of various kinds. In weighing up the overall effect of psychiatry, including its diagnostic approach, it is important to ensure that both positive and negative effects of its practices are respected and that both sides of the balance are taken into account. However, when psychiatry is practised in settings that are alien to the culture – in multicultural societies of the West and in non-western settings – a simple balance is insufficient. The culture of psychiatry itself must be analysed first for bias and second for its effect in undermining culture and social systems in places where psychiatry is imposed.

Chapter 8

Asian and African 'Therapy' for Mental Health

Although biomedical psychiatry within the overall aegis of western – sometimes called 'allopathic' – medicine is now practised worldwide, other indigenous systems of what are sometimes called 'folk-ethnopsychiatry' by anthropologists (Blue and Gaines, 1992) still persist in many parts of the world, although more so in non-western countries than in the West.

This chapter describes in brief some systems of helping people in trouble – medical or otherwise – that amount to 'therapy' originating in Asian and African cultural settings, in so far as they apply to matters of 'mind' or (what in the West are seen as) mental health problems. The emphasis is on examining the interface between psychiatry and systems indigenous to Asian and African cultures that may address the sort of problems that western, biomedical system attempts to do. It should be noted that pre-Columbian Native American traditions are as rich as those from Asia and Africa and there are many other traditions such as those from Australia and New Zealand that may be usefully explored. But these are not considered in this book for the sake of brevity.

Asian approaches

Aspects of diagnosis and treatment (in western terms) that may be applicable to healing and medical systems in Asian cultures are varied and complex. However, certain basic principles are evident: First, medical illnesses and practices to deal with them are not entirely separate from religious problems and religious practices; second, psychology, philosophy and religion are closely interconnected if not integrated – a fact that is particularly evident in the case of Buddhism, which, in western terms, is more of a psychology than a religion (Watts, 1971, 1995); finally, a sense of holism underpins all thinking about the person – and it is a 'holism' that includes the individual, the spiritual world, the physical environment and the cosmos, to a greater or lesser extent. The traditional medical system of Ayurveda is discussed as a system analogous to the medical approach of the West, although the basic premises of the two systems of medicine are very different. Then, some comments are made about therapeutic approaches to mental health problems that seem to address the spiritual dimension of human existence. Finally, 'Tibetan psychiatry', as described by Clifford (1984), is described since it is the nearest practical system outside the West to psychiatry in the way the latter in constituted. Finally there are some comments on Chinese medicine.

Ayurveda

The literature on traditional Ayurveda is derived largely from the writings of Susruta and Caraka – collected in the *Susruta Samhita* and the *Caraka Samhita*, partially translated into English (Sharma and Dash, 1983, 1985; Susruta, 1963). But ideas derived from Ayurveda are mingled with those of Indian philosophy/psychology, ritual and religion – in what Obeyesekere (1977) calls 'a metamedical extension of medical concepts' (p. 155). In other words, the medical approach does not exclude the religious and philosophical dimensions of human existence and experience, although contradictions may be apparent in some aspects. Further, Ayurveda is as much about 'dissertations on correct behaviour' as about medical treatment and prophylaxis; and, from the psychological angle, Ayurveda is a 'repository' of Indian cultural thinking about the human body and the concept of the person (Kakar, 1984, p. 220).

Ayurveda focuses on the person rather than the disease – the person being conceptualized as a totality including physical, psychological, social and metaphysical aspects. And the person is a microcosm of the cosmos. The Ayurvedic notion of a healthy person is pervaded by ideals of moderation, control and responsibility. And the maintenance of good health is inseparable from deliverance from disease. The treatment in Ayurveda for mental disorders is not differentiated from that for bodily illness; and there is no systematic theory of mind and mental processes as there is in western thought, although some forms of therapy for 'restraining the mind' derive from the various schools of yoga. In addition, purification by, for example, purges and enemas, and 'pacification' of the person by decoctions that tranquillize, counteract depression and strengthen the nerves may be used (Kakar, 1984).

The documentation of insanity in Indian Ayurvedic literature has been studied by Haldipur (1984) and Obeyesekere (1977). The former believes that the division of insanity into two broad causal categories of 'humoral' and that caused by 'spirit possession' may be analogous to divisions of illness in western medicine into those having 'constitutional' and 'accidental' causation or into being 'endogenous' and 'exogenous' in type – as in psychiatry. But it would be misleading to present the terminology of one or other system in, as it were, 'alien garb' by emphasizing similarities between them; the basic approach in Ayurveda is very different from that implicit in western definitions of mental disorder. Obeyesekere believes that humoral disequilibrium is referred to in classical Sanskrit as 'anger' or 'excitement'; the aim of Ayurvedic treatment is the calming of this disturbance and restoration of a balance of the humoral state.

In describing the diverse methods of healing concerned with the restoration of mental health and the variety of practitioners using these methods in contemporary India, Kakar (1984) writes that in addition to medical healers such as the *vaids* of Hindu Ayurveda and Siddha systems and the *hakim* of the Islamic *unani* tradition:

> there are palmists, horoscope specialists, herbalists, diviners, sorcerers and a variety of shamans, whose therapeutic efforts combine elements from classical Indian astrology, medicine, alchemy and magic, with beliefs and practices from the folk and popular traditions. And then, of course, we have the ubiquitous *sadhus*, swamis, *maharajs, babas, matas* and *bhagwans*, who trace their lineage, in some fashion or other, to mystical–spiritual traditions of Indian antiquity and claim to specialize (whatever else they might also do) in what in the West in a more religious age used to be called 'soul health' – the restoration of moral and spiritual well-being. (p. 4, italics in original)

Diagnosis in Ayurveda

The *Caraka Samhita* lists three methods for diagnosing illness, divided by Jaggi (1981) into 'judgement of the inspired or the wise (*āptoupadesa*), observation (*pratyaksha*), and inference (*anumāna*)' (p. 136) – analogous to the processes in western psychiatric practice of history-taking, examination and evaluation. Judgement by the specialist is based on history obtained in a comprehensive manner, and inference is concerned with deducing conclusions from the association of the illness with particular events in the patient's life history, diet, character and general conduct. One of the main tools of observation is the monitoring of the *nadi*, which means both pulse and nerves. 'With the proper spiritual imagination, developed through the use of an inner ascetic vision rather than relying on the ordinary eye vision (*netra-chaksu*) alone, the adept can "see" the state of a person's five *bhutas*, three humors and the three mental qualities through the examination of a single *nadi*' (Kakar, 1984, p. 248). But 'diagnosis' in Indian medicine does not mean 'only identifying the disease; it comprises much more' (Jaggi, 1981, p. 140).

A part of an Ayurvedic diagnosis is the deduction of the patient's personality type; this is perceived in relation to the qualities that are traditionally expected, and (as in psychiatry) social desirability is equated, more or less, with health. In an Ayurvedic assessment, the patient's constitution includes their mental state or state of mind, judged against a norm that rests within Indian philosophy and religion. 'Normal mind (*satva*) consists in memory, veneration, wisdom, valour, purity, and devotion to useful work' (Jaggi,

1981, p. 144). Dreams of patients are analysed in assessing mental state in order to determine both diagnosis and prognosis. According to Kakar (1984), Ayurveda recognizes various categories of dreams: some dreams gratify desires that are taboo in the waking state and others depict individual fantasies in dramatized fashion; dreams may foretell the future; and finally, dreams may reflect the disturbance of a particular body humour. *Vaids* maintain that dreaming is the predominant psychic activity even during the waking state, the waking state itself being regarded as delusionary. And Ayurveda has a clear perception of the connections between dreams and bodily processes. Although 'Ayurvedic insights into the working of man's psyche and the causation of mental illness are remarkable achievements', the insistence of Ayurveda on maintaining *wholeness* (body-mind-cosmos) appears to dilute its 'clinical thrust' by its inability to make detailed study of the psyche; consequently, 'mental illness has become the province of many kinds of healers [apart from Ayurvedic physicians] of shamans and exorcists, mystics and astrologers' (Kakar, 1984, pp. 246–7).

Madness or insanity (*unmada*) is diagnosed on the basis of certain 'premonitory symptoms' – premonitions of symptoms rather than symptoms themselves – followed by distinctive features (Sharma and Dash, 1985). The former include 'emptiness of the head', anorexia, 'fatigue, unconsciousness and anxiety in improper situations', various aches and pains and frequent appearance of certain types of dreams; the latter include 'incoherent speech', laughter and dancing in inappropriate situations, emaciation, excitement, 'observance of silence' and aversion to cleanliness. The particular combination of distinctive features denotes the type of insanity but the basic characteristics of insanity are described as follows:

> Due to the perversion of mind, the patient does not think of such things which are worth thinking; on the other hand, he thinks of such things as ought not to be thought of. Due to perversion of intellect, he understands eternal things as ephemeral and useful things as harmful. Due to the perversion (loss) of consciousness, the patient is unable to have perception of burns caused by fire etc. Due to the perversion of memory, the patient either does not remember anything or remembers things incorrectly. Due to perversion of desire, disinclination develops for things desired previously. Due to perversion of manners, the patient, who is otherwise normal, gets enraged. Due to perversion of behaviour, the patient indulges in undesirable activities. Due to perversion of conduct, the patient resorts to such activities as are against the rules prescribed in religious works. (p. 89)

According to Caraka, *unmada* (insanity) is divided into five types on the basis of cause, four caused by vitiation of *dosas* (humours) and one by external factors (Sharma and Dash, 1985; Valiathan, 2003). The latter includes madness caused by possession, described by Wise (1845) as being a separate kind of *unmada*, namely 'devil-madness', which is composed of *bhutonmada* (possession by bad spirits) and *devonmada* (possession by good spirits). Obeyesekere (1977) quotes Susruta as describing another cause of *unmada*, namely sorrow and shock (*sokaya*). Three points should be noted: First, there is no mention of the cardinal symptoms of schizophrenia as described in biomedical psychiatry. Second, *unmada* is accepted as an illness as well as a spiritual possession – the latter initiated by elders, ancestors or such beings as *gandarvas* who affect the patient by touch, *yaksas* by seizure, and *rāksasas* by smell. And, finally, epilepsy is described as a separate disease (Sharma and Dash, 1985).

Treatment in Ayurveda

The *Caraka Samhita* (Sharma and Dash, 1985) describes therapies for all illnesses as divided into three general types: 'Spiritual therapy, therapy based on reasoning (physical propriety) and psychic therapy' (1983, p. 231). All three types of therapy are recommended for most diseases whether mental or physical. The first and last are clearly psychological in the western sense of this word. Spiritual therapy includes incantation of *mantras*, wearing of talismans and gems, auspicious offerings, as well as what may be called religious activity such as the 'observance of scriptural rules, atonement, fasts, chanting of auspicious hymns, obeisance to gods, going on pilgrimage, etc.'; and psychic therapy is described as the 'withdrawal of mind from harmful objects' (1983, p. 231). Physical therapies include herbal remedies, dietary advice and cleansing through massage, fomentations and medicines (drugs in herbal mixtures) administered through the mouth as well as by enema through the rectum or by inhalations through the nose.

In practice, treatment is essentially based on drugs and diet, carefully matched by the physician to the temperament of the patient and geared to an assessment of the manner in which the *dosas* (humours) are affected. If the patient requires care, the attendant (or nurse) must be carefully chosen and the patient too must play an active part in the treatment process. Jaggi (1981) quotes an Ayurvedic text, the *Kusyapa Samhita*, as describing 'four pillars of treatment', namely, physician, medicine, patient and attendant. The patient should possess 'strength of mind, physical vigour, intellect ... [and] ... should have full faith in God, Brahmins, teachers, physicians and friends'; the attendant should be 'one whose passions have been extinguished and possessed of good health and strength ... not suffer from duplicity ... and be tolerant' (p. 157). Obeyesekere (1977) states that the classic texts advise 'harsh measures to control intractable and extreme cases of *unmada*, such as threatening patients with flogging, piercing the patient with pointed instruments, or putting the patient in a dry well with a cover over it', but that 'in the case of *mada* (preliminary stage of insanity) gentle forms of these remedies' should be used while in all instances 'the restoration of serenity of mind' should be the primary aim (p. 160).

It should be noted that the understanding of mind, body and spirit within Ayurveda is holistic in recognizing their oneness and the validity of a meta-physical dimension to the human person. But in most of South Asia spiritual healing is used in conjunction with, or as an alternative to, medical systems. It is probably a fair generalization that the approach to psychological prob-lems within traditional Ayurveda is essentially somato-psychic in practice if looked at in western terms; conversely, psychiatry from an Asian cultural perspective may well appear as a combination of the medical and the spirit-ual, although secularized to an extraordinary extent (see below for meaning of secularization).

Spiritual healing/healing rituals

There are several other healing traditions in the Indian subcontinent apart from medical systems. In fact, healing rituals are the main means by which *unmada* (madness) due to spirit possession is dealt with in the cultural trad-itions of South East Asia. They 'stand out as an uneasy meeting between medical and priestly concerns' (Kakar, 1984, p. 248) – uneasy that is for practitioners of the two very different arts. Although appearing to outsiders as merely counteracting sorcery and/or exorcizing malevolent spirits, heal-ing rituals have a much deeper significance to people brought up within cul-tural traditions where they thrive. They usually involve dancing and music, usually drumming. They are not linked closely to any particular organized religion or medical system but yet they are not 'secular' meaning – accord-ing to a dictionary definition of the word – being 'concerned with the affairs of this world' (Pearsall and Trumble, 1995, p. 1309). They may be described as supernatural but, more appropriately, as spiritual; spirituality is discussed in Chapter 5.

Another type of healing in South Asia involves the work of astrologers and fortune-tellers. These specialists are usually consulted for opinions on what the future may bring, auspicious times for people to undertake cer-tain actions (such as journeys) and likely outcomes in the case of personal issues. When consulted, astrologers/fortune-tellers tend to explore various aspects of their clients' lives, their worries and fears, and their hope and wishes. Pugh (1983) calls the work of astrologers/fortune-tellers 'astrol-ogical counselling'.

Although non-medical healing traditions of India may appear analogous to western psychotherapy/counselling they are fundamentally different (Kakar, 1984): The latter, underpinned by a tradition of introspection aimed at knowing oneself and characterized by scrutinizing 'events' and 'adventures' of one's own life, differs from the Indian tradition of examining one's self by meditative procedures of self-realization; and the 'self' of Indian thinking is 'uncontaminated by time and space' while the western 'self', explored by introspection, is made up of deeds and emotions set in history (pp. 7–8).

In addition to specific practices conducted by specialists, healing may occur in the context of worship at religious shrines and establishments, usually temples, mosques and churches, especially ones that specialize in dealing with people who are seen as mad. It is well known that there are many such places in South Asia with long-established reputations for therapeutic qualities in relation to mental health problems. Anthropologist Skultans (1980) studied such a centre, the Abbasai temple in Phaltan, a small town in Maharashtra (India), and wrote up in the anthropology journal *Man*. Although interesting and informative, this report, like others, does not provide details of the process of healing in terms of the nature of the therapies used. A recent study by psychiatrists of temple healing in South India is described in Chapter 9 but again the nature of the therapy as such is not specified.

'Tibetan psychiatry'

The influence of Ayurveda entered Tibet along with Buddhism around AD 650 and reached Indonesia, Cambodia, Burma and Sri Lanka in the first millennium AD (Jaggi, 1981). Tibetan medicine developed into a comprehensive holistic system by about the eighth century AD and continues to be practised in Tibet (how widely is not known), Nepal and, more recently, among Tibetan communities in India. In her book *Tibetan Buddhist Medicine and Psychiatry*, Terry Clifford (1984) writes: 'Tibetan Buddhist medicine is a fascinating and complex interweaving of religion, mysticism, psychology, and rational medicine' (p. 7). It is because of this peculiar amalgam that Clifford calls it 'Tibetan psychiatry', but its theory and practice are very different to biomedical psychiatry – see below. Essentially, Tibetan medicine brings together three remedial approaches: The *dharmic* or religious alluding to the Buddhist concept of realizing the nature of mind; the *tantric* or yogic referring to spiritual practices for self-healing; and the *somatic* or regular based on the Indian Ayurvedic system of medicine.

The causes of disease in Tibetan medicine are conceptualized in terms of innumerable subtle interwoven factors; according to Rinpoche and Kunzang (1973) these are of two general types – long term and immediate: The former stems from ignorance giving rise to anger, desire and 'mental darkness', the three 'poisons' of the mind, which are related to changes in the three humours namely, bile, air and phlegm; and the latter arise from environmental changes or various other causes such as the overuse of sense organs, unhealthy diet and bad medicine. Each disease is caused by the imbalance of the humours, sinful actions in one's previous lives or a mixture of both. The diagnostic procedure determines the kind of disease, the cause of the disease in the particular individual and the constitution of the individual developing the disease.

'Tibetan psychiatry' has a complex system of classification of demons that cause different types of disorders (Clifford, 1984): 'To the Tibetans, "demon" is a symbolic term representing a wide range of forces and emotions which are normally beyond conscious control and all of which prevent wellbeing and spiritual development'; and the Tibetan psychiatrist reckons that mental illness results from 'leading a life that runs counter to one's inherent disposition' resulting in 'poisons' and 'air disturbances' that cause insanity (pp. 137–48). According to Clifford, it is possible to identify three basic categories of mental illness in Tibetan medicine, expressed in terms of psychological characteristics of (1) fear and paranoia, (2) aggression, and (3) depression and withdrawal. The Tibetan view of insanity in its relationship to enlightenment is described in Chapter 2.

The treatment programme for a psychiatric case in the Tibetan tradition includes a variety of interventions: Ritual exorcism, mantras and other religious practices, special tantric measures to counteract demons and the practice of the *Dharma*, change of diet and environment, acupuncture and, most especially, herbal medicines. In determining the exact combination lies the expertise of the Lama-doctor who could be likened to a psychiatrist in the western biomedical tradition.

The similarity of the Tibetan system to biomedical psychiatry is that it is an amalgamation of what would be seen in western terms as religious practice allied to metaphysical ideas about mental illness, drug therapy and psychotherapy. But there are important differences between Tibetan psychiatry and biomedical psychiatry that developed in the West. First, as Chapter 3 shows, what happened in the West is that a medical system took over and secularized human matters concerned with morality, beliefs, thinking and feeling; Tibetan psychiatry never did aspire to be a secular discipline. Second, psychiatry derives its power by taking political control over lunatics, while the importance of 'Tibetan psychiatry' depends (wherever it still functions) on its roots in Tibetan culture including its religious tradition. Finally, Buddhist *dharma* is accessed by contemplation while psychotherapy is a matter of influence being exerted by 'specialist' therapist re-educating clients. In effect the system does not really qualify as a form of psychiatry.

Chinese medicine

A variety of medical systems, conforming to a basic pattern, based on an understanding of the human condition that reflects Chinese philosophy and tradition – especially the Taoist concept of yin and yang – are generally called 'Chinese medicine'. The classic work for Chinese medicine is *Nei Ching*, translated into English as *The Yellow Emperor's Classic of Internal Medicine* (Veith, 1966).

Kaptchuk (2000) a western authority on Chinese medicine states: 'The logic of Chinese Medicine is organismic or synthetic, attempting to organize symptoms and signs into understandable configurations. The total configurations, the patterns of disharmony, provide the framework for treatment. Therapy then attempts to bring the configuration into balance, to restore harmony to the individual'. A doctor of Chinese medicine seeks to identify patterns of disharmony, similar to what biomedicine calls diseases; 'but they are different from diseases because they cannot be isolated from the patient in whom they occur.' In Chinese medicine, a symptom 'is not traced to its cause, but is looked at as a part of a totality ... [and] ... illness is situated in the context of a person's life and biography' (pp. 4–7). According to Hammer (1990), Chinese medicine classifies the aetiology of disease into three main categories: 'Foremost of these is the "emotions", the "Internal Demons": anger, grief, fear, joy, compassion, anxiety, and worry ... [and] ... Internal Demons are responsible for alterations in the energy system of a person, affecting to one extent or another the mind, the body and the spirit' (p. 2).

During the time of Mao Zedong (Tse-Tung), the various strands of Chinese medicine were regularized in one system – Traditional Chinese Medicine (TCM). Comparing TCM and western (allopathic) medicine is difficult because they different in logical structure: The former does not deal with causation of illness but analyses the physiological and psychological state of a person in order to identify a pattern of disharmony that describes a situation of imbalance in the individual; in the latter, the ostensible aim of treatment is to counteract or eliminate the cause(s) of illness, although much of what passes for psychiatric treatment is geared to the suppression or control of symptoms and/or behaviour. In practice, therapy administered by a TCM physician covers advice on ways of life and diet, together with herbal remedies, massage and acupuncture; the exact mixture depends on the type and form of disharmony to be counteracted (Kaptchuk, 2000). A slightly different view is proposed by Hammer (1990) who believes that (from a western viewpoint) TCM can be seen as entirely 'psychological' – having a similar basis to psychotherapy.

African approaches

Although colonialists, missionaries and anthropologists have described healing practices in Africa, many of their observations are presented in negative terms such as paganism, fetishism, voodoo and black magic. In fact there is at present a lack of a proper unprejudiced understanding of various strands of African medical systems, beliefs and practices. Forms of therapy for 'mental illness', however there were conceptualized, flourished in ancient Egypt as a part of religious healing (Nasser, 1987) and there was a cultural continuity between Egypt and the rest of Africa (Asante, 1985). The remnants of this tradition that have survived the European onslaught surely continue awaiting proper exploration and understanding.

There is a dearth of documentation for western readers concerning the variety of healers practising in African societies today. Another problem in drawing any firm conclusions from the available descriptions of religious and medical healing currently practised in Africa, and culturally indigenous to that continent, is that the descriptions are often distorted by condescension and insensitivity reflected, for example, in the name 'witch doctor' (Gelfand, 1964) usually ascribed to practitioners of all types of African indigenous healing – a nosology that implies, erroneously, a similarity between them and the stereotype of malevolent European witches of the Middle Ages.

According to Mbiti (1990), everywhere in Africa, medicine-men are concerned with both sickness and misfortune; they have knowledge about herbs and other substances used in curing the sick but also have techniques for preventing misfortune, using spiritual methods. Since disease and misfortune are both seen as religious experiences, the medicine-man is in effect 'both doctor and priest'. But in many African villages, 'he is the friend of the community ... accessible to everybody and at almost all times, and comes into the picture at many points in individual and community life'. African medicine-men undergo formal or informal training. Among the Azande (in Sudan) training is formalized being 'long and expensive' and medicine-men form associations or corporations. But even when not formalized, training always 'involves some kind of apprenticeship' (pp. 162–5).

Canadian psychiatrist, Raymond Prince (1964), who worked in West Africa for many years, states: 'The therapy of Yoruba healers is often effective. The relative importance of the magical (or other psychotherapeutic) factors and the physiological factors in healing is difficult to determine because in almost all the cases I studied the two elements were intertwined' (p. 110). Prince goes on to describe the successful treatment by a *babalawo* of a 'severe neurotic' who had not been helped by several western practitioners.

Janzen (1979) has described the healing culture called *ksi-nsi* practised in the southern part of the Democratic Republic of Congo (DRC) then called Zaire – a system that had survived in spite of the severe suppression of indigenous cultural practices during colonial times. Illnesses were perceived as being caused by witchcraft, magic or God, but at the time of writing (in 1979) a 'demystification' in the perception of illness had occurred: 'The mystical cause of witchcraft is substituted in diagnosis by an analysis of social relations either within the kin set or beyond it' (p. 211). Changes in political and administrative power structure in the DRC since the 1960s has resulted in a medical pluralism where the techniques of the traditional healers, interventions aimed at straightening out social problems, purification and initiation (for example, through washing or anointing) and western medicine are practised side by side in the country. In this setting, the illness of an individual is usually managed by a group of relatives who rally for the purpose of sifting information, lending moral support, making decisions and arranging details of therapeutic consultation.

Nigerian psychiatrist Lambo (1969) writes that African traditions attribute the causation of illness to both natural and supernatural or spiritual factors, the balance between them varying across tribes: 'The idea of natural causation reaches its highest peak among the Masai of East Africa who seldom attribute disease to spiritual agency and only very rarely to human intervention' (p. 205). The treatment of an illness is determined by its cause; non-supernatural illnesses are treated with 'rational' treatment using medicaments, but the treatment of supernatural ailments requires a combination of 'rational' and 'preter-rational' treatment. Lambo makes the following generalization about differences between the ideologies underlying western and African medical traditions:

> Reality in the western world has gone the way of attempting to master things; reality for the African traditional culture is found in the region of the soul – not in the mastery of self or outer things, but in the acceptance of a life of acquiescence with beings and essences on a spiritual scale. In this fashion only is the traditional culture mystic. Not because of any prelogical function of mind but merely because the African is the possessor of a type of knowledge that teaches that reality consists in the relation not of men with things, but of *men with other men, and of all men with spirits*. (p. 207, italics in original)

The Yoruba are a major Nigerian ethnic group. The traditional Yoruba worldview is that there are three interconnected states of being, the unborn, the living and the ancestors; and everything living or inanimate is imbued with a spirit (Plastow, 2009). This spirit or vital force can be harnessed by 'distillation' by the specialist through 'contagion' or 'incantation' (Ayoade, 1979, p. 50). Distillation involves the use of objects that have been in contact with the person or thing possessing the essence, and the incantation involves pronouncing certain words in certain ways. The Yoruba tradition of medicine addresses the 'whole person', physical and spiritual, recognizes confession of sin – whether real or imaginary – as vital to the resolution of illness and involves the extended family in therapy (Obembe, 1983). According to Ayoade (1979), traditional Yoruba medicine recognizes three broad categories of disease – supernatural, non-supernatural and God-caused. Although a variety of strategies are used for curing illnesses, such as medication and exorcism, harnessing of inner forces – spirits – plays an important part in dealing with illness.

Even though a specific system of knowledge or therapy analogous to that within psychiatry cannot be extracted out of the African traditions of medicine, philosophy and religion that have been documented, it is clear that African ways of thinking about mental and psychological matters (in western terms) are very different from those in the West. In that sense, an African system is there to be discovered and documented. The main characteristics of such a system should include a sense of unity of the spiritual and material worlds, perhaps akin to a feeling alluded to in contemporary literature as 'magic realism', where naturalistic detail is combined with imaginative elements of fantasy (Pearsall and Trumble, 1995).

Cross-cultural collaboration

Since different cultural traditions have developed diverse approaches to what is mental and what is illness, what happens in many countries is that practitioners of various types work in parallel and the clients choose one or other type – or both or several – at the same time. The obvious approach then would be to strive for collaboration between various systems. But, there are several hindrances to such a vision being realized: First is the cultural arrogance amounting sometimes to racism whereby practitioners of one cultural tradition belittle those from another, the winner being determined by power. And since government sponsorship and promotion is usually for biomedical psychiatry (see Chapter 9), power generally favours western biomedicine. Second is the fact that the worldviews on which the various systems are based are very different, and that the differences are complicated by value judgements linked to perceptions of what is scientific and what is not. Finally, there is an inherent contradiction in collaboration because of the assumption that both cultural relativity (where very different systems are seen as equivalent) and psychological universalism (where a universally applicable basis for human psychology is assumed) can be worked with *simultaneously* (Kakar, 1984). The following paragraphs note a few instances where attempts at practical collaboration have been attempted between practitioners versed in biomedical psychiatry and those using other systems.

Collaboration between systems requires, first and foremost, a mutual respect for each other by the people who work – or try to work – together. And this 'respect' must be built into the structure of the programme or joint system that is evolved, otherwise the more powerful or prestigious system is likely to override the other(s) and 'collaboration' becomes a means of imposing one on the other. To ensure this does not happen, both short- and long-term effects of the collaboration must be considered. Collaborative structures must be examined at a very basic level, with genuine understanding of the political forces that usually keep western approaches on top; and in most instances there should be inbuilt anti-racist measures to counteract the devaluation of anything that is seen as not being derived from European culture. Otherwise, collaborative ventures in the mental health field, as in any other, are likely to become a mere tool for the imposition of western thinking.

One of the earliest attempts by a western-trained psychiatrist to work in conjunction with African healers was by Adeoye Lambo. Dr Lambo founded a day hospital at Aro in western Nigeria which developed into a unique system of 'boarding out' patients in the neighbouring villages and collaborating with local healers in providing care and treatment. Unfortunately, this tender plant of collaboration between an African indigenous system and western biomedical psychiatry appears to have withered over the years. Similar attempts were pioneered by Tigani El-Mahi in the Sudan (*Lancet*, 1964) but again did not survive very long. Patel (1995) has described largely unsuccessful efforts to establish collaboration between traditional healers and biomedical psychiatric practitioners in Zimbabwe concluding that 'the two types of health professionals will not be able to work together' (p. 316). Use of acupuncture for mental illness in China is discussed in Chapter 11. It is known that Ayurvedic doctors and western-type psychiatrists work in geographical proximity to each other in Bangalore (India) but, apparently, do not collaborate.

Although it is difficult to envisage close cooperation between practitioners of western and other systems because of the conceptual gulf between them (see Chapter 2), this does not mean that an individual patient or family does not move around between different types of healers, or use different systems of psychiatry/healing concurrently. In non-western countries such mobility is probably the rule, rather than the exception. Lorna Amarasingham (1980), an anthropologist, has described and analysed the case of a Sri Lankan patient being taken to a number of healers in seeking treatment for 'madness'. Two fortune-tellers were consulted first, then a practitioner of healing rituals who conducted two such rituals, the second of which involved masked dancers; next, an Ayurvedic physician was consulted and made a diagnosis of 'wind-bile madness' caused by an imbalance of the humours. Ayurvedic treatment by decoction or headpack resulted in a lessening of symptoms but the family continued their efforts to help the patient by making propitiation to 'the gods' at an important temple. Later, when an apothecary (pharmacist) gave the patient some pills that helped even further, the relatives took her to a western-type hospital. She was admitted to hospital, diagnosed as suffering from paranoid schizophrenia, and treated with phenothiazine medication.

The illness of the patient described in the previous paragraph was described (by her relatives) as 'weakness of the nerves and brain'; and she was discharged improved but noted in the hospital records to 'retain ideas of a culture-bound nature' (Amarasingham, 1980, p. 80). The view of the family was that both western medicine and astrological forces were powerful in effecting a recovery. They felt that hospital treatment worked because a ritual had already been held. Amarasingham makes the following observation:

> All the healers, with the exception of the Western physicians, share a method in which the confirmation or disconfirmation of the diagnosis rests with the patient. While the diviners, exorcist and Ayurvedic physician are all recognized as having the power to detect causes unknown to the family, the family can recognize or reject these causes. The 'burden of proof' rests on the healer to make his description of the situation 'match' the actual situation of the family. (p. 84)

Although the western-type hospital 'operates within a system of medicine which is hidden from the patient's understanding', both the patient and her family were pragmatic in their approach, taking from each system, including the western one, whatever suited them (p. 84).

The case described above is far from unique; the author is aware that this type of shopping around by users of services and their relatives is the norm in many parts of Sri Lanka and India, even today (June 2009). He is also aware of anecdotal evidence of benefit from healing rituals and Ayurveda – without western medicine being involved at all – for people with problems that fall within the realm of both psychoses and neuroses in the psychiatric nomenclature.

The case reported earlier shows how service users (consumers of services) may bring about a successful outcome if there is sufficient variety of services available for them to choose from and they have the financial means to make the choices. In a situation where there is little information on what type of approach is best anyway, this may well be the best system to promote in the present circumstances. In theory, a collaborative system, where service users and their families find the most effective therapies that suit them, should work equally well *and* be cost-effective. But, in the view of the author, this is not feasible at present for reasons considered earlier; what usually happens when biomedical psychiatry tries to work with 'other' approaches is that it dominates and excludes or distorts the 'other'.

Summary

In the earlier part of the book, psychiatry is envisaged as being composed of practices that have developed within a western medical tradition

(Chapter 2). This chapter shows that mental health problems are addressed in other traditions too, possibly equally effectively. Attempts to amalgamate western biomedical psychiatry and non-western approaches to mental health have been largely unsuccessful. The challenge for the world of mental health is to face up to the diversity available and if possible build systems for mental health that are universally applicable.

Chapter 9

Mental Health in Low- and Middle-Income Countries

In the post-colonial era when the cold war was in full swing the term 'third world' was given to countries that did not fall into one or other power block. Then, as economic development was seen as the way forward for all countries, the world was roughly divided into 'developed' and 'underdeveloped'/'developing' nations. More recently a classification has been introduced by the World Bank of categorizing countries on the basis of gross national income (GNI) per capita, calculated using the World Bank Atlas method (http://www.worldbank.org): Using 2007 GNI per capita incomes, low-income countries (LIC) have $935 or less; lower middle-income countries (LMC) $936–$3705; upper middle-income countries (UMC) $3706–$11,455; and high-income countries (HIC) $11,456 or more (World Bank, 2008). Examples of the groupings based on GNI are as follows:

- LIC includes Afghanistan, Bangladesh, Cambodia, Congo Republic (Zaire), Haiti, Kenya, Nepal, Pakistan, Tanzania, Uganda, and Uzbekistan.
- LMC includes Albania, Angola, China, Guatemala, India, Iraq, Nicaragua, Peru, Sri Lanka, and West Bank and Gaza (Palestine).
- UMC include Argentina, Brazil, Chile, Czech Republic, Jamaica, Malaysia, Mexico, Poland, Russian Federation, South Africa, Suriname, St Vincent and Grenadines, and Turkey.
- HIC include Australia and New Zealand, Canada, Germany, Israel, Ireland, Saudi Arabia, Trinidad & Tobago, USA, UK and other West European countries, United Arab Emirates, Qatar, Kuwait.

In line with some recent books dealing with mental health – for example, *World Mental Health Casebook* by Cohen *et al.* (2002) – this chapter will use the junction between LMC and UMC as the dividing line between poor and rich countries referring to the former as low and middle-income (LM) countries and the latter as middle and high-income (MH) countries. Most of the former are non-western in cultural background and have suffered from colonialism. Some countries, such as China and India, are developing economically at a faster rate than others, but even there the majority of people are poor and systems for mental health care leave much to be desired.

Introduction

In many LM countries, general health and welfare services are underdeveloped and under-resourced; further, whatever mental health systems that exist within the state sector are largely based on western models of mainly institutional care. Since most of these countries have their own independent governments, one might think that indigenous medical and religious systems for promoting mental health are being developed but unfortunately this is not the case. Where mental health services are developed, they are usually based on biomedical psychiatry which is nearly always available free or at subsidized rates at the point of access. Also, since most non-governmental agencies (NGOs) involved in this field are resourced by western countries, they too turn to biomedical approaches for whatever services they support. Often, traditional asylums – now called mental hospitals – dating from the colonial era still exist, sometimes run down and neglected but far too often unchanged in organization. But together with these, there are a few innovative projects that are conceptualized and developed by local people based on local needs assessments and/or community priorities. Unfortunately, there is very little information on these local projects in the literature. However, the author has observed some of the work in Sri Lanka personally and has been involved in some recent developments in that country; and this chapter will draw on this personal knowledge.

Some of the English language publications that address the special needs and contexts of LM countries include *World Mental Health. Problems and Priorities in Low-Income Countries* by Robert Desjarlais *et al.* (1995), *World Mental Health Casebook. Social and Mental Programs in Low-Income Countries* edited by Alex Cohen *et al.* (2002) and *Meeting the Mental Health Needs of Developing Countries. NGO Innovations in India* edited by Vikram Patel and R. Thara (2003). The first and second of these books deal with overall problems in general without describing mental health projects as such. The third consists of descriptions of projects around mental health that draw upon the experience of workers in the field but it is only about India. Also, there have been two recent papers in the English language literature reporting religious healing in South India (Halliburton, 2004; Raguram *et al.*, 2002).

Interest in service provision

Interest in examining cross-national differences in mental health as a prelude to promoting mental health services dates to WHO research studies of 1960s and 1970s such as the IPSS described in Chapter 7. Being based on traditional epidemiological approaches with ethnocentric assumptions, they are seriously flawed and do not provide a true indication of what is required for improving mental health in developing countries. Clearly, what is needed must (a) be based on an understanding of how local people understand 'mental health' and (b) take on board both indigenous ways of dealing with what may be construed as ill health or illness as well as knowledge from western systems of mental health care, where appropriate.

The broad guidelines for health care enunciated at the Alma Ata Conference in 1978 (WHO/UNICEF, 1978) reconfirmed at Riga in 1988 (WHO, 1988) define health as 'a state of complete physical, mental and social well-being' (1988, p. 7). *The World Health Report 2001* (WHO, 2001) points to the following principles for good systems of mental health care: Continuity of care, wide range of services, partnerships with patients and families, involvement of the local community and integration into primary health care. The report supports the importance of understanding and integrating local knowledge and, in the case of African and Asian countries, 'working with traditional healers' (2001, p. 58). The strategy for South East Asia (WHO Regional Office for South-East Asia, 2008) emphasizes the need for community-based mental health programmes that are 'culturally and gender appropriate and reach out to all segments of the population, including marginalized groups' (p. 1). In other words, the tendency today is to move away from formal mental health services linked to finding and treating 'illness', towards a public health and welfare model.

Although WHO now emphasizes community care and a public health model for LM countries, it is not clear from its publications how this should be converted into policies and practical service development; this may reflect a division of opinion on where exactly *mental health care* as a category should fall, that is, as an extension of a mental illness service or within a broader framework of welfare and psychosocial health. For example, a recent paper from WHO quoting Saraceno (2004) points out that if medical care is separated from psychosocial care, '*mental health* care services may inadvertently promote exclusively biological care for the severely mentally ill by drawing human resources skilled in non-biological interventions away from formal mental health services' (van Ommeren *et al.*, 2005, p. 71, italics in original). But there are some problems in terminology used by WHO that may well indicate conceptual cultural issues around mental health. WHO's emphasis on well-being has given rise to theoretical objections to the use of the well-being concept in relations to health (see Carlisle and Hanlon, 2008). Also, the apparent reluctance of WHO to move too far away from the traditional medical approach to mental health as the absence of 'illness' may reflect political forces within the organization itself; for example, there are issues around funding from the pharmaceutical industry being funnelled to WHO through patient organizations (Day, 2007) – and this industry has a vested interest in promoting biomedical psychiatry (Chapter 3). The reality on the ground is that resource-poor, LM countries look to WHO for guidance and sources of funding for developing mental health services; and, whatever the reasons for the apparent muddle at WHO, there appears to be a discrepancy between 'talk' and 'walk' when it comes to WHO experts advising low-income countries (see below).

WHO helps Asian and African countries by providing support for individual projects and advice to governments in developing policies as well as developing individual services (see WHO, 2002). A problem that seems to occur is that consultants sent by WHO do not often implement the sort of changes that WHO itself advocates in its reports (see above). Quite often, experts from western countries tend to impose models and ideologies derived from their own experiences in the West without much sensitivity to local cultures and customs. Local politics and local vested interests too play a part in this; for example, local professional establishments often favour services that imitate those in the West that they have been taught to regard as scientific and modern; and local professionals are usually unfamiliar with service users playing a role in mental health development. But in spite of all this, there are local professionals and community workers in many countries striving hard to provide culturally sensitive services and these people tend to be in local NGOs. But even in NGOs, discrepancies arise between intent and action.

The dependence of many LM countries on the work of NGOs is a major problem. In many places, services provided by NGOs are not coordinated; they often compete with one another and do not share information and know-how. Many NGOs are controlled and directed from outside the countries they serve and even in the case of those controlled locally, they are dependent to a large extent on funding from western countries. Foreign controlled NGOs tend to be geared to interests and priorities set by funding agencies that usually favour promoting particular philosophies and approaches that reflect needs or attitudes in donor countries rather than the needs of the receiving countries. So anti-stigma campaigns, individual rights and de-institutionalization (see Scull, 1984) are pushed as the main thrust of some NGO work or even that of WHO, ignoring (a) the connection of stigma with the biomedical model (see Chapter 2); (b) the tendency for community rights to be as important as individual rights for people from non-European cultures (Chapter 5); and the lack of welfare systems and sometimes grinding poverty in many developing countries that mitigate against people being able to lead productive lives in their own community. Other systems that are sometimes promoted without proper regard to local conditions all of which the author has knowledge of include: General Practitioner (GP) centred treatment – ignoring the fact that in many LM countries GP services are fee-paying while hospital services are free; day-hospital-based group therapy – although group therapy may not be culturally appropriate; and CBT in settings where individualized focus on sorting out thinking patterns may contradict religious beliefs. Moreover, many systems underpinned by biomedical, diagnosis-based systems of mental health care clash with local cultural patterns.

Current scene

People who receive services for mental health access one or more of a mixture of agencies and people as shown in Table 9.1. Most LM countries suffered from oppression and underdevelopment between the mid-eighteenth to mid-twentieth centuries. An early attempt, actually during colonial occupation, to draw on western knowledge and expertise while addressing local conditions and illness behaviour was the Aro project in Nigeria described in Chapter 8. There, biomedical therapy and medical investigations were combined with therapy from indigenous healers, religious services and social activities. A different approach is described by anthropologist Gananath Obeyesekere (1977) at a Buddhist temple at Neelamahara, about 20 miles from Colombo, Sri Lanka, which had a reputation for Ayurvedic treatment of *unmada* (equivalent to mental illness). At this centre, clients, usually with their carers, were accommodated in a local village in a boarding-out scheme and attended upon by the healer-priest. Neelamahara thrived as a centre for the healing of mental illness well into the 1980s. The author has been told that the Buddhist monk who established the centre died in 1986 but his main pupil continued the tradition by treating patients at Maharagama which is about 30 miles from Colombo until he too died in 2006.

It is well known that that there are numerous centres in Asian and African countries where 'mad' people are taken for cures – usually around a temple, mosque or church – although there are hardly any recent reports on these services in medical or psychiatric journals except for two papers (Halliburton, 2004; Raguram *et al.*, 2002) referred to later when efficacy of

Table 9.1 Provision of mental health care in developing countries

Statutory (state funded) services
 mainly institutions
Indigenous practitioners
 mainly private
Healing
 private healers, healing centres, mainly religious
NGOs
 funded by western sources, mainly foreign controlled
Humanitarian agencies
 psychosocial programmes

systems is discussed. Many years ago Field (1960) described Ashanti shrines in Ghana which people with 'fear and guilt frenzies' and people who 'are indistinguishable from classical schizophrenics' benefitted from attending (1960, p. 1045).

It is necessary at this point to sound a word of warning about the danger of being carried away by idealizing what may happen in LM countries. The reality for people who are very disturbed mentally – psychotic in the language of psychiatry – in many LM countries is that they are tied up, or physically controlled in some way in order to prevent uncontrolled behaviour (Gilbert, 2002; and personal communications to author from various sources), at least until they can be transported to a mental hospital, if one is available. Conditions at healing centres, too, may be inhumane; on a visit in January 1998 to a religious institute in Kerala (South India) renowned for helping people with insanity, the author observed mentally disturbed people being housed in cages in the grounds of the institution, cared for by relatives sitting outside the cages. (Also in the grounds of the institution were many small dwellings built for other 'mad' people waiting for help.) It is likely that small doses of psychotropic medication may well have enabled such people to be physically free, as they would undoubtedly be in most developed countries where psychiatric units are easily available.

The information available on currently active innovative centres for mental health care in LM countries is very limited. Two examples, Sri Lanka and China, are used to illustrate the sort of problems facing non-western LM countries today. The information presented is from personal observations of the author together with published material in the English language literature.

Sri Lanka as an example

An indigenous medical system, Ayurveda (see Chapter 8), has been practised in Sri Lanka for many hundreds of years. It was promoted by the state before colonial occupations began in the later eighteenth century. It continued to flourish under the Portuguese and Dutch (although not state-supported) mainly because these colonial powers were not interested in servicing the medical needs of the people apart from their own nationals (Uragoda, 1987). But as state sponsorship of western medicine developed under British rule (Britain captured the whole island in 1815), Sri Lanka experienced a decline of Ayurveda. But in the early twentieth century there was some revival of interest in Ayurveda as part of a political movement and this led to a modicum of government support for Ayurveda, although the main thrust of the government was – and still is – the promotion of allopathic (western) medicine. Today (June 2009), allopathic medicine and

Ayurveda function separately as institutional forms, Ayurveda losing out in funding and status; and the two sets of practitioners occupy separate social spaces. But most Sri Lankans use both systems without any real conflict (Waxler-Morrison, 1988), 'interchangeably and also in tandem' (Jones, 2004, p. 104).

Although the bulk of organized medical care in the statutory sector in Sri Lanka is based on allopathic medicine – which in the case of mental health is a narrow biomedical psychiatry – there are government supported Ayurvedic medical centres in some areas. The extent to which the latter provide help for people with mental health problems is not known. In practice, people suffering from mental health problems (usually accompanied by their carers) consult and obtain help from a variety of professionals apart from physicians practising Ayurveda or allopathic medicine; they include specialists in exorcism and other forms of healing (Amarasingham, 1980; Kusumaratne, 2005; Vogt, 1999; Wijesekera, 1989) as well as astrologers, who provide what Pugh (1983) calls 'astrological counselling'. In fact in most of South Asia, forms of medicine and healing rituals exist side by side and are used by most people without experiencing any conflict, one merging into the other in practical terms (see Amarasingham, 1980; Waxler-Morrison, 1988). Although astrologers are easily available and relatively inexpensive, other forms of healing are becoming increasingly expensive to access because their therapies involve setting up elaborate rituals. This is driving people to access biomedical psychiatry.

Mental health care based on western-type institutions was first introduced to Sri Lanka by the British colonial government in the 1840s and the main mental hospital, Angoda Hospital, opened in 1926 (Uragoda, 1987). Today (June 2009), statutory mental health services are based mainly at this hospital and two others (all near Colombo), and small units in provincial general hospital psychiatric units, where also outpatient clinics are conducted. The current approach is largely biomedical and institutional, although some changes are being made to encourage recovery through integration of patients into the community. The Sri Lankan Department of Health, with help from WHO, produced a new *Mental Health Plan* (Mental Health Directorate, 2006) which is being gradually implemented. This addresses basic issues of management, organization and human resources development; and envisages several new inpatient units being built in towns across the country, the training of 'psychiatric social workers' and 'specialised psychosocial counsellors', and the prospect of 'a broad range of rehabilitation and psychosocial services' being developed in the future (p. 5). Two government 'rehabilitation units' have been established in the south of the island but few patients sent there have actually been able to leave the institutions.

Some NGOs provide community services, the best known being *Nest* (Fernando, 2005b) and *Basic Needs Sri Lanka* (Weerackody and

Fernando, 2009): The former runs a series of houses across the country from which community workers conduct outreach support for vulnerable people; and the latter aims to influence attitudes of communities towards mental illness and to mobilize the families and communities to take a more responsible role in the care of mentally ill instead of incarcerating them in hospitals or sometimes in their own dwellings. Also, *Nest* runs an occupational therapy centre in one of the mental hospitals near Colombo and *Basic Needs Sri Lanka* runs a horticultural unit adjoining the main mental hospital at Angoda near Colombo. There is a day centre in Colombo and there are resource centres, located near Kandy in Central Province and Jaffna in the Northern Province (Rodrigo, 1999), all run with the help of NGOs. In addition, a number of so-called humanitarian agencies (NGOs) have been carrying out various forms of psychosocial programmes in areas affected by conflict and (since 2005) in tsunami-affected regions of the country.

Non-medical healing practices in Sri Lanka antedate Ayurveda and even antedate the introduction of Buddhism in the third century BC. These practices have been described by Pertold (1930), Wirz (1954), Obeyesekere (1981) and Kapferer (1991). However, the descriptions are of little value for extracting any lessons about 'therapy' analogous to that in western systems. The ceremonies themselves usually involve dancing where masked actors depict demonic figures supervised by a specialist called a *kattadiya*.

Beatrice Vogt (1999), a psychotherapist who studied healing systems in Sri Lanka in the 1980s, identifies three forms of healing ritual commonly used there: (a) *Pirit* is a monastic ritual, sometimes also conducted by lay persons, and performed at significant events (such as burial or birth preparations) as well as illness. (b) In *puja* (offering ceremony), a group (of family, friends or well-wishers) offers a ritual act of generosity towards, for example, a monastic community or towards gods. (c) The *tovil* is a public healing ritual held in the house of a patient that involves dancing and drumming. It may also incorporate a *puja* to gods. As noted earlier, astrological counselling (Pugh, 1983) is also accessed by Sri Lankans.

Kusumaratne (2005) describes the practice of a healer – a *kattadi mahattaya* – practising a form of exorcism in the hamlet of Homagama with a population under 40,000. (The same person also practises as a physician specializing in the treatment of snakebite.) It seems that this healer dealt with 25 cases of witchcraft, 50 cases of demon possession and 60 family disputes during a period of three months using various types of *thovil* ceremonies (Kusumaratne, 2005, pp. 132–4). So, to judge from the extent of this healer's practice, it would seem that mental or psychological problems among many Sri Lankans may well be dealt with predominantly by Ayurvedic physicians or healing of some sort, relatively few people with such difficulties receiving psychiatric therapies.

The recent social disruption arising from conflict and political violence in Sri Lanka (see Meyer, 2006 for summary) has resulted in some interest in the resilience and coping mechanisms used by people living in areas most affected by disruption. According to Gombrich and Obeyesekere (1988), a way of dealing with inner conflict or social stress available in the Buddhist tradition (which is pervasive in most of the country even among non-Buddhists) is to 'withdraw one's attention from the external world and meditate. Another is to evade the harsh realities of daily life in ecstatic emotion, the love of god' (1988, pp. 14–15). Kakar (1984) points out that identification with gods and goddesses enables experience of inner states of consciousness – perhaps a form of 'therapy' in the western idiom. Patricia Lawrence (2000, p. 2003), an anthropologist, has described how, in the face of the suffering resulting from political violence in eastern Sri Lanka, traumatized people obtain protection and healing from Hindu goddess cults and local oracles – mainly people who have been empowered through possession. A current programme of research and capacity building is exploring the question as to what types of interventions are seen as valuable by the people themselves (see Weerackody and Fernando, 2008 for a field report).

China as an example

Traditional Chinese Medicine (TCM) does not recognize a separate category of mental illness (Chapter 8), and so health of the mind as separate field for service provision did not occur until late 1800s when foreign missionaries began establishing asylums for the insane in China. The following account of recent history of mental health service provision in China is based on reports by Chang and Kleinman (2002) and personal observations by the author and matters reported to him informally.

Widespread disruption and war during first part of the 1900s prevented much development in China in any field of health. By 1948 there were around sixty psychiatrists and five psychiatric hospitals (1100 beds) for 500 million people. By end of 1959 this had increased by nineteen times. Russian neuropsychiatric models were in use – biological and Lysenko-Behavioural. During the cultural revolution which caused massive social disruption from 1965 to 1969, 'mental illness' was seen as deviancy or wrong political thinking and psychiatry held to be unnecessary. Also religious institutions were suppressed as 'superstition', social sciences were banned and there was hardly any development in the discipline of psychology although it was not actually banned. So China in the 1980s was in a very different condition socio-politically to, for example, India, Sri Lanka and other South Asian countries. From the 1980s onwards, there was an extension of state-funded mental illness services, modelled on western lines. By 2002, there were about 150,000 beds and 13,000 mental health professionals in the whole country, with a population of about one billion. But once market forces came on the scene and fee-for services was introduced in the late 1990s, 30 per cent of beds became empty. The author was told in 2001, that many admissions to the mental hospitals at that time were through police intervention. Anyway hospitals were then (and still are) concentrated in urban locations; cooperative medical schemes instituted in the Maoist period have virtually collapsed and rural social welfare has declined in rural areas.

Alongside all the social-political changes in China, some novel experiments in mental health care have been reported (Chang and Kleinman, 2002; Chang *et al.*, 2002; Desjarlais *et al.*, 1995). The best known is a unique type of community care which has been dubbed the 'Shanghai Model' since it began in the urban area of Shanghai in the 1950s. This model is based on three-tiers of levels of care – community, district hospital and municipal hospital – and is said to deal with rehabilitation of people suffering from 'mental retardation', psychosis and epilepsy. As the cooperative medical care system and barefoot doctor schemes had broken down in the 1990s with charges for services being introduced, the 'guardianship network model' for mental health care has spread reputedly to other cities, although there is little reliable information on this. Innovations have been added to the original system – for example, of guardianship networks apparently geared mainly to maintaining public security and having home-based 'sick beds' attached. In urban areas too outpatient psychiatry is growing for 'psychosocial problems' and substance abuse problems. The extent to which Chinese people have returned to religious and other spiritual forms of therapy are not known. Since religious activity was suppressed during Maoist times, it is safe to assume that forms of healing that may have been seen as religious or stemming from superstition play little part in modern China.

Efficacy of different systems

It is worth noting that serious doubts about the value of predominantly biomedical psychiatry in the UK, in particular when applied to people from Britain's minority ethnic groups, have been the subject of much concern (see Bhui and Olajide, 1999; Fernando, 2003; Fernando and Keating, 2009b; Ingleby, 2004; Ramon and Williams, 2005; Tew, 2002). For this reason and because of the cultural and socio-political diversity across the world, and the differences in access to resources between rich and poor countries, developing mental health services in South Asia or other non-western setting is not a simple matter of transferring established strategies commonly used in high-income countries of the West. Mental health is not just a *technical* matter but is tied up with ways of life, values, and worldviews that may vary significantly across cultures.

Comparing systems of mental health care across cultures is difficult if not impossible because of the disparities of definition of, for example, mental health and illness and variations in illness behaviour (see Chapters 2, 3 and 8, and parts of Chapter 1). However, two recent articles throw some light on this matter.

A study of healing at a Hindu temple in Tami Nadu (South India) visited by people who want help with mental health problems (usually with their carers) was published in the *British Medical Journal* (Raguram *et al.*, 2002) – the first such study to be printed in a prestigious British medical journal. The authors had elicited the views of both the patients and their carers about their experiences and also made psychiatric assessment (of the patients) on a standard scale before and after their stay at the temple. The findings are that (a) most of the patients studied suffered from psychotic illness and (b) showed a degree of improvement (judged by reduction of psychiatric symptoms and their own expressed views) that matched that generally achieved by traditional biomedical therapy: 'Healing temples may constitute a community resource for mentally ill people in cultures where they are recognised and valued' (p. 40). The author has visited a similar place – a mosque near Trivandrum in Kerala (South India) – and has heard of many others in South Asia that provide healing often by service-users just 'being there' (Fernando, 2004, p. 25). The nature of healing at these centres is unclear but if they are effective from a service-user and carer perspective they must be considered at least as a valuable resource.

The journal *Transcultural Psychiatry* carried a paper by Halliburton (2004), a psychiatrist from USA, reporting research into experiences of 100 people who accessed treatment in three forms of therapy in Kerala (South India) – Ayurvedic, biomedical psychiatry and religious healing at three locations namely a Hindu temple, Muslim mosque and a Christian church, all of which had reputations for healing people who suffer from mental illness. Patients of all three systems were interviewed about their illness histories, the process of therapy-seeking and other issues. The research also involved discussions with over twenty healers. All the patients had similar mixtures of symptoms and were diagnosed (in the allopathic psychiatric system) as suffering from schizophrenia or other severe mental disorder. Similar proportions of patients benefitted from each form of therapy. Follow-up six to nine months after the initial assessments showed that no significant difference in outcome of three therapies. But there were several instances where patients (with their carers) had changed therapies. Having not benefitted from one they had changed to a different one and then benefitted. So availability of several different types of therapy with the means for people (service-users and their families/carers) to shop around and find the one that suited them best produced an overall improvement rate that was superior to that in a setting where only one type of therapy was available. The lesson from this study may point to a policy that could be applied universally – backing user-choice (Fernando, 2005c).

Situation on the ground; pluralism

In most of South Asia, people with mental health problems obtain help, if any at all, through informal family networks; attending statutory services, usually run on psychiatric lines; therapy from indigenous physicians; centres of healing; religious institutions where they could consult priests or other religious leaders; and help of healers of various types. The reality in many African and Asian countries is that (a) systems of religion and indigenous medicine are closely related, if not co-incident, and these, together with biomedical psychiatry and spiritual healing – which may or may not be part of 'religion' – form the main sources for the alleviation of mental suffering (see Chapters 2 and 8) and (b) biomedical psychiatry is available to a minority of people who suffer from mental health problems. Although the efficacy of any of the systems accessed by people in LM countries is not known, it should be noted that the imposition of biomedical psychiatry in non-western cultural settings is fraught with problems and dangers to the societies concerned (see Chapter 7).

In South Asia, the main system of indigenous medicine accessed by local people is Ayurveda (see Frawley, 1989; Obeyesekere, 1977), in China it is TCM (see Hammer, 1990; Kaptchuk, 2000), and in Africa there are a variety of systems (see Ademuwagun *et al.*, 1979; de Jong, 1987; Lambo, 1965; Last and Chavunduka, 1986; Prince, 1964). Further, since (what in the West are seen as) mental health problems are often seen in spiritual terms, it is commonly the custom for people in South Asia to turn to healing rituals as well as both indigenous and western (allopathic) medical systems, quite often concurrently – not as alternatives but part of a pluralistic system of help and support for people in trouble (Halliburton, 2004; Nichter, 1980; Sachs, 1989; Waxler, 1984; Waxler-Morrison, 1988) – something that the author could attest to. This is illustrated, for example, by a case study of a mental patient in Sri Lanka described by Amarasingham (1980) referred to in Chapter 8.

Challenges and limitations

There are no easy answers to the question as to what type of mental health system should be promoted in developing, non-western countries. The challenge is to build mental health services based on principles and practices that are both consistent with indigenous traditions and worldviews but yet calling on methods and experiences of value from both their own traditional sources and from western scientific knowledge and practice – and

Table 9.2 Building mental health services in developing countries

Challenges	Limitations
Cultural acceptability	Economic restraints
Incorporation or support of indigenous medicine and healing systems	Low political priority for mental health
	Paucity of social welfare networks
Adaptation of western systems where necessary	Shortage of trained professionals
Sustainability and affordability	Brain drain of trained professionals
Link to general rural development and poverty reduction	Stigma arising from medical model for 'madness'
	Foreign control and inappropriate agendas

to do so in a context where resources are scarce, poverty often endemic and social welfare minimal (Table 9.2). To achieve this aim, the author's opinion is that the process for development should take on board aspects of community development (CD) (see Jones, 1983) and/or participatory rural appraisal (PRA) (see Chambers, 1983, 1997), both of which depend on mobilizing and supporting communities, together with ideas based on educational approaches of, for example, Paolo Freire (1996) or on spiritual/ religious approaches indigenous to the countries themselves and consistent with the cultures of the people. Underlying all is the need for development to be sustainable (see Warburton, 1998) with implications for justice and equity (see Sachs, 1997). The need for services to be consistent with the cultural ambiance of the country is often accepted without opposition but how this is put into practice is worth considering.

The biggest issue on the ground for achieving some way of combining different approaches is around power, allied to the status and the inherent attitudes of professionals groomed in western education; unfortunately power works to give priority to anything 'western' (see Chapter 8) – reinforced by the fact that development is dependent to a large extent on financial assistance from western countries. Also, mental health development cannot be seen outside of general development – social, political and economic. And in poor countries economic development and industrialization, in whatever form that takes place, should be accompanied to a greater or lesser extent with rural development – changing the lives of the vast majority of people who live in the rural countryside or small towns. A discussion of more general development is outside the remit of this book.

There are many limitations to mental health development in developing countries some of which (e.g., attitudes among professionals derived from colonial times) have been referred to already. Allied to this is the dependence for development on foreign aid and the consequent control exercised by western agencies on the nature of development, especially their promotion of western styles of mental health care. Economic restraints are one of the major limitations to development in any field, but should be less so as time goes on in countries where economies are growing fast, such as China and India. But here, and in all countries, low political priority given to mental health is a limitation to development. Clearly, development must go hand in hand with training of professionals; unfortunately, the emigration of trained professionals to the West is a problem that is difficult to limit unless western countries play a part in limiting this or compensating developing countries for the brain drain. The paucity of social welfare schemes means that the concept of mental health must be sufficiently wide to address social welfare. Finally, there is the issue of stigma. A case was made in Chapter 2 for stigma being intimately tied up with the biomedical concept of mental illness. The problem is that in developing mental health services, incorporating – even in a small way – western ideas of 'mental illness' may increase stigma. Although it may not be possible to fully address the lessons enunciated in Chapter 2 – that to get rid of stigma we need to get rid of the genetic-biomedical model of mental illness – giving indigenous medical systems and healing the priority that they deserve anyway could be a way of minimizing stigma.

Summary

Mental health services in non-western developing countries should be 'home-grown', suited to the cultural context and needs of the communities themselves, and not just copies of systems in western developed countries. They need to be developed against a background of knowledge about the culturally determined meaning of 'mental health' in the countries concerned and care should be taken to avoid imposing unmodified models derived from psychiatry and western psychology; the particular danger is that western biomedical approaches are taken as the standard mainly because they are often assumed to be 'scientific' and 'modern'. However, approaches developed in the West may play a part in service development, particularly when they are rethought from the perspectives of transcultural psychiatry. An approach that may be useful is to make community consultation the starting point of all development; then, western expertise could be brought in an advisory role rather than a decision-making or determining role.

Developing community-based mental health services

In the course of a recent programme in Sri Lanka consultations were carried out to explore perceptions of well-being in areas of conflict and disaster.

As a result of this work, a possible way forward for mental health development has emerged. In order to advance a broad, culturally appropriate approach to building mental heath services in close collaboration with people concerned, Weerackody and Fernando (2009) propose three overlapping stages: (i) dialogue and consultation with communities; (ii) capacity building with local mental health workers; and (iii) integration of the system into social welfare and health structures. In the first stage, they propose using tools derived from PRA (see Chambers, 1997) to allow a 'bottom-up' consultation process with communities in locations where development is to take place. In the second stage, they suggest capacity building of local agencies through training in their abilities to consult adequately and blend the results of their consultations with training provided by western agencies adept in approaches of transcultural psychiatry. In the final stage, they suggest that knowledge and experience should be integrated into a sustainable and effective system of community care linked to the health and social care systems in the district, sustainability being ensured by linking the system from the start with a community facility, such as a religious centre or community organization. The final outcome could be a process for building a community-care system that may vary from place to place; this process could be a model for building care systems across the country, geared to needs of different locations. The model proposed may not be the best, but if mental health development in developing countries is to advance, a people-sensitive model for work is urgently needed. Otherwise, the result may well be an imposition of western-dominance posing as 'development'.

Chapter 10

Mental Health of Refugees in High-Income Countries

A major feature of the past two decades has been the massive forced migration of people because of war, natural disasters and poverty, in spite of restrictions enforced on travel across national borders, especially those of countries in the European Union (EU). Today large numbers of people are either 'internally displaced persons' (IDPs) or live in foreign countries as 'asylum seekers' or 'refugees'. The United Nations High Commissioner for Refugees (UNHCR, 2008) estimates 51 million IDPs worldwide, 26 million displaced as a result of armed conflict and another 25 million displaced by natural disasters, and 16 million refugees of which about 1.6 million live outside their regions of origin. Although the underlying causes for this massive number of people fleeing from, or evicted from, their homelands are complex – civil war, ethnic conflict, famine poverty and natural disaster – they could be envisaged largely as the legacy of 300 years of European expansion into Africa, Asia and America with its human rights abuses, stealing of property and land, and cultural, political and economic under-development of Asia and Africa, added to by the post-war colonization of Palestine by European settlers and the more recent invasion of Iraq by some western nations.

The term 'refugee' is used in this chapter to mean both officially rec-ognized refugees and unofficial refugees namely, asylum seekers who have overstayed although failing in their application for refugee status or leave to remain and people who have immigrated without permission from relevant authorities. The chapter is largely about issues concerning mental health of refugees living in UK, especially London, as an example of high-income, relatively rich, 'developed' western country (see Chapter 9 for discussion of division into high-, middle- and low-income countries); they have come mainly from countries undergoing turmoil in Asia (including the Middle East), Africa and South America. Many issues around race and culture that apply generally in the mental health field are dealt with in Chapters 2, 3 and 4; and issues of psychological trauma and some aspects of providing help for people affected by armed conflict are considered in Chapter 6. This chapter should be taken in conjunction with these earlier chapters, especially Chapter 6.

Introduction

In the UK, a person is recognized as a refugee only when their application for asylum has been accepted by the Home Office or they are granted leave to remain. So the term refugee is a legal term and not something that points to them as *people*. The Refugee Council (UK) (2008) states that (a) asylum seekers represented just 0.025 per cent of the total number of people who entered UK in 2005; (b) the UK is home to less than 3 per cent of the world's refugees – around 290,000 out of 8.4 million worldwide; and (c) three-quarters of the world's refugees live in developing countries, Europe looking after just 18 per cent. Nearly all refugees and asylum seekers living in the UK have left their homes in Asia and Africa because of armed conflict and/or expulsion, some having experienced significant personal trauma both physically and psychologically; and others have left because of extreme poverty and/or harassment because of their political, religious or personal beliefs or activities.

Many refugees and asylum seekers in the UK come with a history of personal trauma before their departure from home ('pre-migration') for which they may well require specific psychological help (see Chapter 6); in addition they may have encountered many hardships during their journeys to UK sometimes through many countries, often in hiding; and finally they may face many stressors in the place that they consider one of safety – the UK.

In general terminology, asylum seekers and refugees form part of what are currently described in the UK as 'black and minority ethnic' (BME) people (see Fernando and Keating, 2009a) and therefore suffer from the problems faced by BME people, but there are significant additional factors impinging on mental health that apply to refugees and asylum seekers: They are nearly all relatively recent arrivals in the country and mostly feel marginalized from mainstream and from settled BME people; many lack family connections in the country and are sometimes fearful of communicating with their kinfolk in other countries for a variety of reasons; most find difficulties in grasping the English language especially in terms of nuances of language, and all suffer a feeling of deprivation at being forced to migrate, rather than choosing to do so. But overriding all these considerations is the fact that most refugees and asylum seekers who manage to make it to the UK have within themselves, especially when they are able to connect with others of a similar background and/or origin, an underlying resilience and strength of personality – a characteristic of struggle against adversity. This resilience needs to be respected, honoured, supported and drawn out when services to help refugees and asylum seekers are being devised.

Meaning of mental health

Refugees come from a variety of cultural backgrounds and so carry a diversity of ideas and perceptions of what it is to be mentally healthy (see Chapter 2). Current discourses in mental health, especially those derived from traditional western psychiatry and psychology that inform services, do not apply or at least only apply piecemeal. Earlier chapters in this book, especially Chapter 7, have drawn attention to the ways in which cultural differences and racism impact on the mental health scene; all this applies in high intensity and very importantly in the case of most refugees. So, great care has to be taken in labelling problems of refugees. A diagnosis that often comes to mind when someone who is a refugee is identified as having a mental health problem is PTSD; it was pointed out in Chapter 6 that the use of this diagnosis has drawbacks: (a) It takes attention away from the complexity of social, personal and psychological problems that refugees face and for which they require help; and (b) sets the discourse on mental health of refugees in a paradigm that obscures the strength and resilience of many refugees.

Discrimination, racism and social exclusion

Chilean refugees who came to the UK fleeing the Pinochet regime in the 1970s were generally welcomed and were included rapidly in the social and political life of the nation (Wallace, 2003). But most migrants to UK who have arrived in relatively large numbers since the 1960s, whether seeking asylum or for economic/personal reasons, have not been generally welcome: 'The mass influx of non-white immigrants did not sit well with large numbers of British public. The "colour" question became an important part of the political discourse of the period' (RAL, 2007). However, some negative reactions to the arrival post-2003 of Polish and other (racially) white East Europeans who came as of right as citizens of countries of the European Union, as described by Slack (2007), suggest that skin-colour racism may not be the only basis of hostile attitudes towards people seen as foreigners. But, there is no evidence so far that non-white immigrants to UK face much lasting discrimination and the absorption into British society of East European migrants who decide to remain in the UK appears to be progressing without much difficulty.

Many immigrants and some British minorities seen as 'the other' face discrimination arising from racism, cultural arrogance, stigma and so on. While discrimination is stressful and frustrating for anyone to face, it causes additional confusion when it is unexpected and occurs in a context where the victims see the country – the host community – as a place of safety, as indeed many refugees do. For refugees who have experienced persecution and worse in the past, the experience of discrimination brings back fears and insecurities that they thought they had left behind. For someone who has faced psychological trauma, discrimination is a 're-traumatization', no less.

Exile and loss

Many migrants, especially those forced to migrate, 'are permanently undermined by the loss of something left behind forever' (Said, 2001, p. 173) – their homes. Many writers and people who work with refugees recognize the importance of 'loss' in their lives – often a sense of loss that they never get over but have to learn to live with. In fact it goes back to the formulation by Freud (1917) in *Mourning and Melancholia* of loss being the basis of depression: 'Exile and the memory of trauma and loss is an experience of bereavement many times over' (Moorehead, 2006, p. 215). Eisenbruch (1991) suggests that the concept of 'cultural bereavement' is preferable to PTSD as a label for the complex mixture of what amount to normal reactions to loss in cultural contexts where reliving the past may be desirable: 'Cultural bereavement can help clinicians working with refugees to separate signs of pathology – reliving of the past, for example – from signs of a consistent and culturally normal relationship between the person's past and present' (p. 677).

The concept of home is tied up with roots, belonging and identity – and identity is not a simple concept (see Chapter 1). Eva Hoffman (1999) points out that 'there are two kinds of homes: the home of our childhood and origin, which is given...and the home of our adulthood, which is achieved only through an act of possession, hard-earned, patient, imbued with time, a possession made of our choice, agency, the labor of understanding, and gradual arrival'. To someone who does not migrate the two concepts of 'home' coincide more or less. For Hoffman, the experience of *enforced* exile (as opposed to voluntary migration) 'accentuates the potency of what is given, of the forces that have shaped us before we can shape ourselves' (1999, p. 60). Many migrants attempt to hold on to both home of origin and adopted home via 'the myth of return' (Cohen and Gold, 1997; Ganga, 2006) – the notion, often held deep down and sometimes not even acknowledged to themselves, that one day they will return 'home'. This may prevent fully adapting to the new life in the country of adoption or, on the other hand, enable the migrant to live through multiplicity of identities and homes, more suited (than a single identity) for a world of cultural diversity (Chapter 1).

Migration always requires psychological and social adjustments. Forced migrants have to go through these forcibly as it were. Being exiled from home has been considered traumatic in all societies. In medieval Europe, exile was one of the worst punishments for misdemeanour and there is large literature – usually in fiction – around exile which is nearly always seen as something negative when set against a highly charged concept of home, family and community, and the implied notion of separation being pathological. More recently the view has grown that there is another perspective on having many homes, a positive advantage in being rootless well enunciated by Hoffman (1999) in its application to migrants in Europe.

The western world today, especially in cities such as London, requires from its inhabitants an ability to adapt to changing circumstances and to find one's way through complex and confusing demands. Society in places like London are far from stable in the sense of (say) English village life in the Middle Ages or life in many rural areas of the world. Two groups of forced migrants have been adept at making good in urban British cities in two waves of recent migration, Ashkenasi Jews at the turn of the nineteenth into twentieth century (Kushner, 2006) and East African Asians in the 1960s (Herbert, 2006). In the case of the former, although settled in Eastern Europe for generations, they carried in their minds an imaginary 'Israel' 'as less a geographic and more a spiritual territory' (Hoffman, 1999, p. 41); the latter, although having homes in Kenya, had lived in Africa as 'Asians' who (at least in imagination) had homes in India too. Loss of home was real enough to both groups but in many instances home is something variable, not fixed, something that is more alive in their minds than in geographical reality. In Hoffman's view, exile can be a positive advantage – a strength.

Resilience in the face of trauma and exile

Muecke (1992), writing over a decade ago, is critical of the tendency in the USA for research into health of refugees and planning of services for them to be on a paradigm of pathology or 'problems', forgetting their resilience and also excluding refugees themselves from the debates. Muecke calls for a paradigm for refugee health that is 'primarily concerned with refugees as extraordinarily resilient human beings' and she argues that 'construing refugee "patients" and research "subjects" as resilient and as mutual participants could allow them latitude to reformulate their assumptive worlds as they need, and could inform health practice and research with unconventional perspectives needed to alleviate suffering among refugees' (p. 521). To some extent, there has been a shift in the past few years towards this sort of paradigm in the discourse about mental health of refugees. And it was noted in Chapter 5 that, although the concept has not caught on in general mental health discourse, resilience is a fairly prominent theme in talking about the effects of trauma on people exposed to armed conflict and disaster (see Goodkind *et al.*, 2004; Hart *et al.*, 2007; Kostelny and Wessels, 2004). The ecological framework for developing mental health services for refugees promoted by Miller and Rasco (2004) acknowledges the remarkable resilience of most refugees, pointing out that this resilience is evident in the development of refugee community organizations (RCOs) and collective coping is a common sight in many high-income countries. However, it must be admitted that many psychiatric clinics in the USA and UK still persist in promoting the deficit-approach through focusing on trauma clinics and overusing the PTSD model for assessing mental health problems of refugees.

Summary

The chapter has set psychological and emotional issues in a context of resilience because this is the approach that the author thinks should be followed in devising ways of helping refugees to deal with aftermath of (pre-migration) experience often construed as 'trauma' (discussed in Chapter 6); the hardship of getting to a place of safety (journey of migration); and facing the stressors of settling into a country that a person chooses as the second home, be it on a permanent or temporary basis. The first aim of services to help refugees should be that of providing a home – or something as near to home as possible. Then, aims of therapy, support and guidance that the host communities give to refugees must be structured in the idiom of resilience. Although the model to work with would initially focus on resilience of the individual, community resilience must be considered if at all possible. Thus, the second aspect of help for refugees is around family and community. Whatever their initial contacts in the country of adoption, refugees like everyone else need and seek companionship and friends and (if possible) family to live with or to be in communication with. Reconstituting families, easing communication of refugees with their kin who may well be in other countries must be high on the list of priorities. A feature of refugee life in UK is the existence of RCOs which often form the surrogate family when family is missing or unavailable. Many RCOs are ethno-specific in that they cater for one particular ethnic group or part of an ethnic group. That is often their strength. Statutory and voluntary organizations need to see RCOs as the 'community' to work with in helping and supporting refugees. Clearly there is a place for individual therapy; if refugees see their problems in an individualized fashion or suffer from serious (personal) emotional disturbance; the need for personalized therapy must be allowed for. So the third aspect of helping refugees in the mental health field is personal therapy.

The refugee experience often leaves issues that become transgenerational. Moorehead (2006) generalizes in a way that may be too extreme but are pertinent: 'Like the children of holocaust survivors, the children of refugees grow up in a world circumscribed by fear, unrealistic expectations and over protectiveness with parents whose profound sense of powerlessness in the face of annihilation and loss expresses itself often as self-blame and guilt' (Moorehead, 2006, p. 215). The children of refugees' families are therefore at risk on a long-term basis. Keeping lines open for them to seek help if and when ready may well be all that helping agencies can do.

Refugees who have managed to reach a potentially safe place are people like everyone else – but people who have faced complex problems over prolonged periods in situations that many people in the host community (that gives them refuge) find hard to comprehend or make sense of. What they seek and deserve are acceptance, understanding and the opportunity to make a new life – find a new home – or, if they wish, return to an earlier home when conditions allow. What is central is the security that goes with the concept of home, and mental health needs often derive from this need. What others can provide in supporting refugees in maintaining their mental health is limited but may well be crucial: Support should be structured in terms of *their* needs and *their* wishes and not on the basis of preconceived ideas about trauma, stress and mental illness; and needs should be addressed in a framework that includes attention to personal suffering they carry, discrimination they face, loss and exile they are contending with – all within an overarching knowledge of resilience.

Chapter 11

Prospects for Plurality in Therapies for Mental Health

Earlier chapters make the case against applying biomedical psychiatry across the world as a total package; clearly, it would be equally unwise to think that ways of dealing with emotional stress and/or maintaining mental health developed in non-western cultures can be applied *in toto* outside the cultures that they grew up in. This chapter discusses the transcultural portability of fragments of cultural systems in the shape of what may be called 'technologies' concerned with mental health – a term that, broadly speaking, means 'any tool or technique, any product or process, any physical equipment or method of doing or making, by which human capability is extended' (Schon, 1967, p. 1); in the context of mental health this refers to ways of handling stress, counteracting what may be conceived as mental illness, and promoting well-being, spiritual development, and recovery from emotional crises. This chapter should be seen as a prelude to Chapter 12 where ideas of unity and amalgamation across racial and cultural barriers are taken further.

Introduction

The question of extracting techniques from a total system such as psychiatry, religion or spiritual healing is problematic for two main reasons: First, there is the problem of defining the limits of a technique as distinct from its context – of separating its form from its content. For example, does a technique of exorcism include all the rituals that go with it or only some? Can ECT be transported without taking with it the concept of 'endogenous depression' and, more importantly, the concept of dealing with certain problems as illness? Second, there is the problem of evaluating the effectiveness of a technique when the aim of using it may be different in the host culture from that in its culture of origin. For example, the aim of western psychotherapy is often conceptualized in terms of a person becoming self-reliant and independent while, in a different culture, such qualities may be seen as a sign of deviance or even illness. Spiritual growth through self-denial may be valued in one society but seen as nonproductive and maladaptive in a different society. The problems may be even more complex and serious: For instance, a process of exorcism that is concerned with elimination of evil influences may be seen in western culture – or rather by most people exposed to western culture – as a sign of malevolence or even illness in the exorcist; while the use of electric shocks or powerful psychotropic drugs when, for example, people hear 'voices' may be seen in an African or Asian tradition as unethical – and even malevolent – interference with spiritual experiences or beliefs. On the whole, it is easier to delineate and conceptualize the transport of pre-dominantly physical techniques such as drug or herbal therapy, compared with methods that involve psychological or spiritual matters, although the difference is one of degree only.

Unfortunately, there is no reliable literature to fall back on for the topic discussed here. There are reports of eastern techniques, such as medita-tion, being used in western psychotherapy (Carrington, 1982) and psych-iatry (West, 1979) and of eastern ideas being used to develop a special type of psychotherapy, namely transpersonal psychotherapy (Vaughan and Boorstein, 1982), but no real discussion of the difficulties inherent in inte-grating one process or system with another. A form of CBT that claims to incorporate Buddhist mindfulness, 'Mindfulness cognitive behavioural therapy' (MCBT) (Crane, 2009), is offered at a price by many commer-cial organizations and even referred to in the latest psychiatric textbook (Gelder *et al.*, 2009). This appears to be a mixture of Buddhist mindfulness, which is about non-judgmental observation of one's thoughts in meditation (Gunaratne, 2002), and CBT where the focus is on restructuring thinking patterns (Fennell, 2009; Scott and Beck, 2008) – as described in Chapter 7. As there is an obvious contradiction between mindfulness and CBT, the alleged combination cannot be a true amalgamation.

Psychiatric techniques

In considering cross-cultural transfer of techniques of treatment in bio-medical psychiatry, it is necessary, first and foremost, to side-step the pre-sent system of diagnosis and assessment in psychiatry in order to get at those aspects of psychiatric practice that may be portable. But there is one exception: psychiatry can contribute significantly, with few reservations, to useful global knowledge in the identification of any illness, mental or otherwise, caused by clear-cut organic pathology. The organic disorders in psychiatric nosology are the diseases caused by physical, structural or bio-chemical factors, the major ones being chronic brain syndrome – various forms of dementia, especially Alzheimer's disease – epilepsy, nutritional dis-orders that may cause emotional disturbance and endocrine dysfunction. Knowledge about these disorders is likely to be applicable in large measure across cultures and races, for any distortions caused by cultural and racial biases can be checked out and removed fairly easily. In the case of functional disorders – which is where biomedical psychiatry comes into play – biases are too well integrated into the culture of the subject to be amenable to such action (see Chapters 2 and 3).

Physical treatment

In general, techniques of physical treatment are interventions that may be used for suppressing and/or distorting various human experiences, modalities and behaviour. Biomedical psychiatry has experience in the use of a large number of drugs and other physical treatment such as ECT. They are generally used empirically, meaning that their use is based on knowledge from experience alone. In preparing these techniques for transportation cross-culturally, each treatment must be analysed in terms of its effect on particular forms of distress rather than in terms of ethnocentric illness models; they must be seen as directed at particular perceptions, such as 'hearing voices'; biological functions, such as sleep and appetite; and behaviour, such as excitement or excessive slowness. Once analysed in this way, the specific circumstances, if any, in which each intervention is needed in the 'new', host culture can be evaluated. The aim is to match a particular intervention to a type of perception, biological dysfunction or behaviour and then to match its use to the relief of distress in individuals or communities seen as integral units within the host cultures. Clearly, the use of the item of treatment in the host culture may be very different from its use in the culture of origin.

The above approach to biomedical psychiatric techniques of physical treatment means that they are not transported cross-culturally as treatment of (diagnosed) illness but as interventions in specific situations. In this way, it is conceivable that most psychotropic drugs, and even ECT, may be used pragmatically across cultures for the alleviation of distress, control of behaviour or suppression of perceptual experiences. But, as they become established in a host culture, their use should be incorporated into the host culture without discounting the value of other forms of intervention, and without interfering with culturally consonant practices or treatment techniques. By avoiding the process of diagnosis, the 'alien' physical technologies of psychiatry can thus diffuse into the host culture and become incorporated into it to be used as, and if, the need arises. In summary, since physical treatments are generally used empirically anyway, they are usable without the need for a diagnostic rationale for their use. As such, they can be transported cross-culturally, once they are evaluated in terms of their individual effects rather than in terms of treating diagnosed illness.

Psychological therapies

Western psychotherapies are geared to cultural needs in the West and consist of individualized therapies of one sort or another. In exploring commonalities in psychotherapy across cultures, Prince (1980) chooses as his starting point 'the mobilization of the healing forces of the patient'; he then goes on to consider the variety of ways in which people try to draw on their 'endogenous healing mechanisms' and suggests that 'most of the treatments that the healers offer are simply an exaggeration or extra development' of these mechanisms (p. 297). The following suggestions are offered as speculations about transferring technologies for psychological therapies across cultures: The emphasis in western psychotherapy on the client gaining insight – usually meaning cognitive understanding – should be discarded as a culture-bound phenomenon that is unlikely to have much meaning as an indication of benefit in other cultures; but the importance of the 'therapeutic relationship' established between the therapist and client is a concept that may be universally useful – but not if it is conceptualized in terms of 'transference', since this, too, has a meaning specific to (western) psychoanalytic psychotherapy. Clearly, the qualities in this relationship that are therapeutic must be culture-specific, but its overall importance in therapy is likely to be universally valid.

The minutiae of psychoanalytic theory, such as the oedipal complex, are unlikely to be applicable universally in the highly ethnocentric form that they are used, although some aspects of the general approach of the (western) psychoanalyst in evaluating infantile behaviour may be useful in the understanding of adult behaviour in other cultures also. Certain aspects of behaviour therapy may be extractible for use across cultures; but here too, they must be integrated into the cultural system of the patient and behaviour judged in terms of that culture. And, as in the case of interventions with drugs and other physical treatments, psychological therapies too could be used pragmatically according to personal and/or community need or preference rather than as treatment for specific illness.

Various systems of family therapy have developed recently in Europe and North America. This phenomenon may be a corrective reaction to the emphasis on the 'individualization' of western cultures (Triandis, 1995); but it is nothing new for healers in Africa and Asia to involve the family and to take a wide view of problems presented to them as illness. Although family therapies in the West are geared to western models of family structure and functioning, it is possible that certain ways of analysing families – especially systemic models – may be transportable across cultures. But great care is needed. Annie Lau (1986), a practitioner of transcultural family therapy, recommends the clarification of cultural assumptions about families before applying the basic approach of a western family therapist: While accepting the assumption that an individual's problems can be helped by treating the entire family as a unit, the therapist must reinforce what is considered to be competent family functioning and discourage patterns of behaviour that are dysfunctional in the culture of the individual or family being treated and not that which the therapist comes from.

Data analysis and legal framework

It has been noted earlier (Chapters 4, 7 and 9) that psychiatric systems for analysing people through diagnosis of illness constructed within western culture are not just of limited use cross-culturally, but may well be very destructive if imposed on to other cultures. However, some aspects of methodology derived from statistical theories used in psychiatric settings for collecting, quantifying and analysing data may well be usable universally, once valid observations sensitive to culture and free of racist bias have been made. Thus, ways of ordering some types of outcome data – so long as they are obtained in a culturally appropriate manner – may be useful in analysing the effectiveness of interventions for mental health. Even the emphasis on objectivity characteristic of the western, scientific approach may be applicable cross-culturally in limited ways in evaluating specific matters related to mental health. But great care needs to be taken to ensure that 'objective' criteria in a western sense are not applied to questions of feeling, belief and spiritual values, and that the western reductionist approach (Chapter 2) is not allowed to distort the knowledge about ways of working for mental health in other cultures.

It must be admitted that the rights and welfare of people are not always dependent on laws and regulations. However, a legal framework is generally an essential prerequisite for fair and humane treatment of people who are seen as deviant or mad. Fundamental tenets embodied in mental health legislation in Western Europe and North America may be usefully transported cross-culturally for integration into legal systems elsewhere, although such a manoeuvre is not a simple matter; the laws must be integrated into legal systems in other countries and in line with what is practicable and enforceable. A detailed examination of this legal field is beyond the remit of this book.

Herbal remedies

Treatment with herbs may seem, at first sight, to have a similar basis to drug therapy; after all some drugs were originally merely purified extracts of plants. But herbs are not usually used in Ayurvedic or Chinese medicine in the way that drugs are used in western medicine and biomedical psychiatry. In Chinese medicine, for example, herbs do not target specific conditions or symptoms; the aim of herbal therapy, like all other therapies, is to rebalance disharmonies in bodily rhythms (Kaptchuk, 2000). Moreover, herbs are seldom used singly; different herbs are carefully blended in a balanced mixture to fit the precise disharmony that is diagnosed. In Tibetan medicine, which has been influenced by both Chinese and Indian medical systems, 'it is not so much the presence of one particular ingredient but the particular combination of many ingredients that provides the desired therapeutic effect' (Clifford, 1984, p. 115). The oldest known system of herbal medicine is the ancient Vedic system of the Indian tradition which predates Ayurveda. In describing a particular Vedic herbal remedy, Jaggi (1981) states:

> The herbs are propitiated and also appeased for being uprooted. The high cost of the medicinal preparation and the deep knowledge of the physician are emphasized upon. His closeness to the healing divinities is publicised. Lastly, after the administration of the drug, it is forcefully suggested that 'the herbs have driven away all defects of the body whatever'. (p. 21)

In modern Ayurveda, herbal remedies are suited to the individual who takes them, as well as being geared to the diagnosis in terms of imbalance rather than specific cause. They are usually combined with diet and other remedies. Sometimes, the way that herbs are grown and picked is considered important. In Tibetan medicine, the state of mind of the physician when preparing a medicine 'adds a crucial factor to the effectiveness of the medicine' (Clifford, 1984, p. 122). Finally, herbs may be taken by mouth as pills or concoctions, inhaled after being burned, or even massaged into the body; the exact method is often as important as the herbs that are used.

Thus, when used in its original context, herbal remedies are not just individual substances for specific needs (as drugs are in western medicine) but are part of a larger system of healing. If transported into a culturally western medical setting and used in the way that drugs are used in the West, the basis of the treatment may be lost. It may be argued from a scientific standpoint that such a change would merely separate the therapeutic effects of the herbal remedy from placebo effects. But, in the field of mental health, one cannot meaningfully dismiss placebo effects as being fundamentally different from, or less important than, therapeutic effects. The mere empirical use of herbs as substances which may affect the mind through biochemical means should be avoided. There may be some gain in research, using perhaps both quantitative and qualitative methods, into the use of herbs in the setting of biomedical psychiatry, so long as the methods of combining herbs are honoured, some attempt is made to understand the use of herbs in their original cultural context, and the use of herbal remedies is accepted as a means of balancing different emotions, rather than suppressing symptoms of pathological conditions.

Acupuncture

The use of acupuncture, and the associated technique of moxibustion, must be seen in the context of Chinese medicine based on Chinese philosophy, epitomized by the concept of a balance of yin and yang – distinctive but inseparable poles of life energy which are in dynamic balance. Chinese medicine is not concerned with cause and effect but with relationships, contexts and patterns of events. When an illness is diagnosed, the Chinese physician does not look for causes but for disharmony between a person's environment, emotional attitude and way of life. By inserting needles at carefully selected points along a system of meridians traversing the human body, acupuncture aims to rebalance those aspects of the body's yin and yang whose harmonious proportion and movement have become disordered (Kaptchuk, 2000). The points on the surface of the body at which acupuncture needles are applied are related to pathways (meridians) that carry *qi*, a type of energy, unifying all parts of the body into a harmonious whole. Acupuncture is carried out in combination with dietary advice, physical exercise and advice on correct living; it is part of a comprehensive system of medicine very different in approach from biomedicine of the West.

According to Ratnavale (1973) writing during the time of Mao Zedong (Tse-Tung), doctors at the Shanghai Psychiatric Institute told him that acupuncture had replaced ECT. Later, Dunner and Dunner (1983) reported that various psychiatric institutes in China, modelled on western lines and using American diagnostic systems and drug therapy, used electrical stimulation by acupuncture needles placed in the forehead that induce convulsions; clearly a way of giving ECT rather than the use of acupuncture. However, when the author visited China in 2001, he was told by staff of a large mental hospital in Beijing that not only was acupuncture not being used at all, but ECT was indeed being used quite extensively. There are reports from China of trials of acupuncture for the treatment of depression diagnosed according to DSM criteria (ARRC, 2002; Luo *et al.*, 1990). And a report from USA of a pilot randomized controlled trial of acupuncture for the treatment of depression claims that acupuncture is superior to non-specific treatment (Allen *et al.*, 1998).

Clifford (1984) states that the acupuncture points recognized in Tibetan medicine for the treatment of psychiatric disorders are on the top of the skull and base of the neck. It is possible that further research into the empirical use of acupuncture, based perhaps on its use in Tibetan medicine, may prove to be of advantage in the West in using acupuncture as an empirical technology. However, it is unlikely that its use can be integrated into psychiatric practice unless the theory of disease in the latter is greatly modified.

Yoga

Yoga, the 'way', is the term given to a form of Indian psychology as well as to systems of what might be called self-purification. Yogic powers are no myth and they should not be seen as magical or supernatural. They arise from practices – yogic practices – that are a matter of application and training. Some comments about yoga may be appropriate in the context of mental health.

The ultimate goal of yoga is liberation and an eightfold path to liberation has been described (Safaya, 1976): (1) abstention (*yama*) (2) observance (*niyama*) (3) posture (*asana*) (4) regulation of breath (*pranayama*) (5) withdrawal of the senses (*pratyahara*) (6) contemplation (*dharana*) (7) fixed attention (*dhyana*) and (8) deep meditation (*samadhi*). The first five are external or indirect means or aids, while the last three are internal or direct aids. Different teachers of yoga emphasize various aspects of this basic approach, concentrating on particular practices. Bhakti yoga concentrates on love and devotion, raja-yoga on meditation, karma-yoga on (good) works, jnana-yoga on understanding and hatha-yoga on utilizing physical (somato-psychic) forces. Systems of yoga are expressed in metaphorical, sometimes picturesque, presentations. For example, in 'kundalini-yoga' the centre of psychic energy is depicted as a coiled serpent resting within the human being. Here yogic practices are designed to awaken the Kundalini which gradually unfolds to reveal one's inner self, which is akin to as the basic reality of the universe.

In purely practical terms, a system of yoga is a discipline consisting of exercises of the mind and body; thus, yoga as a means of keeping mentally healthy seems to have great potential as a portable technology that may be isolated from its cultural medium. In fact it is as a basic system of keeping healthy and fit that yogic exercises are often practised in India in the present day (Sen, 1961). Hatha-yoga has already been taken up in the West as a system for keeping physical health and clearly has a future for integration into psychiatry. It may be considered (in western terms) as a somato-psychic therapy – a way of influencing the mind by training the body.

Japanese psychotherapies

Various forms of religious psychotherapy – as distinct from religious practice per se – which have emerged during the twentieth century in Japan have been written about in the English language literature. Some are seen as cults – for example, *Gedatsukai* or 'a society for deliverance' also called the 'Salvation Cult' (Lebra, 1982, p. 269) – but others which are more acceptable to psychiatry, such as Morita therapy (Kora and Sato, 1958; Murase and Johnson, 1974) and *naikan* therapy (Murase, 1982), are recognized as treatment. Clearly, all Japanese psychotherapies have roots in Zen Buddhism and Shintoism but seem to be less mystical and exotic to western thinking than are Indian and African healing systems – for both racial and cultural reasons (as noted below). From a western psychological viewpoint, they appear to be based on self-reconstruction of personality, although meditation, possession rituals and the consumption of health foods are all used.

Morita therapy was developed in the 1920s in a western medical model of illness but emphasizing Japanese cultural traditions. It has undergone some change over the years and is now used in Japan entirely for a narrowly defined personality type, the *shinkeishitsu* type, who might be seen as suffering from *shinkeishitsu* neurosis. There are two steps in Morita therapy: first, absolute bed-rest, and second, gradual adaptation to outer reality by physical work in groups (Fujita, 1986). Correspondence with the therapist by means of a written diary which is corrected by the therapist is an important part of the highly structured regime in Morita therapy. *Naikan* therapy uses meditation for 'observing oneself' for guilt and gratitude and it is carried out under the direction of an interviewer who visits the client periodically. According to Murase (1982): 'The role of the interviewer is quite different to that of the ordinary professional counselor or therapist. His primary function is to directly supervise the client in a very specific routine of concentration on his past. His main concern is that the client follows instruction and reflects successfully on the topics assigned for self-examination'. The basic ethos of both *naikan* therapy and Morita therapy is 'accepting things as they are' – summarized by the Japanese word *sunao*, which implies 'a harmonious and natural state of mind vis-à-vis oneself and others' (Murase, 1982, pp. 308–27).

Morita therapy has been transported to the USA and utilized in an educational model rather than a medical one; it is used on an outpatient basis, without bed-rest, for the treatment of 'a broad spectrum of clients – from the neurotic to the normal, and some borderline psychotics and depressed clients as well' (Reynolds, 1988, p. 257). It is significant that after transportation from its cultural roots, it is the practical methodology of Morita therapy that is used and not the explanatory model underlying the system. It may be significant that it is a Japanese system of psychotherapy, not an Indian or African one, that has taken root in American psychiatry. The significance may lie in the fact that as Japan has become industrialized and, more importantly, 'Americanized' since the end of the Second World War, the Japanese have been increasingly seen as 'western' and 'white'. As such Japanese systems become more acceptable – even 'modern'.

Healing and liberation techniques

People around the world use various means – therapies – for dealing with problems that affect them. These may be social and/or interactional involving other people – for example, in exorcism rituals – or they may be for the individual to practise alone – such as meditation, although this may involve other people as teachers, facilitators or gurus. The self-help, healing methods considered in this chapter are those regarded, at least in their original forms, as being derived from the culture of the society they belong to. Prince (1976) argues that all people everywhere have certain 'endogenous' healing capacities of a self-help type and that healing techniques, whatever they consist of, are all 'simply manipulations and elaborations of these endogenous healing mechanisms' (p. 116). He goes on to argue that the most important healing mechanisms of self-help involve altered states of consciousness – as in dreams, dissociated states, a variety of religious experiences, mystical states and psychotic reactions. This section aims to consider first, the question of meditation as a possible technology for psychiatric healing. Second, dreams and trance states will be discussed briefly in the same context; and finally, some comments will be made about exorcism.

The attainment of a mystical experience through meditation is a therapeutic venture that is attained by practice and training. States of 'ecstasy' and trance states are similar, although the means for reaching them may be different. One of the most universal of self-help techniques for achieving mystical experience, and one that has been avidly taken on by western 'scientific' authorities for investigation and use, is meditation. Exorcism is also universally seen in various religious contexts; it is the kind of procedure that is particularly associated with the activity of shamans or priests of various cultures. Trance states may be induced or occur seemingly spontaneously; and dreams, though more clearly spontaneous, may be seen as vehicles of divine communication and/or means of healing. Although healing and (spiritual) liberation characterize much of how mental health problems are dealt with in many parts of the world, most of the literature on their techniques refer to practices in eastern cultures; inevitably, much of this section is about practices in these traditions.

Meditation

All the major religions, except Zoroastrianism, appear to have religious practices that may be subsumed under the general rubric of meditation techniques (Prince, 1976). Although meditation is particularly associated with Buddhism, 'the belief that the higher spiritual life can be lived only in and through meditation' is applicable to the traditions of the Hindus, Taoists, Sufis and Christian contemplatives (Conze, 1959, p. 98), as well as those of pre-Columbian North America (Freuchen, 1959) and Africa (Katz, 1973). In all these traditions, the experience of an altered state of consciousness induced by meditation is not an end in itself but closely linked to the attainment of what can be loosely described as 'liberation' or 'enlightenment'. There is a considerable body of information on meditation in the Buddhist tradition in which various techniques (of meditation) are practised. In presenting these for western readers, Edward Conze (1959) notes that the psychological constitution of the subject must be suited to the technique chosen. Further, there are progressive steps to be followed leading to meditation, such as the restraint of the senses (holding back from attachment to sense objects), moderation in eating and avoidance of sleep: 'With your senses turned inward, unmoved and well-controlled, with your mind undistracted, you should walk about or sit down at night'. Then, with a 'mindfulness' of all activities, the subject goes into 'seclusion'; 'sitting cross-legged in some solitary spot, hold your body straight, and for a time keep your attention in front of you...then force your wandering mind to become wholly occupied with one object' (pp. 105–8). This 'object' may be a 'mantra' (word of power) suited to the individual.

Zen meditation emphasizes the importance of sitting while meditating to deal with repentance and destruction of sins. It may use a type of riddle or paradox to which there is no answer in the ordinary sense, called a *koan* – such as, 'what is the sound of one hand clapping'. The teaching is that 'the practice is the enlightenment' – but this should not be taken to mean that meditation is purposeless. Nor has it got a purpose in the ordinary sense of the word. In Zen meditation, the 'Buddha-nature' is not something to be attained or awaited but to be realized (Conze, 1959, p. 99). In general, 'being without thoughts is the object of Zen meditation; the control of body and mind is only a method of reaching it. When body and mind have been controlled, then from the ensuing absence of thoughts are born naturally and rightly brilliant understanding'; the ultimate state is one of 'perfect Buddha-wisdom, reading of the scriptures and devotion, asceticism and austerities' (Amakuki, 1959, p. 138).

In ascribing the use of meditation according to the type of person who meditates, Buddhist theory has a complex way of evaluating 'types'. Conze (1959) quotes a teacher of meditation, Buddhaghosa, as delineating six types of persons for this purpose, each identified by a dominant quality. Thus, there are people dominated by greed, hate, delusion, faith, intelligence and discursiveness. These dispositions are determined by the person's postures, attitudes and behaviour as well as 'the kind of mental Dharmas which are found in him'. Certain mental states are supposed to be found in particular types of people. For example, the 'hate-type' is characterized by anger, grudges, belittling the worth of others, and so on; the 'delusion-type' by sloth, worry, perplexity, obstinacy and tenacity; the person ruled by discursiveness shows excessive talkativeness, fondness for society and a dislike of wholesome practices; and those ruled by faith are generous and are desirous of seeing holy men and hearing the dharma (teaching). The content of the meditation and the way it is carried out are geared to 'counteract some given fault', or to be 'particularly beneficial to some given type'. Thus, the 'greed-type' person may have to meditate on ten repulsive things (e.g., ten aspects of decomposing corpses) and to recollect what belongs to the body, and those ruled by discursiveness are instructed to be mindful of respiration and concentrate on a small object (pp. 117–21).

The approaches to meditation, as described very briefly above, have been translated into western 'exercises' or 'clinical tools'. As such, they have achieved a vogue in some circles, including psychiatric ones. Transcendental meditation, or TM, a 'standardized form of mantra meditation which has been adapted for Western use...consists of the individual sitting upright with eyes closed, silently repeating the mantra', without calling on the subject to make any effort at concentrating or preventing attention wavering and thoughts intruding (West, 1979, pp. 457–8). Zen meditation, which has received much attention in the West as a technique separated from its philosophical and cultural base, is seen as the (mere) practice of 'zazen' (sitting meditation) maintaining 'a quiet awareness' (Watts, 1962).

As a therapeutic intervention, meditation differs in several important respects from conventional psychotherapy, which seeks to pinpoint conflicts that are often of an unconscious nature, and then attempts to bring into play the conscious integrative functions of the ego. Unlike psychotherapy, meditation does not provide any conceptual handle with which to reorganize one's cognitions of self. The rational elements of the psychodynamic psychotherapies and/or cognitive and behavioural therapies are conspicuously absent in meditation, and the interpersonal elements take a back seat as well. In a fundamental sense, one is alone with oneself during meditation, while simultaneously removed from the verbal-conceptual world.

If meditation is separated from its cultural roots and examined as a form of psychotherapy it may well be seen as a purposeless indulgence or, at best, a technique for inducing a special type of mental state. In the medical model of biomedical psychiatry, this mental state, the 'altered state of consciousness' induced by meditation, is a *treatment* equivalent to a drug or ECT, or a course of psychotherapy. Even when it is not practised as *treatment*, it is perceived and used as a way of counteracting undesirable feelings. Used in this way, meditation may serve a limited purpose – but a very different one from its original purpose in Buddhist tradition.

Clearly, there is a vast difference at a very basic level between meditation as treatment in a western medical model and its place in the Buddhist tradition, as a process used for healing or liberating. In transporting it across into western society from other cultures, it must be integrated into the former in order to fulfil a function, for when used in isolation from a function, it is unlikely to serve a purpose in a meaningful way. It is conceivable that meditation can be incorporated into western culture if taken on its own merits as a process for self-understanding, rather than as a psychological or psychiatric treatment. But for this to happen, the strict illness model of emotional distress must be abandoned; spiritual needs and ethical considerations must be a part of the process of achieving liberation or cure. It cannot be used in isolation but only in concert with insights from Chinese and Indian philosophies, which underlie the use of mystical states. It is such insights that have given rise to 'new' approaches in psychotherapy, such as 'transpersonal psychotherapy' (Vaughan and Boorstein, 1982), 'psychosynthesis' (Assaglioli, 1975) and 'enlightenment intensive' (Graham, 1986).

Trance states, ecstasy and dreams

Healing ceremonies involving ecstasy and trance are widely practised throughout the world. In parts of South America, drug-induced ecstasies are carried out in the course of healing ceremonies. The plants and fungi that are used for this purpose contain various hallucinogens including mescaline, D-lysergic acid and psilocybin (Schultes, 1969). Dobkin De Rios (1972) describes one such ceremony in north-east Peru in which the visions experienced by the patients are interpreted by the therapist (shaman) who may take the drugs himself. In reviewing the available information about the 'great shamanic tradition' of the Americas, Prince (1980) describes the 'democratization of shamanism' (p. 329); by this he means that among some indigenous American groups, contact with the 'spirit-world' through dreams or induced visions becomes a part of everyday practice in order to keep (mentally) healthy – akin to the use of yoga in India.

Unlike the case with mystical states, full memory is usually not retained of experiences under a trance state, although there may be a hazy recollection of what happens during it. In western culture, and hence in psychiatry, such states are seen as being associated with loss of 'ego control'; and they are seen as pathological because domination by the conscious ego – commonly called self-control – is important in that culture. Prince (1976) delineates two broad patterns: In one, the healer alone dissociates and in the other the client, or both healer and client, dissociate(s). When the healer alone dissociates, the power of the healer is affected by suggestion, the power being greatly augmented when a supernatural spirit is seen to speak through the healer. Prince (1980) points to a distinction between shamanic ecstasy and a dissociated state: In ecstasy there is loss of motor power but intense subjective experience of a visionary nature that can subsequently be remembered and reported on by the shaman. On the other hand, in the dissociated state the subject engages in highly coordinated motor activity but has amnesia for the period of the altered state.

The use of dreams for therapeutic purposes is a part of the western psychiatric tradition and it is relatively common for dreams to be seen as related to illness in many parts of the world (Prince, 1980). The tradition of healing by 'temple incubation', widespread in ancient Egypt and Greece, involved sleeping in a room of a temple in order to have dreams with healing powers; a remnant of this tradition persists in Morocco, according to Prince (1980). But it is in north-east America, among the Iroquois, that dream fulfilment is described as having been a complex and important healing process even into the eighteenth century, and still surviving in some form today (Wallace, 1958).

Exorcism

Various types of exorcism are carried out all over the world by practitioners called by the general term 'shamans' unless they are within the Judeo-Christian culture in which case they are referred to as priests or rabbis. In many cultures, possession is attributed to something evil or at least unwanted – usually a demon or spirit – akin to 'conflicts' or deeper disturbances of the psyche or noxious biochemical events postulated in western psychology and psychiatry. The process of removing the unwanted demon or influence is, broadly speaking, a form of exorcism. Hence, if there is a belief in illness being caused by the possession of a person by one or more forces, be they extrinsic or intrinsic, counteracting the malign (pathological) factor by exorcism may be as logical as treatment with psychotherapy or medication to counteract psychopathology. Thus, a shaman may be perceived as performing similar functions to those of a psychologist or psychiatrist.

Wherever it is practised, each technique for exorcism is deeply involved in the cultural roots that give it form and meaning. It is difficult to see how any particular type of exorcism can be extracted from its culture to be applied as a technology in a different culture. However, compromises may be possible in the case of people who maintain their own cultures in predominantly western societies. Here, exorcism rituals may have to be adapted to become acceptable to the wider society. This is not a matter of cross-cultural transfer of a technique but the elaboration and development of cultural forms to deal with changes in society. How this is done is likely to vary from society to society but assumes an acceptance of many cultural forms without racist value judgements being attached to them.

Summary

This chapter takes a pragmatic approach in trying to dissect from (western) biomedical psychiatry culturally transportable 'bits' of the discipline, and to extract from other cultures those techniques that may be concerned with the maintenance of mental health (in a wide sense) or counteracting problems that are seen (in western terms) as 'mental illness' for transport to a western context.

Notwithstanding the drawbacks and problems, sometimes a technology may be portable across cultures if uprooted carefully and with an understanding of its place in the home culture, and transplanted with an equally sympathetic understanding of its place and need in the host culture. It is important that a technology introduced into a culture fits into it and is absorbed by it; and such a transplanted technology should be given time to grow and become incorporated (or rejected). Some technologies are more portable than others. In general, limited aspects of yoga and acupuncture from eastern systems of medicine may be integrated into (western) biomedical psychiatry without too much difficulty; similarly, drug therapy and possibly ECT from (western) biomedical psychiatry may be portable for integration into other systems of healing. However, a medical model of illness in western terms is a hindrance to cross-cultural sharing of techniques and ideas, and if psychiatry is to acquire and use techniques from non-western cultural sources, *and* vice versa, it must move away from its present position on defining illness.

Chapter 12

Mental Health for All

The purpose of the final chapter is twofold. First, it aims to get beyond the long-standing conflict between concepts of cultural relativism and universality in questions of mental health (Chapters 2, 7 and 8), while facing up to the reality of racism, ethnic loyalties and the many social and political issues that complicate the picture. Second, the chapter attempts to develop ways of working with people with mental health problems that have universal applicability, countering the globalization of ideologies around mental health that actually means the imposition of western cultural concepts on the back of what is seen as 'scientific knowledge' fed by the power of pharmaceutical companies. It is constructed in four sections, redefining mental illness, restructuring mental health, mental health promotion and developing systems that promote change.

Redefining mental illness

The fact that both 'illness' and 'madness' are concepts that are recognized the world over suggests that some universal agreement may be possible on what is, and is not, essentially illness or madness. But when the WHO attempted to develop a common language for defining mental illness that cuts across culture – as in its research study IPSS described in Chapter 7 – what actually happened was that real cultural differences were ignored and, even more importantly, western ideas were imposed across the world with racist perceptions dominating the process. It seems that issues of power interacting with complex cultural variations in the understanding of health, illness and madness preclude progress in a search for a common language for defining mental illness across cultures – or even for a universally applicable theory or model for analysing questions of illness and health in the mental sphere – such as 'systems theory' which was suggested by Capra (1982) for this purpose. However, some cross-cultural communication on concepts of mental health and the definition of common aims in this field with universal and cross-cultural relevance are both necessary if only because human beings are united by a common ancestry and have to live together on one small planet.

The first stage in redefining illness is to address the issue of its presumed aetiology. Instead of a genetic determinant, cause or predisposition, a genetic

It can set the scene for a change of direction by, for example, controlling the indiscriminate sale of powerful psychotropic drugs, which are presented by commercial interests as the 'scientific' approach to establishing mental health, and by introducing proper standards for assessing their usefulness in countries of the third world. The practical projects undertaken by WHO in the mental health field should be aimed primarily at identifying and alleviating stress, rather than diagnosing and treating mental illness based on biomedical models, and mental health promotion must take into account indigenous systems of therapy and care using local experts in the field – who may well come from the social sciences and religion – supported where necessary by western expertise in organization. Research promoted by WHO should be directed at evaluating ways of helping people with mental health problems, which are culturally consonant and tuned to the real needs of the people in the countries concerned. And, most importantly, WHO must eliminate racial bias at all levels with careful regulation of its research projects, of the selection of 'experts' who provide consultative advice and organize the delivery of services and of the staffing of the WHO itself. If WHO takes on both anti-racism and cultural sensitivity, many ways of promoting universal mental health would emerge. It is essentially political will led by international organizations that is needed to begin with.

Changes at a national level must take place in both the rich western countries – the developed world – and resource-poor, third world. In general, the former provide 'aid' in various forms to the latter. Over the past forty years, western technology has helped to build dams, factories, irrigation works, and so on in the third world, but vast numbers of people in those countries still cannot earn a living. Schumacher (1973) has pointed out that western high technology is actually exacerbating the plight of the world's poor by distorting their economies and misusing their resources. Applying this view to the mental health field, current western intervention in the third world seems to be creating mental ill health through its economic and political pressures and, at the same time, failing to promote mental health by encouraging and supporting high-tech psychiatry that uses inappropriate methods of diagnosis and treatment. Further, the imposition of psychiatry may actually cause cultural damage by medicalizing human suffering and tying remedies to the purchase of expensive drugs from western countries. If western aid in the mental health field is to address the needs of the people it is supposed to help, the following principles enunciated by Schumacher should be followed: First, aid programmes must be located in villages and towns, where most of the poor live; second, the programmes should not require much financial capital investment and must be sustainable within the resources available; third, new training should be minimal; and finally – most importantly – maximum use should be made of local talent and resources. A model for mental health development in non-western, third world is discussed in Chapter 9.

A change in the policies of aid-giving countries must be matched by changes in the attitudes of governments and mental health professionals in non-western, low-income countries. The assumption of western superiority in *everything* – an attitude that is rife in many parts of Asia and Africa – must be seriously confronted and changed in a realistic fashion. The baby should not be thrown out with the bathwater by attempting to deny real advantages to African and Asian countries that accrue from, for example, obtaining western help for industrial development or the improvement of medical services. But the limitations of western expertise in the field of mental health care and in particular the ethnocentricity of western biomedical psychiatric practice must be faced. The sort of change in the ethos and structure of aid indicated here would lead to biomedical psychiatry becoming involved in the third world on the basis of mutual benefit with a give and take of knowledge about mental health, rather than involvement as an expertise. And so a sense of mutual respect may emerge between rich and poor, western and non-western, black and white, north and south.

A new psychology

The restructuring of mental health at a personal level must be concerned with developing a form of psychology that is sufficiently flexible to understand mental health and ill health cross-culturally. The aim is not to build bridges between culturally distinct psychological-philosophical systems but to evolve strategies to promote interaction between cultural systems that result in a better understanding *on both sides*, so that culture will be a part of that understanding and not something that divides people. At a theoretical level at least, a truly universal psychology is possible on a basis of the similarity of concepts and ideas in modern physics, on the one hand, and the traditional ways of thinking of India and Africa, on the other. For this to work out in practice, it is necessary to think in terms of a coming together of *Ancient Wisdom and Modern Science*, to quote the title of a book edited by Stanislav Grof (1984). But this is a vision for the distant future and this section is concerned with the here and now.

Welwood (1979) suggests that a combination of 'the experiential, holistic, and enlightenment-oriented traditions of the East with the precision, clarity, skepticism, and independence of Western methods could lead to a new kind of psychology that transcends cultural limitations' (pp. xv–xvi). The danger here to be guarded against is that eastern ideas may become perverted into 'mental health gimmicks' rather than providing an alternative vision of the human condition (Cox, 1977, p. 75). A true and lasting amalgamation of East and West, North and South for a new approach in psychology must find a way of honouring diversity, providing, as it were, 'a neutral meeting ground' where practitioners of different systems of knowledge about human being could come together and work out common understandings – or differences in understanding – of the human condition, of human consciousness and human behaviour. This psychology would need to include knowledge from a variety of sources as well as a framework for people to reach out beyond (for example) ego or self, in order 'to realize a more ecological relationship with the world around them' (Welwood, 1979, p. 225).

In such a broad-minded psychology, research methodology would be wide-ranging and not just tied to objectivity. In clinical work (of psychologists), meaning would be paramount; altered states of consciousness seen as valid human experience; and the division into normality and pathology abolished. Thus, for example, people who hear voices or have intensely meaningful experiences will no longer be seen as pathologically 'hallucinated' or 'suffering' from symptoms of 'passivity feelings'; the concept of illness may be retained but will relate to disturbances of balance within individuals, within families and within societies, in a context of their relationship with the universe. Religion and psychiatry will not be considered in separate compartments, but as one system that deals with all aspects of human existence.

Anti-racism

Racism has to be dealt with systematically and deliberately *in practical terms*. Strategies must be aimed at both the practices that are racist and the thinking that underlies them. Attempts to change racist attitudes must go hand in hand with the implementation of strict codes of practice to counteract racism in behaviour. And there is the issue of institutional racism. Facing up to this subtle but very pernicious variety of racism requires careful planning with long-term strategies. Anti-racism in this context may be more about building up strengths of black people and changing power structures than about working with people who form the dominant groups in society.

Mental health promotion

Promoting mental health as a practical proposition may be considered at two levels, the 'mega' level of international or national policies and the 'micro' level of the individual and the family. These two overlap when communities wider than the family are considered. And questions of health cannot be considered in isolation from economic and political matters, and this applies particularly to the third world.

Macro-level engagement

Although the concept of mental health in both theory and practice has major problems when compared with that of physical health, primary health care (PHC) is generally conceptualized as being directed towards mental well-being, in addition to physical and social well-being. Mental health promotion within PHC at a national level must be based on several basic principles (Morley *et al.*, 1983).

First, the community's human, financial and material resources need to be mobilized for PHC activities – not just to ease government resource constraints but to help the community achieve a sense of responsibility. Second, the community should be involved in every stage of the project – the initial assessment and definition of problems, planning, implementation and evaluation. Third, political commitment to social equity is 'an essential starting point for a successful PHC programme'. Fourth, 'universal coverage by health services and the integration of health with other sectors of development' are more important than high capital investment or technical sophistication. Fifth, people affected by health care systems should have an effective voice in decision-making, with women being 'in the front line'. Finally, a 'technical fit' is required between the health care that is provided and based on appropriate epidemiological analyses that are approved by the community affected. Projects need to focus on 'important conditions for which affordable solutions exist' (Morley *et al.*, 1983, pp. 325–6).

The principles given above were developed with the third world in mind but are universally applicable and issues of race and culture must be addressed when they are applied. First, racist ideology may be manifest in judgements that are made or imposed from without. It is all too easy for western aid-giving agencies or western experts to allow their preconceptions to affect the judgement of, for example, who forms the 'community' that is listened to. Political commitment may be compromised by governments which have to bow to pressures for maintaining western systems of health care because they are judged as superior for racist reasons alone and/or promoted for reasons of economic gain of, for example, western pharmaceutical companies. Epidemiological analyses may be forced into models determined by western experts bringing over concepts, such as 'depression' and 'schizophrenia' that may be irrelevant to the cultural setting concerned; the result would be an imposition of western models of mental health and 'therapy' with consequent damage to indigenous ways of coping and caring.

Mental health promotion programmes in the third world must start off with clear policies on their aims *before* seeking help or advice from western countries. And the basis for any programme should be the evaluation and development of culturally consonant systems of care based on an understanding of how their own people perceive mental health needs – explored by qualitative methods of research, such as participatory rural appraisal (Chambers, 1997) referred to in Chapter 9. Once this is done, help may be sought for planning ways and means of carrying out the programme. However, in the present circumstances, countries of the third world should steer clear of any involvement with multinational organizations with an interest in the manufacture of drugs. This is not to imply that drug usage should be excluded as a means of alleviating mental distress, but mental health programmes should be protected from the pressures that economic interests may exert. Experts from the West should not be shunned but must be carefully monitored for their ability to keep to the primary aims of the mental health programme. And they should at all times work under the supervision of local experts with a knowledge of the culture and an ability to tease out racist viewpoints.

Micro-level engagement

The focus here is primarily on basic needs of individuals and families in terms of adequate housing, food, gainful employment for adults and proper education for children, harmonious relationships within families and communities, and a sense of fulfilment and feelings of ethical and spiritual well-being in the individual person. The promotion of mental health at this level overlaps with primary health promotion considered above, but also includes the need for personal services for preserving mental health – whether this is seen as treatment, counselling, liberation or spiritual enlightenment. The systems of help that a person has access to must be indigenous to their cultures and sensitive to issues of racism. But health promotion must reach beyond culture and race to be geared to the needs of the individual and family. These needs would naturally vary according to place and time but also according to the person. For example, an African in Nairobi, a European in London and a Native American in Washington will all have very different life experiences and hence very different needs. But it is equally important to realize that, although focused on the individual, mental health promotion at the micro level cannot and must not ignore the overall social, economic and political aspects of the society in which the person lives.

Developing systems that promote change

The problems resulting from adherence to biomedical psychiatry are discussed in several chapters of this book. Ways of promoting change systemically are far from clear. This section aims to provide possible ways forward taken from leads developed in family therapy and child and adolescent mental health services (CAMHS) – in some ways subspecialities of main-stream psychiatry which have latterly gone their own way in some areas.

Systemic family therapy

In the mid-1980s, DiNicola (1985) argued that family therapy and tran-scultural psychiatry covered similar terrains and Palazzoli (1986) sug-gested that the two fields of study – those around family therapy and transcultural psychiatry – may enrich each other. But at that time there were serious barriers evident between the two because family therapy seemed tied to concepts of the traditional western family and its sup-posed values. However, there has been a movement within family ther-apy towards systemic formulations, shifting the emphasis in family work away from individuals (involved in families) towards seeing families as systems of interactions – at least as foci for interventions when things go wrong (Hoffman, 1981). The approach in systemic formulations is to see problems as lying not in individual pathology but in malfunction-ing of (what should be) balanced interactions. Thus, diagnosis is of the faults in the system, not an illness in an individual or even in family pathology as such. In addition to systemic thinking, family therapy in the USA began to address issues of racism and multiculturalism in the later 1980s onwards. In Britain this tendency has been much less marked although some places such as the Marlborough Family Centre has made some moves in this direction (see Malik *et al.*, 2009). The two books that stand out, both published in the USA, are *Black Families in Therapy, a Multisystemic Approach,* second edition, by Nancy Boyd-Franklin (2003) and *Re-Visioning Family Therapy,* second edition, edited by Monica McGoldrick and Kenneth Hardy (2008).

Kleinman (1977) has proposed what he calls 'the new transcultural psychiatry' (p. 3) in which culturally determined explanatory models form the context for an ethnographic assessment that gives a culturally meaning-ful understanding of symptoms (see Chapter 2). What a systemic approach would bring to general psychiatry is that, apart from seeing an individ-ual's perceptions, emotions and behaviour in terms of their symbolic mean-ing, their problems will be understood as reflecting their positions vis-à-vis various systems: Primary is the family system, but other systems too are important – the judicial, the educational and even the psychiatric system; combining all these in a multisystemic approach on the lines suggested by the family therapists Boyd-Franklin and Shenouda (1990) is what should be aimed at. So, people with problems – as everyone else – will be seen as being located in a multiplicity of systems and interventions ('therapies') would focus on altering balances in each system.

In a predominantly multisystemic approach, individualized diagnosis would lose its significance even if it continues to be used. And the dominant approach would allow more easily the incorporation of cultural understanding and issues about discrimination that people face in the various systems – in fact allow the full impact of institutional racism to be encapsulated into a total understanding. Instead of disorders of thought, belief, relationships and behaviour, analysed as personal illness, such problems would also be seen in terms of relationships connecting with a variety of systems and their meanings could be evaluated in a multisystemic framework. Although this section cannot explore the multisytemic approach in depth, it is proposed here as a way forward towards dropping the illness model and still have a sound base for psychiatric practice.

Choice and partnership working

A recent development in service structures for dealing with children and adolescents, referred to as CAMHS in the UK, has seen several innovative approaches relating to the structure of services and their management. The example the author wishes to quote is called 'The Choice and Partnership Approach' (CAPA) (Kingsbury and York, 2006). Although devised for CAMHS, some of its elements could be applied to a general mental health service.

The crucial interaction is the first meeting, the choice appointment, between the family referred for assessment and the clinical team or professional allocated to meet them: 'In contrast to a traditional assessment model that may be experienced as a semi-structured interview from an "expert with power", families should experience from us a facilitative, conversational curiosity that draws on their strengths' (Kingsbury and York, 2006, p. 74). At this meeting, service user(s) and staff get together to workout, and reach a consensus on, what the 'needs' and 'wants' are – the needs being mainly based on the perceptions of the clinical team and the wants on how the service user/users perceive(s) the situation. The choice appointment is a one-off occasion to be followed, after a break of a week to allow the service users to consider matters, by a 'partnership' meeting if the service users wish to proceed. The partnership is then developed between the service users and the clinician(s) designated to take it on. 'All contacts asessments and interventions should be delivered in Partnership appointments that maintain the stance of informed choice and collaborative work with children and families. This means keeping their choices in mind and reconsidering the choices as the intervention progresses' (Kingsbury and York, 2006, p. 74). CAPA places the service users in the centre of the stage and the professional interventions are guided by what the service users want. The therapeutic alliance is more equal that it might be in the traditional doctor-patient (or professional-client) situation. Also CAPA is aimed at building the capacity of families to be in charge of their own lives, minimizing dependence on therapies or therapists.

Transfering CAPA to a general adult mental health service requires some adjustments because (a) families may not always be available or involved as they would be in the case of children; and (b) adult services contain a social control element associated with risk assessments in keeping with (in the UK) obligations embodied in the Mental Health Act. However, the major problem in applying CAPA to an adult service would be the medical dominance in these services with a powerful adherence to a need for diagnosis, not just for statistical purposes but as drivers for interventions that are planned; and diagnosis, and 'assessments' on which they are based, by their very nature (see Chapters 2 and 3), top-down actions that disempower service users and invalidate the choice and partnership on which CAPA is based. So shifting to a CAPA-like approach in general mental health services would require careful strategies for change, and special attention being paid to the issue of imposed, that is compulsory, treatment implicit in mental health services provided in most countries – something that is being emphasized in the UK via changes in the legislation referred to in Chapters 3 and 5.

Summary

The ideas presented in this chapter are tentative suggestions for changing traditional ways of thinking about mental health – whether seen in relativist or universalist terms – so that an understanding of the subject may have truly universal relevance as well as cultural validity free of racism. Although mental health is a very personal matter in the sense that it can never be defined in exactly the same terms for any two people, it is also never purely personal; it is impossible to formulate the mental health of an individual in terms of the person concerned alone or that of a society isolated from contact with all other groups of people. In broad terms, the concept of mental health is not unlike that of happiness or sorrow; it is not a matter that can be defined in isolation from its context. The concept of well-being is as close as one can get to a definition of mental health that is universally applicable. Also well-being and ill-being are 'words with equivalents in many languages' (Chambers, 1997, p. 9).

An understanding of race and culture is necessary for a discussion of mental health on a global scale, but human beings are really of one race and their diverse cultures may be seen as different paths taken by them for the same basic reasons – in order to live together in relative peace, in communion with one another and in harmony with the environment and within each person. Basic human needs and concerns are probably similar, if not the same, the world over. In order to understand this unity, a realistic approach must be taken to the problems arising from differences in culture and the divisions arising from racism. The paradox that mental health is different because of culture and race and yet the same irrespective of culture and race is the reality.

Bibliography

Aakster, C. W. (1986) 'Concepts in Alternative Medicine', *Social Science and Medicine*, 22(2), 265–73.

Adams, G. L., Dworkin, R. J. and Rosenberg, S. D. (1984) 'Diagnosis and Pharmacotherapy Issues in the Care of Hispanics in the Public Sector', *American Journal of Psychiatry*, 141, 970–4.

Adebimpe, V. R., Chu, C. C., Klein, H. E. and Lange, M. H. (1982) 'Racial and Geographic Differences in the Psychopathology of Schizophrenia', *American Journal of Psychiatry*, 139, 888–91.

Ademuwagun, Z. A., Ayoade, J. A. A., Harrison, I. and Warren, D. M. (eds) (1979) *African Therapeutic Systems* (Waltham, MA: Crossroads Press).

Ajdukovic, D. and Ajdukovic, M. (2003) 'Systemic Approaches to Early Interventions in a Community Affected by Organized Violence' in R. Ørner and U. Schnyder (eds) *Reconstructing Early Intervention after Trauma* (Oxford: Oxford University Press), pp. 82–92.

Allen, J. J. B., Schnyer, R. N. and Hitt, S. K. (1998) 'The Efficacy of Acupuncture in the Treatment of Major Depression in Women', *Psychological Science*, 9(5), 397–401, cited in Acupuncture Research Resource Centre (2002).

Allon, R. (1971) 'Sex, Race, Socio-economic Status, Social Mobility, and Process-Reactive Ratings of Schizophrenia', *Journal of Nervous and Mental Disease*, 153, 343–50.

Allport, G. (1954) *The Nature of Prejudice* (New York: Doubleday).

Amakuki, S. (1959) 'Zen Meditation' in E. Conze (ed.) *Buddhist Scriptures*, trans. E. Conze (Harmondsworth: Penguin), pp. 134–44.

Amarasingham, L. R. (1980) 'Movement among Healers in Sri Lanka: A Case Study of a Sinhalese Patient', *Culture, Medicine and Psychiatry*, 4(1), 71–92.

Anderson, B. (1991) *Imagined Communities, Reflections on the Origin and Spread of Nationalism* (London and New York, Verso).

Andreasen, N. C., Carpenter, W. T., Kane, J. M., Lasser, R. A., Marder, S. R. and Weinberger, D. R. (2005) 'Remission in Schizophrenia: Proposed Criteria and Rationale for Consensus', *American Journal of Psychiatry*, 162, 441–9.

Angermeyer, M. C. and Matschinger, H. (2005) 'Causal Beliefs and Attitudes to People with Schizophrenia. Trend Analysis Based on Data from Two Population Surveys in Germany', *British Journal of Psychiatry*, 186, 331–4.

Anon. (1851) 'Startling Facts from the Census', *American Journal of Insanity*, 8(2), 153–5.

APA (American Psychiatric Association) (1980) *Diagnostic and Statistical Manual of Mental Disorders, DSM-III*, 3rd edn (Washington: APA).

APA (American Psychiatric Association) (1994) *Diagnostic and Statistical Manual of Mental Disorders. DSM-IV*, 4th edn (Washington: APA).

Appleby, L. (2008) 'Services for Ethnic Minorities: A Question of Trust', *Psychiatric Bulletin*, 32, 401–2.

Ardrey, R. (1967) *The Territorial Imperative* (London: Collins).

Argyle, M. (1975) *Bodily Communication* (London: Methuen).

ARRC (Acupuncture Research Resource Centre) (2002) *Depression, Anxiety and Acupuncture. The Evidence for Effectiveness.* (London: British Acupuncture Council) Available: http://www.acupuncture.org.uk. Accessed: 30 May 2009.

Asante, M. K. (1985) 'Afrocentricity and Culture' in M. K. Asante and K. W. Asante (eds) *African Culture: The Rhythms of Unity* (Westport, CT: Greenwood Press), pp. 3–12.

Asante, M. K. and Asante, K. W. (1985) 'Preface', in M. K. Asante and K. W. Asante (eds) *African Culture: The Rhythms of Unity* (Westport, CT: Greenwood Press), pp. ix–x.

Assaglioli, R. (1975) *Psychosynthesis: A Manual of Principles and Techniques* (New York: Hobbs Dorman), cited by Graham (1986).

Audini, B. and Lelliott, P. (2002) 'Age, Gender and Ethnicity of Those Detained under Part II of the Mental Health Act 1983', *British Journal of Psychiatry*, 180, 222–6.

Ayalon, O. (1998) 'Community Healing for Children Traumatized by War', *International Review of Psychiatry*, 10, 224–33.

Ayoade, J. A. A. (1979) 'The Concept of Inner Essence in Yoruba Traditional Medicine' in Z. A. Ademuwagun, J. A. A. Ayoade, I. Harrison and D. M. Warren (eds) *African Therapeutic Systems* (Waltham, MA: Crossroads Press), pp. 49–55.

Babcock, J. W. (1895) 'The Colored Insane', *Alienist and Neurologist*, 16, 423–47.

Bagley, C. (1971) 'Mental Illness in Immigrant Minorities in London', *Journal of Biosocial Science*, 3, 449–59.

Bak, M., Krabbendam, L., Janssen, I., de Graaf, R., Vollebergh, W. and van Oz, J. (2005) 'Early Trauma May Increase the Risk for Psychotic Experiences by Impacting on Emotional Response and Perception of Control', *Acta Psychiatrica Scandinavica*, 112, 360–6.

Balfour, J. G. (1876) 'An Arab Physician on Insanity', *Journal of Mental Science*, xxii, 241–9.

Banton, M. (1987) *Racial Theories* (Cambridge: Cambridge University Press).

Banton, M. and Harwood, J. (1975) *The Race Concept* (London: David & Charles), cited by Husband (1982).

Barzun, J. (1965) *Race: A Study in Superstition* (New York and London: Harper and Row).

Barzun, J. (2000) *From Dawn to Decadence: 500 years of Western Cultural Life 1500 to the Present* (New York: HarperCollins).

Baumann, G. (1996) *Contesting Culture, Discourses of Identity in Multi-ethnic Britain* (Cambridge: Cambridge University Press).

Baxter, J., Kingi, T. K., Tapsell, R. and Durie, M. (2006) 'Māori' in M. A. Oakley Browne, J. E. Wells and K. M. Scott (eds) *Te Rau Hinengaro: The New Zealand Mental Health Survey* (Wellington, NZ: Ministry of Health), pp. 139–78. Available: http://www.moh.govt.nz/moh.nsf/pagesmh/5223. Accessed: 20 October 2008.

Bayer, R. (1981) *Homosexuality and American Psychiatry: The Politics of Diagnosis* (New York: Basic Books).

BBC News (2008) 'Schizophrenia Term Use Invalid', *BBC News on line*. Available: http:// news.bbc.co.uk. Accessed: 5 August 2008. Also see http://www.caslcampaign. com. Accessed: 10 June 2009.

Bean, R. B. (1906) 'Some Racial Peculiarities of the Negro Brain', *American Journal of Anatomy*, 5, 353–415.

Bebbington, P. E. (1978) 'The Epidemiology of Depressive Disorder', *Culture, Medicine and Psychiatry*, 2, 297–341.

Beiser, M. (1987) 'Commentary on Culture-bound Syndromes and International Disease Classifications', *Culture, Medicine and Psychiatry*, II, 29–33.

Benedict, P. K. and Jacks, I. (1954) 'Mental Illness in Primitive Societies', *Psychiatry*, 17, 377–84.

Bentall, R. P. (1990) *Reconstructing Schizophrenia* (London and New York: Routledge).

Bentall, R. P. (2003) *Madness Explained* (London: Allen Lane).

Ben-Tovim, G., Gabriel, J., Law, I. and Stredder, K. (1986) *The Local Politics of Race* (London: Macmillan).

Bernal, M. (1987) *Black Athena: The Afroasiatic Roots of Classical Civilisation*, vol. 1 (London: Free Association).

Berreman, G. D. (1960) 'Caste in India and the United States', *American Journal of Sociology*, 66(2), 120–7.

bhabha, homi (1994) *The Location of Culture* (London: Routledge).

Bhugra, D., Leff, J., Mallett, R., Der, G., Corridan, B. and Rudge, S. (1997) 'Incidence and Outcome of Schizophrenia in Whites, African-Caribbeans and Asians in London', *Psychological Medicine*, 27, 791–8.

Bhui, K. (2002) 'London's Ethnic Minorities and the Provision of Mental Health Services' in K. Bhui (ed.) *Racism and Mental Health Prejudice and Suffering* (London: Jessica Kingsley), pp. 139–87.

Bhui, K. and Olajide, D. (1999) *Mental Health Service Provision for a Multi-cultural Society* (London: Saunders).

Biko, S. (1971) 'White Racism and Black Consciousness', paper given at a conference sponsored by The Abe Bailey Institute for Inter-racial Studies held at Cape Town in January 1971, reprinted in A. Stubbs (ed.) *Steve Biko. I Write What I Like. A Selection of His Writings* (Harmondsworth: Penguin), pp. 75–86.

Birman, D. and Tran, N. (2008) 'Psychological Distress and Adjustment of Vietnamese Refugees in the United States: Association with Pre- and Postmigration Factors', *American Journal of Orthopsychiatry*, 78(1), 109–20.

Bisson, J. and Andrew, M. (2007) 'Psychological Treatment of Post-traumatic Stress Disorder (PTSD)', *Cochrane Database of Systematic Reviews*, Issue 3. Art. No.: CD003388. DOI: 10.1002/14651858.CD003388.pub3.

Bisson, J. and Deahl, M. (1994) 'Psychological Debriefing and Prevention of Post-Traumatic Stress – More Research Is Needed', *British Journal of Psychiatry*, 165, 717–20.

Bleuler, E. (1950) *Dementia Præcox or the Group of Schizophrenias*, trans. J. Zitkin (New York: International Universities Press). Originally published in 1911.

Bloch, S. and Reddaway, P. (1984) *The Shadows over World Psychiatry* (London: Gollancz).

Blue, A. V. and Gaines, A. D. (1992) 'The Ethnopsychiatric Répertoire: A Review and Overview of Ethnopsychiatric Studies' in A. D. Gaines (ed.) *Ethnopsychiatry. The Cultural Constructions of Professional and Folk Psychiatries* (New York: State University of New York Press), pp. 397–484.

Bolton, P. (1984) 'Management of Compulsorily Admitted Patients to a High Security Unit', *International Journal of Social Psychiatry*, 30, 77–84.

Boyden, J. and Gibbs, S. (1996) '*Children of War: Responses to Psycho-social Distress in Cambodia* (Geneva: UNRISD). Cited in Hart *et al.*, 2007.

Boyd-Franklin, N. (2003) *Black Families in Therapy. Understanding the African-American Experience*, 2nd edn (New York and London: Guilford Press).

Boyd-Franklin, N. and Shenouda, N. T. (1990) 'A Multisystems Approach to the Treatment of a Black Inner-City Family with a Schizophrenic Mother', *American Journal of Orthopsychiatry*, 60(2), 186–95.

Boyle, M. (1990) *Schizophrenia a Scientific Delusion?* (London and New York: Routledge).

Boyle, M. (2002) *Schizophrenia a Scientific Delusion?* 2nd edn (London: Routledge).

Bracken, P. J. (2002) *Trauma Culture, Meaning & Philosophy* (London and Philadelphia: Whurr).

Bracken, P. J., Giller, J. E. and Summerfield, D. (1995) 'Psychological Responses to War and Atrocity: The Limitations of Current Concepts', *Social Science and Medicine*, 40(8), 1073–82.

Bricmont, J. (2007) *Humanitarian Imperialism Using Human Rights to Sell War,* trans. D. Johnstone (New York: Monthly Review Press).

Bright, T. (1586) *A Treatise of Melancholy* (London: Vautrolier).

Brittan, A. and Maynard, M. (1984) *Sexism, Racism and Oppression* (Oxford: Blackwell).

Bromberg, W. and Simon, F. (1968) 'The "Protest" Psychosis. A Special Type of Reactive Psychosis', *Archives of General Psychiatry*, 19, 155–60.

Brown, D. and Pedder, J. (1979) *Introduction to Psychotherapy. An Outline of Psychodynamic Principles and Practice* (London: Tavistock).

Brown, G. W. and Harris, T. (1978) *Social Origins of Depression. A Study of Psychiatric Disorder in Women* (London: Tavistock).

Browne, A. (2000) 'The Last Days of a White World', *The Observer*, 3 September, 17.

Browne, D. (1997) *Black People and Sectioning. The Black Experience of Detention under the Civil Sections of the Mental Health Act* (London: Little Rock Publishing).

Buitrago Cuéllar, J. E. (2004) 'Internally Displaced Colombians: The Recovery of Victims of Violence within a Psychosocial Framework' in K. E. Miller and L. M. Rasco (eds) *The Mental Health of Refugees. Ecological Approaches to Healing and Adaptation* (Mahwah, NJ and London: Erlbaum), pp. 229–62.

Burton, R. (1806) *The Anatomy of Melancholy*, 11th edn (London: Hodson). First published in 1621.

Busfield, J. (1986) *Managing Madness: Changing Ideas and Practice* (London: Hutchinson).

Buunk, B. P. and Gibbons, F. X. (eds) (1994) *Health, Coping and Well-Being* (Mahwah, NJ: Lawrence Erlbaum).

Campling, P. (1989) 'Race, Culture and Psychotherapy', *Psychiatric Bulletin*, 13, 550–1.

Capra, F. (1982) *The Turning Point. Science, Society, and the Rising Culture* (London: Wildwood House).

Carlisle, S. and Hanlon, P. (2008) 'Well-being' as a Focus for Public Health? A Critique and Defence', *Critical Public Health*, 18(3), 263–70.

Carothers, J. C. (1947) 'A Study of Mental Derangement in Africans and an Attempt to Explain Its Peculiarities, More Especially in Relation to the African Attitude to Life', *Journal of Mental Science*, 101, 548–97.

Carothers, J. C. (1951) 'Frontal Lobe Function and the African', *Journal of Mental Science*, 97, 12–48.

Carothers, J. C. (1953) *The African Mind in Health and Disease: A Study in Ethnopsychiatry* WHO Monograph Series No. 17 (Geneva: WHO).

Carpenter, L. and Brockington, I. F. (1980) 'A Study of Mental Illness in Asians, West Indians and Africans in Manchester', *British Journal of Psychiatry*, 137, 201–5.

Carrette, J. and King, R. (2005) *Selling Spirituality. The Silent Takeover of Religion* (London and New York: Routledge).

Carrington, P. (1982) 'Meditation Techniques in Clinical Practice' in L. E. Abt and I. R. Stuart (eds) *The Newer Therapies: A Sourcebook* (New York: Van Nostrand Reinhold), pp. 60–78.

Cartwright, S. A. (1981) (1851) 'Report on the Diseases and Physical Peculiarities of the Negro Race', reprinted from *New Orleans Medical and Surgical Journal*, May 1851: 691–715 in A. C. Caplan, H. T. Engelhardt and J. J. McCartney (eds) *Concepts of Health and Disease* (Reading, MA: Addison-Wesley, 1981), pp. 305–25.

Casciani, D. (2004) 'Islamophobia Pervades UK – report', *BBC News June 2, 2004*. Available: http://news.bbc.co.uk. Accessed: 29 January 2007.

Cashmore, E. (1979) *Rastaman. The Rastafarian Movement in England* (London: George Allen & Unwin).

Census (2001) *Resident Population Estimates for Local Authorities, All Persons, and June 2003 – (for Total Population)* (London: Office for National Statistics). Available: http://www.statistics.gov.uk/census2001. Accessed: 15 October 2006.

Chambers, R. (1983) *Rural Development. Putting the Last First* (London: Prentice Hall).

Chambers, R. (1992) *Rural Appraisal: Rapid, Relaxed and Participatory*, Institute of Development Studies (IDS) Discussion Paper 311 (Brighton, Sussex: IDS).

Chambers, R. (1997) *Whose Reality Counts? Putting the First Last* (London: ITDG Publishing).

Chang, D. and Kleinman, A. (2002) 'Growing Pains: Mental Health Care in a Developing China', *Yale-China Health Journal*, 1, 85–97.

Chang, D. F., Yifeng, X., Kleinman, A. and Kleinman, J. (2002) 'Rehabilitation of Schizophrenia Patients in China. The Shanghai Model' in A. Chen, A. Kleinman and B. Saraceno (eds) *World Mental Health Casebook. Social and Mental Health Programs in Low-Income Countries* (New York, Boston, Dordrecht, London and Moscow: Kluwer Academic), pp. 27–50.

Chaplin, R. (2000) 'Psychiatrists Can Cause Stigma Too', *British Journal of Psychiatry*, 177, 467.

Chase, A. (1997) *The Legacy of Thomas Malthus: The Social Costs of New Scientific Racism* (New York: Alfred Knopf).

Clarke, K. B. and Clarke, M. P. (1947) 'Racial Identification and Preference in Negro Children' in T. M. Newcombe and E. L. Hartley (eds) *Readings in Social Psychology* (New York: Holt, Rinehart and Winston), pp. 169–78.

Clifford, T. (1984) *Tibetan Buddhist Medicine and Psychiatry: The Diamond Healing* (York Beach, ME: Samuel Weiser).

CNN News (2008) *House Apologizes for Slavery, 'Jim Crow' Injustices*, 29 July, Available: http://edition.cnn/2008. Accessed: 20 August 2008.

Cochrane, R. (1977) 'Mental Illness in Immigrants to England and Wales', *Social Psychiatry*, 12, 25–35.

Cohen, A., Kleinman, A. and Saraceno, B. (eds) (2002) *World Mental Health Casebook. Social and Mental Programs in Low-income Countries* (New York: Kluwer Academic/Plenum Publishers).

Cohen, P. (1999) *New Ethnicities, Old Racisms?* (London: Zed Books).

Cohen, R. and Gold, G. (1997) 'Constructing Ethnicity: Myth of Return and Modes of Exclusion among Israelis in Toronto', *International Migration*, 35(3), 373–94.

Connolly, C. J. (1950) *External Morphology of the Primate Brain* (Illinois: Springfield), cited by Carothers (1953).

Conze, E. (1959) 'Meditation' in E. Conze (ed.) *Buddhist Scriptures* (Harmondsworth: Penguin), pp. 98–144.

Cooper, J. E., Kendall, R. E., Garland, B. J., Sharpe, I., Copeland, J. R. M. and Simon, R. (1972) *Psychiatric Diagnosis in New York and London*, Maudsley Monograph No. 20 (Oxford: Oxford University Press).

Cooter, R. (1981) 'Phrenology and British Alienists ca. 1825–1845' in A. Scull (ed.) *Madhouses, Mad-doctors and Madmen: The Social History of Psychiatry in the Victorian Era* (London: Athlone Press), pp. 58–104.

Cornah, D. (2006) *The Impact of Spirituality on Mental Health. A Review of Literature* (London: Mental Health Foundation).

Coulter, J. (1979) *The Social Construction of Mind: Studies in Ethnomethodology and Linguistic Philosophy* (London: Macmillan).

Council of Europe (2003) *Convention of the Protection of Human Rights and Fundamental Freedoms as amended by Protocol No. 11 with Protocol Nos 1, 4, 6, 7, 12 & 13* (Brussels: Registry of the European Court of Human Rights). Available: http://www.echr.coe.int. Accessed: 20 October 2008.

Cox, H. (1977) *Turning East: The Promise and Peril of the New Orientalism* (New York: Simon and Shuster).

Cox, O. C. (1948) *Caste, Class and Race: A Study in Social Dynamics* (Detroit, IL: Wayne State University Press), cited by Cashmore and Troyna (1983).

Craddock, N., Antebi, D., Attenburrow, M-J., Bailey, A., Carson, A., Cowen, P., Craddock, B., Eagles, J., Ebmeir, K., Farmer, A. et al. (2008) 'Wake-Up Call for British Psychiatry', *British Journal of Psychiatry*, 193, 6–9.

Crane, R. (2009) *Mindfulness-Based Cognitive Therapy* (London and New York: Routledge).

Crisp, A. H. (2000) 'Changing Minds: Every Family in the Land. An Update on the College's Campaign', *Psychiatric Bulletin*, 24, 267–8.

CSIP (Care Services Improvement Partnership), NIMHE (National Institute for Mental Health in England) and HCC (Healthcare Commission) (2005) *Count Me In. Results of a National Census of Inpatients in Mental Health Hospitals and Facilities in England and Wales* (London: Healthcare Commission). Available: http://www.healthcarecommission.org.uk Accessed: 25 November 2007.

CSIP (Care Services Improvement Partnership), NIMHE (National Institute for Mental Health in England) and HCC (Healthcare Commission) (2008) *Count Me in 2008. Results of the 2008 National Census of Inpatients in Mental Health and Learning Disability Services in England and Wales* (London: Commission for Healthcare Audit and Inspection). Available: http://www.healthcarecommission. org.uk. Accessed: 5 December 2008.

CSIP (Care Services Improvement Partnership), RCPsych (Royal College of Psychiatrists) and SCIE (Social Care Institute for Excellence) (2007) *A Common Purpose: Recovery in Future Mental Health Services,* Joint position paper 08 (London: SCIE).

D'Andrade, R. G. (1984) 'Cultural Meaning Systems' in R. A. Shweder and R. A. LeVine (eds) *Culture Theory: Essays on Mind, Self and Emotion* (Cambridge: Cambridge University Press), pp. 88–119.

Dalal, F. (1988) 'The Racism of Jung', *Race and Class*, 29(3), 1–22.

Dalal, F. (2002) *Race, Colour and the Process of Racialization. New Perspectives from Group. Analysis, Psychoanalysis and Sociology* (Hove and New York: Brunner-Routledge).

Darwin, C. R. (1871) *The Descent of Man* (London: Murray).

Darwin, C. (1872) *The Expression of the Emotions in Man and Animals* (New York: Appleton), reprinted (London: University of Chicago Press, 1965).

Davies, P. and Gribben, J. (1991) *The Matter Myth. Towards 21st Century Science* (Harmondsworth: Viking Penguin Books).

Davies, S., Thornicroft, G., Leese, M., Higginbotham, A. and Phelan, M. (1996) 'Ethnic Differences in Risks of Compulsory Psychiatric Admission among Representative Cases of Psychosis in London', *British Medical Journal*, 312, 533–7.

Dawkins, R. (1976) *The Selfish Gene* (New York: Oxford University Press).

Day, M. (2007) 'Who's Funding WHO?' *British Medical Journal*, 334, 338–9.

de Jong, J. T. V. M. (1987) *A Descent into African Psychiatry* (Amsterdam: Royal Tropical Institute Publications).

de Jong, K. and Kleber, R. (2003) 'Early Psychosocial Interventions for War-Effected Populations' in R. Ørner and U. Schnyder (eds) *Reconstructing Early Intervention after Trauma* (Oxford: Oxford University Press), pp. 184–92.

de Jong, K., Kleber, R. and Puratic, V. (2003) 'Mental Health Programs in Areas of Armed Conflict: The Médecine Sans Frontières Counselling Centres in Bosnia-Hezegovina', *Intervention: International Journal of Mental Health, Psychosocial Work and Counselling in Areas of Conflict*, 1(1), 14–32.

Dean, G., Walsh, D., Downing, H. and Shelley, E. (1981) 'First Admissions of Native-Born and Immigrants to Psychiatric Hospitals in South-East England, 1976', *British Journal of Psychiatry*, 139, 506–12.

DeGruy Leary, J. (2005) *Post Traumatic Slave Syndrome: America's Legacy of Enduring Injury and Healing* (Milwaukie, OR: Upton Press).

Demerath, N. J. (1942) 'Schizophrenia among Primitives', *American Journal of Psychiatry*, 98, 703–7.

Denier, E. and Oishi, S. (2000) 'Money and Happiness: Income and Subjective Well-Being across Nations' in E. Diener and E. M. Suh (eds) *Culture and Subjective Well-Being* (Cambridge, MS and London: MIT Press), pp. 185–218.

Department of Health (2003) *'Delivering Race Equality: A Framework for Action* (London: Department of Health).

Department of Health (2005) *Delivering Race Equality in Mental Health Care: An Action Plan for Reform Inside and Outside Services and the Government's Response to the Independent Inquiry into the Death of David Bennett* (London: Department of Health).

Department of Health (2007) *Mental Health Act 2007* (Norwich: The Stationery Office).

Desjarlais, R., Eisenberg, L., Good, B. and Kleinman, A. (1995) *World Mental Health. Problems and Priorities in Low-Income Countries* (New York and Oxford: Oxford University Press).

Diener, E. (1984) 'Subjective Well-Being', *Psychological Bulletin*, 96, 542–75.

Diener, E. (2000) 'Subjective Well-Being: The Science of Happiness and a Proposal for a National Index', *American Psychologist*, 55, 34–43.

Diener, E. and Oishi, S. (2000) 'Money and Happiness: Income and Subjective Well-Being across Nations', in E. Diener and E. M. Suh (eds) *Culture and Subjective Well-Being* (Cambridge, MS and London: MIT Press), pp. 185–218.

Diener, E. and Suh, E. M. (2000) 'Measuring Subjective Well-Being to Compare Quality of Life of Cultures' in E. Diener and E. M. Suh (eds) *Culture and Subjective Well-Being* (Cambridge, MS and London: MIT Press), pp. 3–12.

DiNicola, V. F. (1985) 'Family Therapy and Transcultural Psychiatry: An Emerging Synthesis. Part 1: The Conceptual Basis', *Transcultural Psychiatric Research Review*, 22, 81–113.

Diop, C. A. (1967) *Antériorité des Civilisations Nègre: Mythe ou Vérité Historique?* (Paris: Présence Africaine) trans. M. Cook *The African Origin of Civilization: Myth or Reality?* (Westport, CT: Lawrence Hill, 1974).

Dobkin De Rios, M. (1972) *Visionary Vine: Psychedelic Healing in the Peruvian Amazon* (San Francisco, CA: Chandler).

Docarmo, S. N. (2008) *Notes on the Black Cultural Movement.* Available: http://www.bucks.edu/~docarmos/BCnotes.html. Accessed: 19 November 2008.

Dols, M. W. (1987) 'Insanity and Its Treatment in Islamic Society', *Medical History*, 31, 1–14.

Dols, M. W. (1992) *Majnūn: The Madman in Medieval Islamic Society*, D. E. Immisch (ed.) (Oxford: Clarendon Press).

Dominelli, L. (1988) *Anti-racist Social Work. A Challenge for White Practitioners and Educators* (Basingstoke: Macmillan).

Down, J. L. M. (1866) 'Observations on an Ethnic Classification of Idiots', *Lectures and Reports from the London Hospital for 1866*, reprinted in C. Thompson (ed.) *The Origins of Modern Psychiatry* (Chichester: Wiley, 1987), pp. 15–18.

Du Bois, W. E. B. (1970) *The Souls of Black Folk* (New York: Washington Square Press), first published by McClurg, Chicago 1903.

Dummett, A. (1973) *A Portrait of English Racism* (Harmondsworth: Penguin) republished (Manchester: Manchester Free Press, 1984).

Dunner, D. L. and Dunner, P. Z. (1983) 'Psychiatry in China: Some Personal Observations', *Biological Psychiatry*, 18, 799–801.

Dyregrov, A. (1989) 'Caring for Helpers in Disaster Situations: Psychological Debriefing', *Disaster Management*, 2, 25–30.

Eagleton, T. (2000) *The Idea of Culture* (Oxford: Blackwell).

Eisenberg, L. (2000) 'Is Psychiatry more Mindful or Brainier Than It Was a Decade Ago?', *British Journal of Psychiatry*, 176, 1–5.

Eisenbruch, M. (1991) 'Post-traumatic Stress Disorder to Cultural Bereavement: Diagnosis of Southeast Asian Refugees', *Social Science and Medicine*, 33(6), 673–80.

Ellenberger, H. F. (1974) 'Psychiatry from Ancient to Modern Times' in S. Arieti (ed.) *American Handbook of Psychiatry*, 2nd edn (New York: Basic Books), pp. 3–27.

Estroff, S. E. and Zimmer, C. (1994) 'Social Networks, Social Support, and Violence among Persons with Severe, Persistent Mental Illness' in J. Monahan and H. J. Steadmen (eds) *Violence and Mental Disorder. Developments on Risk Assessment* (Chicago, IL: University of Chicago Press), pp. 259–95.

Evarts, A. B. (1913) 'Dementia Precox in the Colored Race', *Psychoanalytic Review*, 14, 388–403.

Eysenck, H. J. (1952) *The Scientific Study of Personality* (London: Routledge and Kegan Paul).

Eysenck, H. J. (1971) *Race, Intelligence and Education* (London: Temple Smith).

Eysenck, H. J. (1973) *The Inequality of Man* (London: Temple Smith).

Eze, E. (ed.) (1997) *Race and the Enlightenment. A Reader* (Cambridge MA: Blackwell).

Fabrega, H. (1991) 'Psychiatric Stigma in Non-western Societies', *Comprehensive Psychiatry*, 32, 534–51.

Fanon, F. (1952) *Peau Noire, Masques Blancs* (Paris: Editions de Seuil) trans. C. L. Markmann, *Black Skin, White Masks* (New York: Grove Press, 1967).

Fanon, F. (1961) *Les Damnés de la Terre* (Paris: Maspero) trans. C. Farrington *The Wretched of the Earth* (New York: Grove Press, 1965).

Favazza, A. R. (1985) 'Anthropology and Psychiatry' in H. I. Kaplan and B. J. Sadock (eds), *Comprehensive Textbook of Psychiatry*, 4th edn, vol. 1 (Baltimore, MD: Williams and Wilkins), pp. 247–65.

Fearon, P., Kirbride, J. B., Craig, M., Dazzan, P., Morgan, K., Lloyd, T., Hutchinson, G., Tarrant, J., Fung, W. L. A., Holloway, J. et al. (2006) 'Incidence of Schizophrenia and Other Psychoses in Ethnic Minority Groups: Results from the MRC AESOP Study', *Psychological Medicine*, 36, 1541–50.

Fennell, M. V. (2009) 'Cognitive Behaviour Therapy for Depressive Disorders' in M. G. Gelder, N. C. Andreasen, J. J. López-Ibor Jr and J. R. Geddes (eds) *New Oxford Textbook of Psychiatry*, 2nd edn, vol. 2 (Oxford: Oxford University Press), pp. 1304–13.

Fernando, S. (1988) *Race and Culture in Psychiatry* (London: Croom Helm), published as paperback by Routledge, 1989.

Fernando, S. (1991) 'Black Europeans', *Openmind*, 54, 15.

Fernando, S. (1998) 'Mental Illness and Criminality' in S. Fernando, D. Ndegwa and M. Wilson (eds) *Forensic Psychiatry, Race and Culture* (London and New York: Routledge), pp. 30–50.

Fernando, S. (2003) *Cultural Diversity, Mental Health and Psychiatry: The Struggle against Racism* (Hove, East Sussex and New York: Brunner-Routledge).

Fernando, S. (2004) 'Just Being There', *Openmind*, 127, 25.

Fernando, S. (2005a) 'Multicultural Mental Health Services. Projects for Minority Ethnic Communities in England' *Transcultural Psychiatry*, 42(3), 420–36.

Fernando, S. (2005b) 'Mental Health Services in Low-Income Countries. Challenges and Innovations' *International Journal of Migration and Social Care*, 1(1), 13–18.

Fernando, S. (2005c) 'Backing User Choice', *Openmind*, 131, 6–7.

Fernando, S. (2006) 'Blowing in the Wind', *Openmind*, 137, 24–5.

Fernando, S. (2007) 'Spirituality across Cultures', in M. E. Coyte, P. Gilbert and V. Nicholls (eds) *Spirituality, Values and Mental Health Jewels for the Journey* (London: Jessica Kingsley).

Fernando, S. (2009) 'Inequalities and the Politics of "Race"' in S. Fernando and F. Keating (eds) *Mental Health in a Multi-ethnic Society. A Multi-disciplinary Handbook*, 2nd edn (London: Routledge), pp. 42–57.

Fernando, S. and Keating, F. (2009a) 'Introduction' in S. Fernando and F. Keating (eds) *Mental Health in a Multi-ethnic Society. A Multi-disciplinary Handbook*, 2nd edn (London: Routledge), pp. 1–10.

Field, M. J. (1960) *Search for Security: An Ethnocentric Study of Rural Ghana* (Evanston, IL: Northwestern University Press).

Flaherty, J. A. and Meagher, R. (1980) 'Measuring Racial Bias in Inpatient Treatment', *American Journal of Psychiatry*, 137, 679–82.

Flaherty, J. A., Naidu, J., Lawton, R. and Pathak, D. (1981) 'Racial Differences in Perception of Ward Atmosphere', *American Journal of Psychiatry*, 138, 815–17.

Foa, E. B. and Cahill, S. P. (2006) 'Psychosocial Treatments for PTSD: An Overview' in Y. Neria, R. Gross, R. Marshall and E. Susser (eds) *9/11: Public Health in the Wake of Terrorist Attacks* (Cambridge: Cambridge University Press), pp. 457–74.

Folkman, S. and Lazarus, R. S. (1988) 'The Relationship between Coping and Emotion: Implications for Theory and Research', *Social Science and Medicine*, 26(3), 309–17.

Foote, R. F. (1858) 'The Condition of the Insane and the Treatment of Nervous Diseases in Turkey', *Journal of Mental Science*, 4, 444–50.

Foucault, M. (1967) *Madness and Civilization. A History of Insanity in the Age of Reason* (London: Tavistock) Originally published in French as *Histoire de la Folie* (Paris: Libraire Plon, 1961).

Foucault, M. (1977) *Discipline and Punish. The Birth of the Prison*. trans. Alan Sheridan (London: Allen Lane). Reprinted 1991 (Harmondsworth: Penguin Books). First published as *Surveiller et punir: Naissance de la prison* by Editions Gallimard (1975).

Foucault, M. (1988) *Politics, Philosophy, Culture. Interviews and Other Writings 1977–1984* (ed. L. D. Kritzman) (London: Routledge).

Frawley, D. (1989) *Ayurvedic Healing. A Comprehensive Guide* (Delhi: Motilal Banarsidass Publishers).

Freire, Paulo (1996) *Pedagogy of the Oppressed* (London: Penguin Books).

Freke, T. and Wa'Nee'Che (Dennis Renault) (1996) *Native American Spirituality* (London: Thorsons – HarperCollins).

Freuchen, P. (1959) *The Book of the Eskimos* (New York: Fawcett) cited by West (1979).

Freud, S. (1913) *Totem and Taboo* (Vienna: Hugo Heller) trans. and publ. in English (London: Routledge and Kegan Paul, 1950).

Freud, S. (1915) 'Thoughts for the Times on War and Death', *Imago*, 4(1), 1–21, trans. J. Strachey in *The Standard Edition of the Complete Psychological Works of Sigmund Freud*, vol. 14 (London: Hogarth Press, 1957), pp. 273–300.

Freud, S. (1917) 'Mourning and Melancholia', trans. J. Strachey in *The Standard Edition of the Complete Works of Sigmund Freud*, vol. 14 (London: Hogarth Press, 1957), pp. 243–58.

Friedli, L. (2008) *Mental Health, Resilience and Inequalities* (Copenhagen: WHO Europe and London: The Mental Health Foundation).

Fromm, E., Suzuki, D. T. and de Martino, R. (1960) *Zen Buddhism and Psychoanalysis* (London: George Allen & Unwin).

Fryer, P. (1984) *Staying Power: The History of Black People in Britain* (London: Pluto Press).

Fujita, C. (1986) *Morita Therapy* (Tokyo: Igaku Shoin) cited by Reynolds (1988).

Fulford, K. W. M. (Bill) and Woodbridge, K. (2007) *Values-Based Practice: Help and Healing within a Shared Theology of Diversity* in M. E. Coyte, P. Gilbert and V. Nicholls (eds) *Spirituality, Values and Mental Health* (London: Jessica Kingsley), pp. 45–57.

Fulford, K. W. M. (Bill), Dickenson, D. and Murray, T. H. (2002) 'Introduction. Many Voices: Human Values in Healthcare Ethics' in K. W. M. Fulford, D. Dickenson and T. H. Murray (eds) *Healthcare Ethics and Human Values: An Introductory Text with Readings and Case Studies* (Malden, MA: Blackwell Publishers), pp. 1–19.

Fulford, K. W. M. (Bill), Thornton, T. and Graham, G. (2006) *Oxford Textbook of Philosophy and Psychiatry* (Oxford: Oxford University Press).

Fuller, C. E. (1959) 'Ethnohistory in the Study of Culture Change in Southeast Africa' in W. R. Bascom and M. J. Merskovits (eds) *Continuity and Change in African Cultures* (Chicago: University of Chicago Press), pp. 113–29.

Gaines, A. D. (1982) 'Cultural Definitions, Behaviour and the Person in American Psychiatry' in A. J. Marsella and G. M. White (eds) *Cultural Conceptions of Mental Health and Therapy* (Dordrecht: Reidel), pp. 167–92.

Gaines, P., Bower, A., Buckingham, B., Eager, K., Burgess, P. and Green, J. (2003) *Mental Health Classification and Outcomes Study: Final Report* (Auckland, NZ: Health Research Council). Available: http://www.hrc.govt.nz. Accessed: 20 October 2008.

Galappatti, A. (2003) 'What Is a Psychosocial Intervention? Mapping the Field in Sri Lanka', *Intervention: International Journal of Mental Health, Psychosocial Work and Counselling in Areas of Conflict*, 1(2), 3–17.

Galappatti, A. (2005) 'Psychosocial Work in the Aftermath of the Tsunami: Challenges for Service Provision in Batticaloa, Eastern Sri Lanka', *Intervention: International Journal of Mental Health, Psychosocial Work and Counselling in Areas of Conflict*, 3(1), 65–9.

Galton, F. (1865) 'Hereditary Talent and Character', *MacMillan Magazine*, 157–66.

Galton, F. (1869) *Hereditary Genius: An Inquiry into Its Laws and Consequences* (London: Macmillan).

Ganga, D. (2006) 'Re-inventing the Myth of Return: Older Italians in Nottingham' in K. Burrell and P. Panayi (eds) *Histories and Memories. Migrants and Their History in Britain,* International Library of Historical Studies 7 (London and New York: Tauris Academic Studies), pp. 114–30.

Gauron, E. F. and Dickinson, J. K. (1966) 'Diagnostic Decision Making in Psychiatry: Information Usage', *Archives of General Psychiatry,* 14, 225–32.

Gelder, M. G., Andreasen, N. C., López-Ibor Jr J. J. and Geddes J. R. (eds) (2009) *New Oxford Textbook of Psychiatry,* 2nd edn, vol. 2 (Oxford: Oxford University Press).

Gelfand, M. (1964) *Medicine and Custom in Africa* (Edinburgh and London: Livingston).

Gilbert, J. (2002) 'Responding to Mental Stress in the Third World: Cultural Imperialism or the Struggle for Synthesis' in D. Eade (ed.) *Development and Culture. Selected Essays from Development in Practice* (Oxford: Oxfam in association with World Faiths Development Dialogue), pp. 155–67.

Gilbert, P. (2007) 'The Spiritual Foundation: Awareness and Context for People's Lives Today' in M. E. Coyte, P. Gilbert and V. Nicholls (eds) *Spirituality, Values and Mental Health* (London and Philadelphia: Jessica Kingsley), pp. 19–43.

Gilroy, P. (1993) *Small Acts. Thoughts on the Politics of Black Cultures* (London: Serpent Tail).

Glover, G. and Malcolm, G. (1988) 'The Prevalence of Depot Neuroleptic Treatment among West Indians and Asians in the London Borough of Newham', *Social Psychiatry,* 23, 281–4.

Goffman, E. (1968) *Stigma. Notes on the Management of Spoiled Identity* (Harmondsworth: Penguin Books).

Goldberg, D. T. (1997) *Racial Subjects: Writing on Race in America* (New York and London: Routledge).

Gombrich, R. and Obeyesekere, G. (1988) *Buddhism Transformed. Religious Change in Sri Lanka.* (Princeton, NJ: Princeton University Press).

Goodenough, W. H. (1957) 'Cultural Anthropology and Linguistics' in P. Garvin (ed.) *Report of the Seventh Annual Round Table Meeting on Linguistics and Language Study,* Georgetown University Monograph Series, *Language and Linguistics,* 9 (Washington, DC: Georgetown University). Cited by D'Andrade, (1984).

Goodkind, J., Hang, P. and Mee, Y. (2004) 'Hmong refugees in the United States: A Community-Based Advocacy and Learning Intervention' in K. E. Miller and L. M. Rasco (eds) *The Mental Health of Refugees. Ecological Approaches to Healing and Adaptation* (Mahwah, NJ: Lawrence Erlbaum Associates), pp. 295–334.

Graham, H. (1986) *The Human Face of Psychology: Humanistic Psychology in Its Historical, Social and Cultural Contexts* (Milton Keynes: Open University Press).

Graham, T. F. (1967) *Medieval Minds. Mental Health in the Middle Ages* (London: Allen & Unwin).

Graves, J. L. (2002) *The Emperor's New Clothes. Biological Theories of Race at the Millennium* (New Brunswick, NJ and London: Rutgers University Press).

Green, E. M. (1914) 'Psychoses among Negroes – a Comparative Study', *Journal of Nervous and Mental Disorder,* 41, 697–708.

Grof, S. (1984) *Ancient Wisdom and Modern Science* (Albany, NY: State University of New York Press).

Grounds, A. (1987) 'On Describing Mental States', *British Journal of Medical Psychology*, 60, 305–11.

Gunaratne, B. H. (2002) *Mindfulness in Plain English* (Boston, MA: Wisdom Publications).

Hacker, A. (1995) *Two Nations. Black and White, Separate, Hostile, Unequal* (New York: Ballantine Books).

Haldipur, C. V. (1984) 'Madness in Ancient India: Concept of Insanity in Charaka Samhita (1st Century A. D.)', *Comprehensive Psychiatry*, 25, 335–43.

Hall, G. S. (1904) *Adolescence: Its Psychology and Its Relations to Physiology, Anthropology, Sociology, Sex, Crime, Religion and Education*, vol. II (New York: D. Appleton).

Hall, S. (1992) 'New Ethnicities' in J. Donald and A. Ratansi (eds) *'Race' Culture and Difference* (London: Sage) pp. 252–9.

Hall, S., Critcher, C., Jefferson, T., Clarke, J. and Roberts, B. (1978) *Policing the Crisis: Mugging, the State, and Law and Order* (London: Macmillan).

Halliburton, M. (2004) 'Finding a Fit: Psychiatric Pluralism in South India and Its Implications for WHO Studies of Mental Disorder', *Transcultural Psychiatry*, 41(1), 80–98.

Halliday, F. (1999) 'Islamophobia Reconsidered', *Ethnic and Racial Studies*, 22(5), 892–902.

Hammer, L. (1990) *Dragon Rises, Red Bird Flies. Psychology and Chinese Medicine* (New York: Station Hill Press).

Harkness, K. L. and Monroe, S. M. (2002) 'Childhood Adversity and the Endogenous Versus Nonendogenous Distinction in Women with Major Depression', *American Journal of Psychiatry*, 159, 387–93.

Harrison, G., Glazebrook, C., Brewin, J., Cantwell, R., Dalkin, T., Fox, R., Jones, P. and Medley, I. (1997) 'Increased Incidence of Psychotic Disorders in Migrants from the Caribbean to the United Kingdom', *Psychological Medicine*, 27, 799–806.

Harrison, G., Ineichen, B., Smith, J. and Morgan, H. G. (1984) 'Psychiatric Hospital Admissions in Bristol II: Social and Clinical Aspects of Compulsory Admission', *British Journal of Psychiatry*, 145, 605–11.

Harrison, G., Owens, D., Holton, A., Neilson, D. and Boot, D. (1988) 'A Prospective Study of Severe Mental Disorder in Afro-Caribbean Patients', *Psychological Medicine*, 18, 643–57.

Harrison, P. (1979) *Inside the Third World: The Anatomy of Poverty* (Harmondsworth: Penguin).

Hart, J., Galappatti, A., Boyden, J. and Armstrong, M. (2007) 'Participatory Tools for Evaluating Psychosocial Work with Children in Areas of Armed Conflict: A Pilot in Eastern Sri Lanka', *Intervention International Journal of Mental Health, Psychosocial Work and Counselling in Areas of Armed Conflict*, 5(1), 60.

HCC (Healthcare Commission) (2008) *The Pathway to Recovery: A Review of NHS Acute Inpatient Mental Health Services* (London: Commission for Healthcare Audit and Inspection). Available: http://www.nimhe.csip.org.uk/silo/files/thepathwaytorecoverypdf.pdf. Accessed: 24 June 2009.

Health Education Authority (1997) *Mental Health Promotion* (London: HEA).

Herbert, J. (2006) 'Migration, Memory and Metaphor: Life Stories of South Asians in Leicester' in K. Burrell and P. Panayi (eds) *Histories and Memories. Migrants and Their History in Britain,* International Library of Historical Studies 7 (London and New York: Tauris Academic Studies), pp. 133–148.

Hern, A., Wicks, S. and Dalman, C. (2004) 'Social Adversity Contributes to High Morbidity in Psychoses in Immigrants – National Cohort Study in Two Generations of Swedish Residents', *Psychological Medicine,* 34, 1025–33.

Herrnstein, R. J. and Murray, C. (1994) *The Bell Curve: Intelligence and Class Structure in American Life* (New York: Free Press).

HMSO (Her Majesty's Stationery Office) (1983) *Mental Health Act 1983* (London: HMSO).

Hobbs, M. and Adshead, G. (1996) 'Preventive Psychological Interventions for Road Crash Survivors' in M. Mitchell (ed.) *The Aftermath of Road Accidents: Psychological, Social and Legal Perspectives* (London: Routledge), 159–71.

Hoffman, E. (1999) 'The New Nomads' in A. Aciman (ed.) *Letters of Transit. Reflections of Exile, Identity, Language and Loss* (New York: The New Press), pp. 35–63.

Hoffman, L. (1981) *Foundations of Family Therapy: A Conceptual Framework for Systems Change* (New York: Basic Books).

Home Department (1999) *The Stephen Lawrence Inquiry. Report of an Inquiry by Sir William Macpherson of Cluny* (London: Stationery Office).

hooks, bell (1994) *Outlaw Culture. Resisting Representations* (New York: Routledge).

Hopper, K. and Wanderling, J. (2000) 'Revisiting the Developed versus Developing Country Distinction in Course and Outcome in Schizophrenia: Results from ISoS, the WHO Collaborative Follow-up Project', *Schizophrenia Bulletin,* 26(4), 835–46.

Howitt, D. (1991) *Concerning Psychology. Psychology Applied to Social Issues* (Milton Keynes and Philadelphia, PA: Open University Press).

Human Rights Act (1998) (London: The Stationery Office (TSO)). Available: http://www.opsi.giv.uk. Accessed: 20 October 2008.

Hunter, R. A. and MacAlpine, I. (1963) *Three Hundred Years of Psychiatry 1535–1860: A History Presented in Selected English Texts* (London: Oxford University Press).

IASC (Inter-Agency Standing Committee) (2007) *IASC Guidelines on Mental Health and Psychosocial Support in Emergency Settings* (Geneva: IASC). Available: http://www.humanitarianinfo.org/iasc. Accessed: 10 June 2009.

Ignatiev, N. (2000) *How the Irish Became White* (New York and London: Routledge).

Ineichen, B., Harrison, G. and Morgan, H. G. (1984) 'Psychiatric Hospital Admissions in Bristol: 1. Geographical and Ethnic Factors', *British Journal of Psychiatry,* 145, 600–4.

Ingleby, D. (1980) *Critical Psychiatry. The Politics of Mental Health* (New York: Pantheon Books). Republished by Free Association Books, London 2004.

Ingleby, D. (2004) *Critical Psychiatry. The Politics of Mental Health* (London: Free Association Books).

Inyama, S. (2009) 'Race Relations, Mental Health and Human Rights – the Legal Framework' in S. Fernando and F. Keating (eds) *Mental Health in a Multi-ethnic Society. A Multi-disciplinary Handbook,* 2nd edn (London: Routledge), pp. 27–41.

Jablensky, A., Schwarz, R. and Tomov, T. (1980) 'WHO Collaborative Study on Impairments and Disabilities Associated with Schizophrenic Disorders', *Acta Psychiatrica Scandinavica*, 62, Suppl. 285, 152–63.

Jackson, S. W. (1986) *Melancholia and Depression from Hippocratic Times to Modern Times* (New Haven, CT and London: Yale University Press).

Jaco, E. G. (1960) *Social Epidemiology of Mental Disorders: A Psychiatric Survey of Texas* (New York: Russell Sage Foundation).

Jaggi, O. P. (1981) *Ayurveda: Indian System of Medicine*, 2nd edn, vol. 4 (Delhi: Atma Ram).

Janzen, J. M. (1978) 'The Comparative Study of Medical Systems as Changing Social Systems', *Social Science and Medicine*, 12, 121–9.

Janzen, J. M. (1979) 'Pluralistic Legitimation of Therapy Systems in Contemporary Zaire' in Z. A. Ademuwagun, J. A. A. Ayoade, I. R. Harrison and D. M. Warren (eds) *African Therapeutic Systems* (Waltham, MA: Crossroads Press), pp. 208–16.

Jarvis, E. (1852) 'On the Supposed Increase of Insanity', *American Journal of Insanity*, 8, 333–64.

Jensen, A. R. (1969) 'How Much Can We Boost IQ and Scholastic Achievement?', *Harvard Educational Review*, 39, 1–123.

Jewkes, R. (1984) *The Case for South Africa's Expulsion from International Psychiatry, United Nations Centre against Apartheid. Notes and Documents* (New York: United Nations).

Johnson, T. M. (1987) 'Premenstrual Syndrome as a Western Culture-Specific Disorder', *Culture, Medicine and Psychiatry*, 11, 337–56.

Jones, J. (1983) *Community Development and Health Issues. A Review of Existing Theory and Practice* (Edinburgh: Community Projects Foundation) cited by MacDonald, 1992.

Jones, Margaret (2004) *Health Policy in Britain's Model Colony Ceylon (1900–1948)* (New Delhi: Orient Longman).

Jones, Maxwell (1968) *Social Psychiatry in Practice* (Harmondsworth: Penguin).

Jones, W. H. S. (1823) *Hippocrates with an English Translation* (London: Heinemann).

Jordan, W. D. (1968) *White over Black: American Attitudes towards the Negro, 1550–1812* (Baltimore, MD: Penguin) cited by Fryer (1984).

Jorm, A. F. and Griffiths, K. M. (2008) 'The Public's Stigmatizing Attitudes towards People with Mental Disorders: How Important Are Biomedical Conceptualizations?', *American Journal of Psychiatry*, 118, 315–21.

Jung, C. G. (1930) 'Your Negroid and Indian Behaviour', *Forum*, 83(4), 193–9.

Jung, C. G. (1964) 'The Dreamlike World of India', reprinted in H. Read, M. Fordham and G. Adler (eds) *Civilization in Transition. Collected Works of C. G. Jung*, vol. 10 (London: Routledge and Kegan Paul, 1964), pp. 515–24, from *Asia* (New York), 1939, 39(1), 5–8.

Kabbani, R. (1986) *Europe's Myths of Orient: Devise and Rule* (London: Macmillan).

Kakar, S. (1984) *Shamans, Mystics and Doctors: A Psychological Inquiry into India and Its Healing Tradition* (London: Unwin Paperbacks).

Kalathil, J. (2007) 'Workshop on Recovery Research' in SPN (Social Perspectives Network) (ed.) *Whose Recovery Is It Anyway?* (London: Social Perspectives Network), pp. 39–42.

Kalikow, T. J. (1978) 'Konrad Lorenz's "Brown Past": A Reply to Alec Nisbett', *Journal of the History of the Behavioral Sciences*, 14, 173–80.

Kamin, L. J. (1974) *The Science and Politics of IQ* (London: Wiley).

Kapferer, B. (1991) *A Celebration of Demons. Exorcism and the Aesthetics of Healing in Sri Lanka*, 2nd edn (Washington: Berg Publishers and Smithsonian Institute Press).

Kaptchuk, T. J. (2000) *Chinese Medicine. The Web That Has No Weaver*, revised and expanded edn (London: Rider).

Kapur, R. L. (1987) 'Commentary on Culture Bound Syndromes and International Disease Classification', *Culture, Medicine and Psychiatry*, 11, 43–8.

Kardiner, A. and Ovesey, L. (1951) *The Mark of Oppression: A Psychosocial Study of the American Negro* (New York: Norton).

Karenga, M. (1982) *Introduction to Black Studies* (Los Angeles, CA: Kawaida Publications).

Karno, M. (1966) 'The Enigma of Ethnicity in a Psychiatric Clinic', *Archives of General Psychiatry*, 14, 516–20.

Katz, R. (1973) *Preludes to Growth: An Experimental Approach* (New York: Free Press of Glencoe), cited by West (1979).

Keating, F. (2002) 'Black-Led Initiatives in Mental Health: An Overview', *Research Policy and Planning*, 20(2), 9–18.

Kennedy, H. (2004) *Just Law. The Changing Face of Justice – and Why It Matters to Us All* (London: Chatto and Windus).

King, M., Coker, E., Leavey, G., Hoar, A. and Johnson-Sabine, E. (1994) 'Incidence of Psychotic Illness in London: Comparison of Ethnic Groups', *British Medical Journal*, 309, 1115–9.

Kingdom, D. and Young, A. H. (2007) 'Research into Putative Biological Mechanisms of Mental Disorders Has Been of No Value to Clinical Psychiatry, Debate', *British Journal of Psychiatry*, 191, 285–90.

Kingsbury, S. and York, A. (2006) *The 7 Helpful Habits of Effective CAMHS and the Choice and Partnership Approach', A Workbook for CAMHS*, 2nd edn (Hampton Wick, Surrey: CAMHS Network). Available: http://www.camhsnetwork.co.uk. Accessed: 3 December 2008.

Kinouani, G., Anon. and Lindsey, L. (2007) 'African Caribbean Perspectives on Recovery' in Social Perspectives Network (2008) *Whose Recovery Is It Anyway?* (London: Social Perspectives Network), pp. 43–5.

Kirmayer, L. J., Lemelson, R. and Barad, M. (2007a) 'Introduction: Inscribing Trauma in Culture, Brain , and Body' in L. J. Kirmayer, R. Lemelson and M. Barad (eds) *Understanding Trauma. Integrating Biological, Clinical and Cultural Perspectives* (Cambridge: Cambridge University Press), pp. 1–20.

Kirmayer, L. J., Lemelson, R. and Barad, M. (2007b) 'Clinical Perspectives on Trauma' in L. J. Kirmayer, R. Lemelson and M. Barad (eds) *Understanding Trauma. Integrating Biological, Clinical and Cultural Perspectives* (Cambridge: Cambridge University Press), pp. 171–7.

Kleinman, A. (1977) 'Depression, Somatization and the "New Cross-Cultural Psychiatry"', *Social Science and Medicine*, 11(1), 3–10.

Kleinman, A. (1978) 'Concepts and a Model for the Comparison of Medical Systems as Cultural Systems', *Social Science and Medicine*, 12, 85–93.

Kleinman, A. (1980) 'Major Conceptual and Research Issues for Cultural (Anthropological) Psychiatry', *Culture, Medicine and Psychiatry*, 4(1), 3–13.

Kleinman, A. (1987) 'Culture and Clinical Reality: Commentary on Culture-Bound Syndromes and International Disease Classifications', *Culture, Medicine and Psychiatry*, 11(1), 49–52.

Kleinman, A. (1988) *Rethinking Psychiatry. From Cultural Category to Personal Experience* (New York: Free Press).

Kleinman, A. (1995) *Writing at the Margin. Discourse between Anthropology and Medicine* (Berkeley and London: University of California Press).

Kleinman, A., Das, V. and Lock, M. (1997) 'Introduction' in A. Kleinman, V. Das and M. Lock (eds) *Social Suffering* (Berkeley and London: University of California Press), pp. ix–xxv.

Kleinman, A. and Kleinman, J. (1997) 'The Appeal of Experience; the Dismay of Images: Cultural Appropriations of Suffering in Our Times' in A. Kleinman, V. Das and M. Lock, M. (eds) *Social Suffering* (Berkeley and London: University of California Press), pp. 1–24.

Kloos, B. (2005) 'Creating New Possibilities for Promoting Liberation, Well-Being, and Recovery: Learning from Experiences of Psychiatric Consumers/Survivors' in G. Nelson and I. Prilleltensky (eds) *Community Psychology: In Pursuit of Well-Being and Liberation* (Basingstoke: Palgrave Macmillan), pp. 426–47.

Konner, M. (2007) 'Trauma, Adaptation, and Resilience: A Cross-Cultural and Evolutionary Perspective' in L. J. Kirmayer, R. Lemelson and M. Barad (eds) *Understanding Trauma. Integrating Biological, Clinical and Cultural Perspectives* (Cambridge: Cambridge University Press), pp. 300–38.

Kora, T. and Sato, K. (1958) 'Morita Therapy: A Psychotherapy in the Way of Zen', *Psychologia*, 1, 219–25.

Kostelny, K. and Wessels, M. (2004) 'Internally Displaced East Tomorese: Challenges and Lessons of Large-Scale Emergency Assistance' in K. E. Miller and L. M. Rasco (eds) *The Mental Health of Refugees. Ecological Approaches to Healing and Adaptation* (Mahwah, NJ: Lawrence Erlbaum Associates), pp. 187–225.

Kovel, J. (1984) *White Racism: A Psychohistory*, 2nd edn (New York: Columbia University Press) reprinted London: Free Association Books, 1988.

Koyré, A. (1954) 'Introduction' in E. Anscombe and P. J. Geach (eds) *Descartes Philosophical Writings* (London: Nelson University Paperbacks for Open University), pp. vii–xliv.

Krabbendam, L. (2008) 'Childhood Psychological Trauma and Psychosis', *Psychological Medicine*, 38, 1405–8.

Kraepelin, E. (1899) *Psychiatrie: ein Lehrbuch fur Studirende and Artze*, 6th edn (Leipzig: Verlag von Johann Ambrosius Barth).

Kraepelin, E. (1913) *Manic Depressive Insanity and Paranoia*, translation of *Lehrbuch der Psychiatrie*, R. M. Barclay, 8th edn, vols 3 and 4 (Edinburgh: Livingstone).

Kraepelin, E. (1919) *Dementia Præcox and Paraphrenia*, trans. R. M. Barclay, edited G. M. Robertson (Edinburgh: Livingstone).

Kraepelin, E. (1920) 'Die Erscheinungsformen des Irreseins', *Zeitschrift für die gesamte Neurologie and Psychiatrie*, 62, 1–29, trans. H. Marshall, reprinted as

'Patterns of Mental Disorder' in S. Hirsch and M. Shepherd (eds) *Themes and Variations in European Psychiatry* (Bristol: John Wright, 1974) pp. 7–30.

Kraepelin, E. (1921) *Manic-Depressive Insanity and Paranoia*, trans. R. M. Barclay and edited G. M. Robertson (Edinburgh: Livingstone).

Kuhn, T. S. (1962) *The Structure of Scientific Revolutions*, 3rd edn (Chicago, IL and London: University of Chicago Press).

Kumar, S. and Oakley Browne, M. A. (2008) 'Usefulness of the Construct of Social Network to Explain Mental Health Service Utilization by the Maori Population in New Zealand', *Transcultural Psychiatry*, 45(3), 439–54.

Kushner, T. (2006) 'Great Britons: Immigration, History and Memory' in K. Burrell and P. Panayi (eds) *Histories and Memories. Migrants and Their History in Britain*, International Library of Historical Studies 7 (London and New York: Tauris Academic Studies), pp. 18–34.

Kusumaratne, S. (2005) *Indigenous Medicine in Sri Lanka. A Sociological Analysis* (Nugegoda, Sri Lanka: Sarasavi Publishers).

Laing, R. D. (1967) *The Politics of Experience* (Harmondsworth: Penguin).

Laing, R. D. and Esterson, E. (1964) *Sanity, Madness and the Family* (London: Tavistock).

Lambo, A. (1964) 'Patterns of Psychiatric Care in Developing African Countries' in A. Kiev (ed.) *Magic, Faith and Healing: Studies in Primitive Psychiatry Today*, Part 4 (New York: Free Press of Glencoe), pp. 443–53.

Lambo, A. (1969) 'Traditional African Cultures and Western Medicine' in F. N. L. Poynter (ed.) *Medicine and Culture* (London: Wellcome Institute of the History of Medicine), pp. 201–10.

Lambo, T. A. (1965) 'Psychiatry in the Tropics', *Lancet*, 2, 1119–21.

Lancet, The (1964) 'The Village of Aro', *The Lancet*, 2, pp. 513–4.

Lane, P. (2007) *The Mental Health and Well Being of Black and Minority Ethnic Elders: A Foundational Report on Research Literature and a Mapping of National Resources* (Birmingham: Care Services Improvement Partnership West Midlands). Available: http://www.westmidlands.csip.org.uk. Accessed: 10 August 2008.

Last, M. (2000) 'Reconciliation and Memory in Postwar Nigeria' in V. Das, A. Kleinmann, M. Ramphele and P. Reynolds (eds) *Violence and Subjectivity* (Berkeley and Los Angeles: University of California Press), pp. 315–32.

Last, M. and Chavunduka, G. L. (eds) (1986) *The Professionalisation of African Medicine* (Manchester: Manchester University Press).

Lau, A. (1986) 'Family Therapy across Cultures' in J. L. Cox (ed.) *Transcultural Psychiatry* (London: Croom Helm), pp. 234–52.

Lawrence, E. (1982) 'In the Abundance of Water the Fool Is Thirsty: Sociology and Black "Pathology"' in Centre for Contemporary Cultural Studies (ed.) *The Empire Strikes Back: Race and Racism in 70s Britain* (London: Hutchinson), pp. 95–142.

Lawrence, P. (2000) 'Violence, Suffering, Amman. The work of Oracles in Sri Lanka's War Zone' in V. Das, A. Kleinman, M. Ramphele and P. Reynolds (eds) *Violence and Subjectivity* (Berkeley and London: University of California Press), pp. 171–204.

Lawrence, P. (2003) 'Kālī in a Context of Terror. The Tasks of a Goddess in Sri Lanka's Civil War' in R. F. McDermott and J. J. Kripal (eds) *Encountering Kālī. In the Margins, at the Centre, in the West* (Berkeley and London: University of California Press), pp. 100–79.

Lawson, W. B., Yesavage, J. A. and Werner, P. D. (1984) 'Race, Violence and Psychopathology', *Journal of Clinical Psychiatry*, 45, 294–7.

Lazarus, R. S., Averill, J. R. and Opton, E. M. Jr (1970) 'Toward a Cognitive Theory of Emotions' in M. Arnold (ed.) *Feelings and Emotions* (New York: Academic Press), pp. 207–32.

Lazarus, R. S., Kanner, A. D. and Folkman, S. (1980) 'Emotions: A Cognitive–Phenomenological Analysis' in R. Plutchnik and H. Kellerman (eds) *Emotion: Theory, Research and Experience*, vol. 1, *Theories of Emotion* (New York: Academic Press), pp. 189–217.

Lazlo, E. (1972) *Introduction to Systems Philosophy* (London: Gordon & Breach) cited by Capra (1982).

Lebra, T. S. (1982) 'Self-reconstruction in Japanese Religious Psychotherapy' in A. J. Marsella and G. M. White (eds) *Cultural Conceptions of Mental Health and Therapy* (Dordrecht: Reidel), pp. 269–83.

Leff, J. (1973) 'Culture and the Differentiation of Emotional States', *British Journal of Psychiatry*, 123, 299–306.

Leff, J. (1981) *Psychiatry around the Globe. A Transcultural View* (New York: Marcel Dekker).

Leighton, A. H. and Hughes, J. M. (1961) 'Cultures as Causative of Mental Disorder', *Millbank Memorial Fund Quarterly*, 39(3), 446–70.

Lewis, A. (1965) 'Chairman's Opening Remarks' in A. V. S. De Rueck and R. Porter (eds) *Transcultural Psychiatry* (London: Churchill), pp. 1–3.

Lewis, G. (1986) 'Concepts of Health and Illness in a Sepik Society' in C. Currer and M. Stacey (eds) *Concepts of Health, Illness and Disease: A Comparative Perspective* (Leamington Spa: Berg), pp. 119–35.

Lewis, N. (1989) *The Missionaries* (London: Arena).

Lewis, N. D. C. (1974) 'American Psychiatry from Its Beginnings to World War II' in S. Arieti (ed.) *American Handbook of Psychiatry*, 2nd edn, vol. 1 (New York: Basic Books), pp. 28–42.

Littlewood, R. and Cross, S. (1980) 'Ethnic Minorities and Psychiatric Services', *Sociology of Health and Illness*, 2, 194–201.

Littlewood, R. and Lipsedge, M. (1981) 'Acute Psychotic Reactions in Caribbean-Born Patients', *Psychological Medicine*, 11, 303–18.

Littlewood, R. and Lipsedge, M. (1987) 'The Butterfly and the Serpent: Culture, Psychopathology and Biomedicine', *Culture, Medicine and Psychiatry*, 11, 289–335.

Loring, M. and Powell, B. (1988) 'Gender, Race and DSM-III: A Study of the Objectivity of Psychiatric Diagnostic Behavior', *Journal of Health and Social Behavior*, 29, 1–22.

Luo, H., Jia, Y., Wu, X. and Dai, W. (1990) 'Electroacupuncture in the Treatment of Depressive Psychosis', *International Journal of Clinical Acupuncture*, 1(1), 7–13. cited in Acupuncture Research Resource Centre (2002).

Lutz, C. (1985) 'Depression and the Translation of Emotional Words' in A. Kleinman and B. Good (eds) *Culture and Depression: Studies in the Anthropology and Cross-Cultural Psychiatry of Affect and Disorder* (Berkeley: University of California Press), pp. 63–100.

MacCann, I. L. and Pearlman, L. A. (1990) *Psychological Trauma and the Adult Survivor: Theory, Therapy and Transformation* (New York and London: Brunner-Mazel).

Malik, R., Fateh, R. and Haque, R. (2009) 'The Marlborough Cultural Therapy Centre' in S. Fernando and F. Keating (eds) *Mental Health in a Multi-ethnic Society. A Multidisciplinary Handbook*, 2nd edn (London and New York: Routledge), pp. 174–86.

Mama, A. (1995) *Beyond the Masks* (London: Routledge).

Marneros, A. (2008) 'Psychiatry's 200th birthday' *British Journal of Psychiatry*, 193, 1–3.

Marsella, A. J. (1978) 'Thoughts on Cross-Cultural Studies on the Epidemiology of Depression', *Culture, Medicine and Psychiatry*, 2, 343–57.

Marsella, A. J. and White, G. M. (eds) (1982) *Cultural Conceptions of Mental Health and Therapy* (Dordrecht: Reidel).

Martín-Baró, I. (1994) 'Towards a Liberation Psychology', trans. A. Aron in A. Aron and S. Corne (eds) *Writings for a Liberation Psychology* (Cambridge, MA: Harvard University Press), pp. 17–32.

Masters, A. (1997) 'Schizophrenia, the Illness' in P. M. Ellis and S. C. D. Collings (eds) *Mental Health from a Public Health Perspective* (Wellington, NZ: Public Health Group, Ministry of Health), pp. 354–74.

Mathew, L. (2008) 'The Unholy Doings of Kerala "Godmen"', *Thainidan News*, 25 May. Available: http://www.thsindian.com. Accessed: 24 October 2008.

Maudsley, H. (1867) *The Physiology and Pathology of Mind* (New York: D. Appleton).

Maudsley, H. (1879) *The Pathology of Mind* (London: Macmillan).

May, R. (2008) 'Recovering Healing Communities' in Social Perspectives Network (ed.) *Whose Recovery Is It Anyway?* (London: Social Perspectives Network), pp. 32–6.

Maziak, W. (2006) 'Health in the Middle East', *British Medical Journal*, 333, 815–6.

Mbiti, J. S. (1990) *African Religions and Philosophy*, 2nd revised and enlarged edn (Harlow, Essex: Heineman).

McDougall, W. (1921) *Is America Safe for Democracy?* (New York: Scribner).

McGoldrick, M. and Hardy, K. V. (2008) *Re-visioning Family Therapy. Race, Culture, and Gender in Clinical Practice* (New York and London: Guilford Press).

McGovern, D. and Cope, R. (1987) 'The Compulsory Detention of Males of Different Ethnic Groups, with Special Reference to Offender Patients', *British Journal of Psychiatry*, 150, 505–12.

McQueen, D. V. (1978) 'The History of Science and Medicine as Theoretical Sources for the Comparative Study of Contemporary Medical Systems', *Social Science and Medicine*, 12, 69–74.

Mental Health Directorate (2006) *The Mental Health Policy of Sri Lanka 2005–2015* (Colombo: Mental Health Directorate, Ministry of Healthcare).

Mental Health Task Force (1994) *Black Mental Health – a Dialogue for Change* (London: Department of Health).

Meyer, A. (1905) 'Discussion on the Classification of the Melancholias', *Journal of Nervous and Mental Disease*, 32, 112–8.

Meyer, E. (2006) *Sri Lanka. Biography of an Island*, revised edn, trans. K. Segond-Baldwin (Dehiwela, Sri Lanka: Viator Publications).

MHAC (Mental Health Act Commission) (1987) *Second Biennial Report 1985–87* (London: HMSO).

MHAC (Mental Health Act Commission) (1989) *Third Biennial Report 1987–1989* (London: HMSO).

MHAC (Mental Health Act Commission) (1991) *Fourth Biennial Report 1989–1991* (London: HMSO).

MHAC (Mental Health Act Commission) (1993) *Fifth Biennial Report 1991–1993* (London: HMSO).

MHAC (Mental Health Act Commission) (1995) *Sixth Biennial Report 1993–1995* (London: HMSO).

MHAC (Mental Health Act Commission) (1997) *Seventh Biennial Report 1995–1997* (London: HMSO).

Miah, M. (2009) 'Barack Obama's Victory. What It Means for Race and Class in America', *New Socialist*, 65, 14–16.

Miles, R. (1982) 'Racism and Nationalism in Britain' in C. Husband (ed.) *'Race' in Britain: Continuity and Change* (London: Hutchinson), pp. 279–300.

Miles, R. (1993) *Racism after 'Race Relations'* (London and New York: Routledge).

Miller, K. E. and Rasco, L. M. (2004) 'An Ecological Framework for Addressing the Mental Health Needs of Refugee Communities' in K. E. Miller and L. M. Rasco (eds) *The Mental Health of Refugees. Ecological Approaches to Healing and Adaptation* (Mahwah, NJ: Lawrence Erlbaum Associates), pp. 1–64.

Mitchell, J. (1983) 'When Disaster Strikes: The Critical Incident Stress Debriefing Process', *Journal of Emergency Medical Services*, 8, 36–9.

Moorehead, C. (2006) *Human Cargo. A Journey among Refugees* (London: Vintage Books).

Mora, G. (1961) 'Historiographic and Cultural Trends in Psychiatry: A Survey', *Bulletin of the History of Medicine*, 35, 26–36.

Morel, B. A. (1852) *Traité des Mentales* (Paris: Masson) cited by Gottesman (1991).

Morgan, R., Mallett, R., Hutchinson, G., Bagalkotte, H., Morgan, K., Fearon, P., Dazzan, P., Boydell, J., McKenzie, K., Harrison, G., Murray, R., Jones, P., Craig, T. and Leff, J. (2005) 'Pathways to Care and Ethnicity 1: Sample Characteristics and Compulsory Admission', *British Journal of Psychiatry*, 186, 281–9.

Morley, D., Rohde, J. E. and Williams, G. (1983) *Practising Health for All* (Oxford: Oxford University Press).

Morrison, T. (1993) *Playing in the Dark Whiteness and the Literary Imagination* (London and Basingstoke: Pan Macmillan).

Moynihan, D. (1965) *The Negro Family in the United States: The Case for National Action* (Washington, DC: US Governmental Printing Office).

Muecke, M. A. (1992) 'New Paradigms for Refugee Health Problems', *Social Science and Medicine*, 35(4), 515–23.

Mukherjee, S., Shukla, S., Woodle, J., Rosen, A. M. and Olarte, S. (1983) 'Misdiagnosis of Schizophrenia in Bipolar Patients: A Multiethnic Comparison', *American Journal of Psychiatry*, 140, 1571–4.

Murase, T. (1982) 'Sunao: A Central Value in Japanese Psychotherapy' in A. J. Marsella and G. M. White (eds) *Cultural Conceptions of Mental Health and Therapy* (Dordrecht: Reidel), pp. 317–29.

Murase, T. and Johnson, F. (1974) 'Naikan, Morita and Western Psychotherapy: A Comparison', *Archives of General Psychiatry*, 31, 121–30.

Murphy, G. (1938) *An Historical Introduction to Modern Psychology* (London: Routledge and Kegan Paul).

Murphy, H. B. M. (1973) 'Current Trends in Transcultural Psychiatry', *Proceedings of the Royal Society of Medicine*, 66, 711–6.

Myers, F., McCollam, A. and Woodham, A. (2005) *National Programme for Improving Mental Health and Well-Being. Addressing Mental Health Inequalities in Scotland. Equal Minds* (Edinburgh: Scottish Executive).

Nasser, M. (1987) 'Psychiatry in Ancient Egypt', *Bulletin of the Royal College of Psychiatrists*, 11, 420–2.

Nelson, G. and Prilleltensky, I. (2005) *Community Psychology in Pursuit of Liberation and Well-Being* (Basingstoke: Palgrave Macmillan).

NHS Management Executive (1993) *Collecting Information about the Ethnic Group of Patients'*, (Letter sent October 1993) (Leeds: Department of Health).

NICE (National Institute for Health and Clinical Excellence) (2007) *Depression (Amended) Management of Depression in Primary and Secondary Care, NICE Clinical Guidance 23 (amended) Developed by the National Collaborating Centre for Mental Health*. (London: NICE). Available: http://www.nice.org.uk. Accessed: 30 May 2009.

Nicholls, V. (2007) 'Connecting Past and Present: A Survivor Reflects in Spirituality and Mental Health' in M. E. Coyte, P. Gilbert and V. Nicholls (eds) *Spirituality, Values and Mental Health* (London and Philadelphia, PA: Jessica Kingsley), pp. 102–12.

Nichter, M. (1980) 'The Layperson's Perception of Medicine as Perspective into the Utilization of Multiple Therapy Systems in the Indian Context', *Social Science and Medicine*, 14B, 225–33.

Nichter, M. (1981) 'Idioms of Distress: Alternatives in the Expression of Psychosocial Distress. A Case Study from South India', *Culture, Medicine and Psychiatry*, 5, 379–408.

NIMH (National Institute of Mental Health) (1971) *Socio-economic Characteristics of Admissions to Inpatient Services of State and County Mental Hospitals, 1969* (Washington, DC: Superintendent of Documents, US Government Printing Office).

NIMHE (National Institute for Mental Health in England) (2003) *Inside Outside Improving Mental Health Services for Black and Minority Ethnic Communities in England* (London: Department of Health).

NIMHE (National Institute for Mental Health in England) (2005) *Making It Possible: Improving Mental Health and Well-Being in England* (Leeds: NIMHE). Available: http://www.csip.org.ul. Accessed: 10 August 2008.

NIMHE (National Institute for Mental Health) / Mental MHF (Health Foundation) (2003) *Inspiring Hope: Recognizing the Importance of Spirituality in a Whole Person Approach to Mental Health* (Leeds: NIMHE).

NIMHE (National Institute for Mental Health England), SCMH (The Sainsbury Centre for Mental Health) and the NHSU (National Health Service University) (2004) *The Ten Essential Shared Capabilities for Mental Health Practice* (London: Sainsbury Centre for Mental Health). Available: www.dh.gov.uk. Accessed: 10 August 2008.

Nobles, W. W. (1986) 'Ancient Egyptian Thought and the Renaissance of African (Black) Psychology' in M. Karenga and J. H. Carruthers (eds) *Kemet and the African Worldview. Research, Rescue and Restoration*, Part 3 (Los Angeles, CA: University of Sankore Press), pp. 100–18.

Norfolk, Suffolk and Cambridgeshire SHA (Strategic Health Authority) (2003) *Independent Inquiry into the Death of David Bennett* (Chairman: Sir John Blofeld) (Cambridge, England: Norfolk, Suffolk and Cambridgeshire Strategic Health Authority).

Nugent, H. (2007) 'Black People "less intelligent" Scientist Claims', *Times on line*, October 17. Available: http://www.timesonline.co.uk/tol/news/uk/article2677098. ece. Accessed: 31 July 2008.

Oakley Browne, M. A., Wells, J. E. and Scott, K. M. (2006) *Te Rau Hinengaro: The New Zealand Mental Health Survey* (Wellington, NZ: Ministry of Health). Available: http://www.moh.govt.nz/moh.nsf/pagesmh/5223. Accessed: 20 October 2008.

Obama, B. H. (2008) 'We the People, in order to Form a More Perfect Union,' Speech delivered on 18 March 2008 in Philadelphia. Available: http://www.huffington-post.com. Accessed: 9 November 2008.

Obembe, A. (1983) 'Nigerian Psychiatry – Past, Present and Future' in S. Brown (ed.) *Psychiatry in Developing Countries* (London: Gaskell and Royal College of Psychiatrists), pp. 4–6.

Obeyesekere, G. (1977) 'The Theory and Practice of Psychological Medicine in the Ayurvedic Tradition', *Culture, Medicine and Psychiatry*, 1(2), 155–81.

Obeyesekere, G. (1981) *Medusa's Hair. An Essay on Personal Symbols and Religious Experience.* (Chicago, IL: University of Chicago Press).

Obeyesekere, G. (1985) 'Depression, Buddhism, and the Work of Culture in Sri Lanka' in A. Kleinman and B. Good (eds) *Culture and Depression* (Berkeley: University of California Press), pp. 134–52.

Omi, M. and Winant, H. (1994) *Racial Formation in the United States, From the 1960s to the 1990s* (New York and London: Routledge).

O'Nell, T. (1989) 'Psychiatric Investigations among American Indians and Alaska Natives: A Critical Review', *Culture, Medicine and Psychiatry*, 13(1), 51–87.

Ørner, R. and Schnyder, U. (2003a) 'Progress towards Reconstructing Early Intervention after Trauma: Emergent Themes' in R. Ørner and U. Schnyder (eds) *Reconstructing Early Intervention after Trauma* (Oxford: Oxford University Press), pp. 249–66.

Ørner, R. and Schnyder, U. (2003b) 'Current Theories and Conceptualizations of Early Reactions to Trauma' in R. Ørner and U. Schnyder (eds) *Reconstructing Early Intervention after Trauma* (Oxford: Oxford University Press), pp. 41–3.

Osborne, F. (1971) 'Races and the Future of Man' in R. H. Osborne (ed.) *The Biological and Social Meaning of Race* (San Francisco, CA: Freeman), pp. 149–57.

Outram, D. (2005) *The Enlightenment*, 2nd edn (Cambridge: Cambridge University Press).

Owens, D., Harrison, G. and Boot, D. (1991) 'Ethnic Factors in Voluntary and Compulsory Admission', *Psychological Medicine*, 21, 185–96.

Palazzoli, M. S. (1986) 'Letter to Editor', *Transcultural Psychiatric Research Review*, 23, 83–4.

Pande, G. C. (1995) 'The Message of Gotama Buddha and Its Earliest Interpretations' in T. Yoshinori (ed.) *Buddhist Spirituality* (Delhi: Motilal Banarsidass), pp. 3–33.

Parker, I. (2007) *Revolution in Psychology* (London: Pluto Press).

Parker, I., Georgaca, E., Harper, D., McLaughlin, T. and Stowell-Smith, M. (1995) *Deconstructing Psychopathology* (London: Sage Publications).

Pasamanick, B. (1963) 'Some Misconceptions Concerning Differences in the Racial Prevalence of Mental Disease', *American Journal of Orthopsychiatry*, 33, 72–86.

Patel, V. (1995) 'Working with Traditional Healers in Harare', *Psychiatric Bulletin*, 19, 315–6.

Patel, V. and Thara, R. (2003) *Meeting the Mental Health Needs of Developing Countries. NGO Innovations in India* (New Delhi and London: Sage Publications).

Pattanayak, R. D. and Pattanayak, S. (2008) 'Biology Is Psychiatry's New Dawn', *British Journal of Psychiatry*, 192, 69–70.

Patterson, O. (1982) *Slavery and Social Death. A comparative Study* (Cambridge, MA and London: Harvard University Press).

Pearsall, J. and Trumble, B. (1995) *The Oxford English Reference Dictionary* (Oxford: Oxford University Press).

Pearson, K. (1901) *National Life from the Standpoint of Science* (London: A. and C. Black) cited by Fryer (1984).

Perkins, R. (2005) 'First Person: "You Need Hope to Cope"' in *Enabling Recovery. The Principles and Practices of Rehabilitation Psychiatry* (London: Gaskell), pp. 112–24.

Pertold, O. (1930) *The Ceremonial Dances of the Sinhalese. An Inquiry into Sinhalese Folk Religion* (Dehiwala, Sri Lanka: Tisara Prakasakayo).

Pieterse, J. N. (1995) *White on Black. Images of Africa and Blacks in Western Popular Culture* (New Haven, CT and London: Yale University Press). Original edition published in Dutch as *Wit Over Zwart: Beelden van Afrika en Zwarten in de Westerse Populaire Cultur* (Amsterdam: Koninklijk Institut voor de Tropen, 1990).

Plastow, J. (2009) 'Background', in W. Soyinka and J. Plastow (eds) *Death and the Kings Horseman with Commentary and Notes*, Methuen Drama Student Edition (London: A & C Black), pp. xvii–xxvi.

Plummer, B. L. (1970) 'Benjamin Rush and the Negro American', *American Journal of Psychiatry*, 127, 793–8.

Porter, R. (2004) *Flesh in the Age of Reason. The Modern Foundations of Body and Soul* (New York and London: Norton).

Power, P., Smith, J., Shiers, D. and Roberts, G. (2006) 'Early Intervention in First-Episode Psychosis and Its Relevance to Rehabilitation Psychiatry' in G. Roberts, S. Davenport, F. Holloway and T. Tattan (eds) *Enabling Recovery. The Principles and Practice of Rehabilitation Psychiatry* (London: Gaskell), pp. 127–45.

Prichard, J. C. (1835) *A Treatise on Insanity and Other Disorders Affecting the Mind* (London: Sherwood, Gilbert and Piper).

Prilleltensky, I., Nelson, G. and Peirson, L. (eds) (2001) *Promoting Family Wellness and Preventing Child Maltreatment: Fundamentals for Thinking and Action* (Toronto: University of Toronto Press).

Prince, R. (1964) 'Indigenous Yoruba Psychiatry' in A. Kiev (ed.) *Magic, Faith and Healing. Studies in Primitive Psychiatry Today*, Part 2 (New York: Free Press of Glencoe), pp. 84–120.

Prince, R. (1968) 'The Changing Picture of Depressive Syndromes in Africa', *Canadian Journal of African Studies*, 1, 177–92.

Prince, R. (1976) 'Psychotherapy as the Manipulation of Endogenous Healing Mechanisms: A Transcultural Survey', *Transcultural Psychiatric Research Review*, 13, 115–33.

Prince, R. (1980) 'Variations in Psychotherapeutic Procedures' in H. C. Triandis and J. Draguns (eds) *Handbook of Cross-Cultural Psychology*, vol. 6 (Boston, MA: Allyn & Bacon), pp. 291–349.

Prince, R. (1983) 'Is Anorexia Nervosa a Culture-Bound Syndrome?' *Transcultural Psychiatric Research Review*, 20, 299–300.

Prince, R. and Tcheng-Laroche, F. (1987) 'Culture-Bound Syndromes and International Disease Classifications', *Culture, Medicine and Psychiatry*, 11, 3–19.

Pugh, J. F. (1983) 'Astrological Counseling in Contemporary India', *Culture, Medicine and Psychiatry*, 7, 279–99.

Race Relations (Amendment) Act (2000) (London: The Stationery Office).

Radhakrishnan, S. (1980) *The Hindu View of Life* (London: Unwin).

Raguram, R., Venkateswaram, A., Ramakrishna, J. and Weiss, M. G. (2002) 'Traditional Community Resources for Mental Health: A Report of Temple Healing from India', *British Medical Journal*, 325, 38–40.

RAL (Researching Asylum in London) (2007) *Commonwealth Migration and Non-European Refugees* (London: RAL). Available: http://www.researchasylum.org.uk. Accessed: 27 October 2008.

Ramon, S. (2005) 'Mental Health Promotion' in S. Ramon and J. E. Williams (eds) *Mental Health at the Crossroads. The Promise of the Psychosocial Approach* (Aldershot, Hants: Ashgate), pp. 185–96.

Ramon, S. and Williams, J. E. (2005) *Mental Health at the Crossroads. The Promise of a Psychosocial Approach* (Aldershot, Hants: Ashgate).

Ratnavale, D. N. (1973) 'Psychiatry in Shanghai, China: Observations in 1973', *American Journal of Psychiatry*, 130, 1082–7.

Read, J., Haslam, N., Sayce, L. and Davies, E. (2006) 'Prejudice and Schizophrenia: A Review of the "Mental Illness Is an Illness Like Any Other" Approach', *Acta Psychiatrica Scandinavica*, 114, 303–18.

Refugee Council (2008) *The Facts about Asylum*. Refugee Council on Line. Available: http://www.refugeecouncil.org.uk. Accessed: 30 November 2008.

Renan, E. (1990) [1882]. 'What Is a Nation?' trans. and annotated M. Thorn, in H. K. Bhabha (ed.) *Nation and Narration* (London: Routledge), pp. 8–22.

Repper, J. and Perkins, R. (2003) *Social Inclusion and Recovery: A Model for Mental Health Practice* (London: Ballière Tindall).

Reynolds, D. K. (1988) 'Review Article', *Culture, Medicine and Psychiatry*, 12, 257–8.

Richards, G. (1997) '*Race*', *Racism and Psychology. Towards a Reflexive History* (London: Routledge).

Rinpoche, R. and Kunzang, J. (1973) *Tibetan Medicine* (London: Wellcome Institute of the History of Medicine).

Roberts, G., Davenport, S., Holloway, F. and Tattan, T. (2006) *Enabling Recovery. The Principles and Practice of Rehabilitation Psychiatry* (London: Gaskell).

Rodrigo, E. K. (1999) 'Mental Health' in Law and Society Trust (ed.) *Sri Lanka: State of Human Rights 1999* (Colombo: Law and Society Trust), pp. 191–213.

Roger, P. (1994) 'Individuality in French Enlightenment Thought: Exaltation or Denial?' in S. Bagge (ed.) *Culture and History. The Individual in European Culture* (Cambridge, MA: Scandinavian University Press), pp. 72–83.

Rose, S., Lewontin, R. C. and Kamin, L. (1984) *Not in Our Genes. Biology, Ideology and Human Nature* (Harmondsworth: Penguin).

Rosen, G. (1968) *Madness in Society* (New York: Harper & Row).

Rosenthal, D. and Frank, J. D. (1958) 'The Fate of Psychiatric Clinic Outpatients Assigned to Psychotherapy', *Journal of Nervous and Mental Disease*, 127, 330–43.

Rothbaum, B. O., Meadows, E. A., Resick, P. and Foy, D. W. (2000) *Effective Treatments for PTSD: Practice Guidelines from the International Society for Traumatic Stress* (New York: Guilford Press), pp. 320–4.

Rousseau, C. and Measham, T. (2007) 'Posttraumatic Suffering as a Source of Transformation: A Clinical Perspective' in L. J. Kirmayer, R. Lemelson and M. Barad (eds) *Understanding Trauma. Integrating Biological, Clinical and Cultural Perspectives* (Cambridge: Cambridge University Press), pp. 275–93.

Roy, C., Choudhuri, A. and Irvine, D. (1970) 'The Prevalence of Mental Disorders among Saskatchewan Indians', *Journal of Cross-Cultural Psychology*, 1(4), 383–92.

Royal College of Psychiatrists (2008) *Fair Deal for Mental Health* (London: Royal College of Psychiatrists).

Rutter, M. (1999) 'Resilience Concepts and Findings: Implications for Family Therapy', *Journal of Family Therapy*, 21(2), 119–44.

Ryle, G. (1990) *The Concept of Mind* (London: Penguin Books). First published by Hutchinson, New York, 1949.

Sachs, L. (1989) 'Misunderstanding as Therapy: Doctors, Patients and Medicines in a Rural Clinic in Sri Lanka', *Culture, Medicine and Psychiatry*, 13, 335–49.

Sachs, W. (1997) 'The Need for the Home Perspective' in M. Rahnema and V. Bawtree (eds) *The Post-development Reader* (London: Zed Books), pp. 290–300.

Safaya, R. (1976) *Indian Psychology* (New Delhi: Munshiram Manoharlal).

Said, E. W. (1994) *Culture and Imperialism* (London: Vintage).

Said, E. W. (2001) *Reflections on Exile and Other Literary and Cultural Essays* (London: Granta Books).

Salih, M. and Samarasinghe, G. (2006) *Localizing Transitional Justice in the Context of Psychosocial Work in Sri Lanka* (Colombo: Social Policy Analysis and Research Centre).

Sampath, H. M. (1974) 'Prevalence of Psychiatric Disorders in a Southern Baffin Island Eskimo Settlement', *Canadian Psychiatric Association Journal*, 19, 363–7.

Saraceno, B. (2004) 'Mental Health: Scarce Resources Need New Paradigms', *World Psychiatry*, 3, 3–6.

Sartorius, N., Gulbinat, W., Harrison, G., Laska, E. and Siegel, C. (1996) 'Long-Term Follow-Up of Schizophrenia in 16 Countries', *Social Psychiatry and Psychiatric Epidemiology*, 31, 249–58.

Sartorius, N., Jablensky, A., Gulbinat, W. and Ernberg, G. (1980) 'WHO Collaborative Study: Assessment of Depressive Disorders', *Psychological Medicine*, 10, 743–9.

Sartorius, N., Jablensky, A., Korten, A., Ernberg, G., Anker, M., Cooper, J. E. and Day, R. (1986) 'Early Manifestations and First-Contact Incidence of Schizophrenia in Different Cultures: A Preliminary Report on the Initial Evaluation Phase of the WHO Collaborative Study on Determinants of Outcome of Severe Mental Disorders', *Psychological Medicine*, 16, 909–28.

Saunders, J. J. (1965) *A History of Medieval Islam* (London and New York: Routledge).

Sayce, L. (2000) *From Psychiatric Patient to Citizen* (London: Macmillan).

Sayce, L. and Perkins, R. (2000) 'Recovery: Beyond Mere Survival', Letter to editor, *Psychiatric Bulletin*, 24, 74.

Scheff, T. J. (1966) *Being Mentally Ill: A Sociological Theory* (Chicago, IL: Aldine).

Schmookler, E. (1996) *Trauma Treatment Manual* (Oregan: Trauma Information Pages). Available: http://www.trauma-pages.com. Accessed: 30 May 2009.

Schon, D. A. (1967) *Technology and Change: The New Heraclitus* (Oxford: Pergamon Press).

Schrank, B. and Slade, M. (2007) 'Recovery in Psychiatry', *Psychiatric Bulletin*, 31, 321–5.

Schultes, R. E. (1969) 'Hallucinogens of Plant Origin', *Science*, 163, 245–54.

Schumacher, E. F. (1973) *Small Is Beautiful: A Study of Economics as If People Mattered* (London: Blond & Briggs).

Scott, J. and Beck, A. A. (2008) 'Cognitive Behavioural Therapy' in R. M. Murray, K. S. Kendler, P. McGuffin, S. Wessely and D. J. Castle (eds) *Essential Psychiatry*, 4th edn (Cambridge: Cambridge University Press).

Scott, R. D. (1960) 'A Family-Orientated Psychiatric Service to the London Borough of Barnet', *Health Trends*, 12, 65–8.

Scull, A. (1984) *Decarceration. Community Treatment and the Deviant. A Radical View*, 2nd edn (Cambridge: Polity Press 1984).

Seabrook, J. (2004) 'Religion as a Fig Leaf for Racism', in *Special Report Race in UK*, Friday 23 July 2004. Available: http://www.guardian.co.uk/race/story. Accessed: 29 January 2007.

Select Committee on Race Relations and Immigration (1977) *The West Indian Community* (London: Her Majesty's Stationery Office).

Selten, J-R., Veen, N., Feller, W., Blom, J. D., Schols, D., Camoenië, W., Oolders, J., van der Velden, M., Hoek, H. W., Vladár Rivero, V. M., van der Graaf, Y. and Kahn, R. (2001) 'Incidence of Psychotic Disorders in Immigrant Groups to the Netherlands', *British Journal of Psychiatry*, 178, 367–72.

Sen, A. (2006) *Identity and Violence. The Illusion of Destiny* (London: Allen Lane).

Sen, K. M. (1961) *Hinduism* (Harmondsworth: Penguin).

Shaikh, A. (1985) 'Cross-Cultural Comparison: Psychiatric Admission of Asian and Indigenous Patients in Leicestershire', *International Journal of Social Psychiatry*, 31, 3–11.

Shalev, A. Y. and Ursano, R. J. (2003) 'Mapping the Multidimensional Picture of Acute Responses to Traumatic Stress' in R. Ørner and U. Schnyder (eds) *Reconstructing Early Interventions after Trauma. Innovations in the Care of Survivors* (Oxford: Oxford University Press), pp. 118–29.

Sharma, R. K. and Dash, V. B. (1983) *Agnivesa's Caraka Samhitā*, Text with English Translation and Critical Exposition, 2nd edn, vol. 1 (Varanasi, India: Choukhamba Sanskrit Series Office).

Sharma, R. K. and Dash, V. B. (1985) *Agnivesa's Caraka Samhitā*, Text with English Translation and Critical Exposition, 2nd edn, vol. 2 (Varanasi, India: Choukhamba Sanskrit Series Office).

Shoenberg, E. (1972) *A Hospital Looks at Itself* (London: Bruno Casirer).

SHSA (Special Hospitals Service Authority) (1993) *Report of the Committee of Inquiry into the Death in Broadmoor Hospital of Orville Blackwood and a Review of the Deaths of Two Other Afro-Caribbean Patients: 'Big, Black and Dangerous?'* (Chairman Professor H. Prins) (London: SHSA).

Silove, D. (2005) 'The Best Immediate Therapy for Acute Stress Is Social', *Bulletin of the World Health Organization*, 83(1), 75–6.

Simon, B. (1978) *Mind and Madness in Ancient Greece. The Classical Roots of Modern Psychiatry* (London: Cornell University Press).

Simon, R. I. (1965) 'Involutional Psychosis in Negroes', *Archives of General Psychiatry*, 13, 148–54.

Simon, R. J., Fleiss, J. L., Gurland, B. J., Stiller, P. R. and Sharpe, L. (1973) 'Depression and Schizophrenia in Hospitalised Black and White Mental Patients', *Archives of General Psychiatry*, 28, 509–12.

Singer, K. (1975) 'Depressive Disorders from a Transcultural Perspective', *Social Science and Medicine*, 9, 289–301.

Skultans, V. (1980) 'The Management of Mental Illness among Maharashtrian Families: A Case Study of a Mahanubhav Healing Temple', *Man (N.S.)*, 22, 661–79.

Slack, J. (2007) 'Polish Immigrants Take £1 bn Out of UK Economy', *Mail on line*, 28 June. Available: http://www.dailymail.co.uk/news/article-464759/Polish-immigrants-1bn-UK-economy.html. Accessed: 30 November 2008.

Smith, G. (2008) *A Short History of Secularism* (London and New York: Cambridge University Press).

Smith, J. W. (2005) *Economic Democracy: The Political Struggle of the Twenty-First Century*, 4th edn (Sun City, AZ: Institute for Economic Democracy Press). Available: http://www.ied.info. Accessed: 8 June 2009.

Smith, P., Dyregrov, A., Yule, W., Gupta, L., Perrin, L. and Gjestad, R. (1999) *Children and Disaster: Teaching Recovery Techniques* (Bergen, Norway: Foundation for Children and War).

Soloff, P. H. and Turner, S. M. (1981) 'Patterns of Seclusion: A Prospective Study', *Journal of Nervous and Mental Disease*, 169, 37–44.

Somasunderam, D. and Sivayokan, S. (2005) *Mental Health in the Tamil Community* (Jaffna, Sri Lanka: Shanthiham).

Soyinka, W. (1999) *The Burden of Memory, The Muse of Forgiveness* (Oxford and New York: Oxford University Press).

Spencer, J. (2000) 'On Not Becoming a "Terrorist". Problems of Memory, Agency, and Community in the Sri Lankan Conflict' in V. Das, A. Kleinmann, M. Ramphele and P. Reynolds (eds) *Violence and Subjectivity* (Berkeley and Los Angeles: University of California Press), pp. 120–40.

SPN (Social Perspectives Network) (2007) *Whose Recovery Is It Anyway?* (London: SPN).

St Clair, H. R. (1951) 'Psychiatric Interview Experiences with Negroes', *American Journal of Psychiatry*, 108, 113–19.

Steadman, H. J. (1983) 'Dangerousness among the Mentally Ill: Art, Magic and Science', *International Journal of Law and Psychiatry*, 6, 381–90.

Steinberg, M. D., Pardes, H., Bjork, D. and Sporty, L. (1977) 'Demographic and Clinical Characteristics of Black Psychiatric Patients in a Private General Hospital', *Hospital and Community Psychiatry*, 28, 128–32.

Stott, D. H. (1983) *Issues in the Intelligence Debate* (Windsor: NFER-Nelson Publishing).

Stubbs, A. (1988) 'Martyr of Hope: A Personal Memoir', in A. Stubbs (ed.) *Steve Biko. I Write What I Like. A Selection of His Writings* (Harmondsworth: Penguin) pp. 174–239.

Stubbs, P. (2005) 'Transforming Local and Global Discourses: Reassessing the PTSD Movement in Bosnia and Croatia' in D. Ingleby (ed.) *Forced Migration and Mental Health. Rethinking the Case of Refugees and Displaced Persons* (New York: Springer), pp. 53–66.

Suh, E. M. (2000) 'Self, the Hyphen between Culture and Subjective Well-Being', in E. Diener and E. M. Suh (eds) *Culture and Subjective Well-Being* (Cambridge, MS and London: MIT Press), pp. 63–86.

Summerfield, D. (1999) 'A Critique of Seven Assumptions behind Psychological Trauma Programmes in War-Affected Areas', *Social Science and Medicine*, 48(10), 1449–62.

Summerfield, D. (2001) 'Does Psychiatry Stigmatise?' *Journal of the Royal Society of Medicine*, 94, 148–9.

Susruta (1963) *Susruta Samhita*, ed. and trans. K. S. Bhisagratne (Varanasi: Chowkambra Sanskrit Series Office).

Sweeting, M. (2006) 'Management of Medication When Treatment Is Failing' in G. Robert, S. Davenport, F. Holloway and T. Tattan (eds) *Enabling Recovery. The Principles and Practices of Rehabilitation Psychiatry* (London: Gaskell), pp. 146–57.

Tapsell, R. and Mellsop, G. (2007) 'The Contributions of Culture and Ethnicity to New Zealand Mental Health Research', *International Journal of Social Psychiatry*, 53(4), 317–24.

Te Puni Kōkiri (1993) *Ngā Ia o te Oranga Hinengaro Māori: Trends in Māori Mental Health: A Discussion Document Te Puni Kōkiri*. Cited in Masters (1997), p. 356.

Tew, J. (2002) *Social Perspectives in Mental Health; Developing Social Models to Understand and Work with Mental Distress* (London Jessica Kingsley).

Tew, J. (ed.) (2005) *Social Perspectives in Mental Health. Developing Social Models to Understand and Work with Mental Distress* (London and Philadelphia: Jessica Kingsley).

Thomas, A. and Sillen, S. (1972) *Racism and Psychiatry* (New York: Brunner/Mazel).

Tischler, G. L. (1987) *Diagnosis and Classification in Psychiatry. A Critical Appraisal of DSM-III* (Cambridge: Cambridge University Press).

Torda, C. (1980) *Memory and Dreams: A Modern Physics Approach* (Chicago, IL: Walters).

Torrey, E. F. (1973) 'Is Schizophrenia Universal? An Open Question', *Schizophrenia Bulletin*, 7, 53–7.

Torrey, E. F. (1987) 'Prevalence Studies of Schizophrenia', *British Journal of Psychiatry*, 150, 598–608.

TRC (Truth and Reconciliation Commission) (2001) *Truth the Road to Reconciliation* (Cape Town: TCR) Available: http://www.doj.gov.za/trc. Accessed: 30 May 2009.

Triandis, H. (1995) *Individualism and Collectivism. New Directions on Social Psychology* (Boulder, CO and Oxford: Westview Press).

Tribe R. and the Family Rehabilitation Centre Staff (2004) 'Internally Displaced Sri Lanka Widows: The Women's empowerment Programme' in K. E. Miller and L. M. Rasco (eds) *The Mental Health of Refugees. Ecological Approaches to Healing and Adaptation* (Mahwah, NJ and London: Lawrence Erlbaum), pp. 161–85.

Tuke, D. H. (1858) 'Does Civilization Favour the Generation of Mental Disease?' *Journal of Mental Science*, 4, 94–110.

Ture, K. and Hamilton, C. (1992) *Black Power. The Politics of Liberation. With New After-Words by the Authors* (New York: Random House).

Tyrer, P. and Steinberg, D. (1998) *Models for Mental Disorder. Conceptual Models in Psychiatry* (Chichester and New York: Wiley).

UNHCR (United Nations High Commissioner for Refugees) (2008) *2007 Global Trends: Refugees, Asylum-seekers, Returnees, Internally Displaced and Stateless Persons* (Geneva: UNHCR). Available: http://www.unhcr.org. Accessed: 10 October 2008.

United Nations (1996) *The Universal Declaration of Human Rights* (Geneva: The Office of the High Commissioner for Human Rights). Available: http://www.unhchr.ch/udhr. Accessed: 20 October 2008.

Uragoda, C. G. (1987) *A History of Medicine in Sri Lanka – from the Earliest Times to 1948* (Colombo, Sri Lanka: Sri Lanka Medical Association).

Valiathan, M. S. (2003) *The Legacy of Caraka.* (Hyderabad, India: Orient Longman).

van de Put, W. A. C. M. and Eisenbruch, M. (2004) 'Internally Displaced Cambodians: Healing Trauma in Communities' in K. E. Miller and L. M. Rasco (eds) *The Mental Health of Refugees. Ecological Approaches to Healing and Adaptation* (Mahwah, NJ and London: Lawrence Erlbaum), pp. 133–59.

van Ommeren, M., Saxena, S. and Saraceno, B. (2005) 'Mental and Social Health during and after Acute Emergencies: Emerging Consensus?', *Bulletin of the World Health Organization*, 83(1), 71–5.

Vaughan, F. and Boorstein, S. (1982) 'Transpersonal Psychotherapy' in L. E. Abt and I. R. Stewart (eds) *The Newer Therapies: A Sourcebook* (New York: Van Nostrand Reinhold), pp. 118–34.

Veith, I. (1966) (trans.) *The Yellow Emperor's Classic of Internal Medicine* (Berkeley: University of California Press).

Vogt, B. (1999) *Skill and Trust: The Tovil Healing Ritual of Sri Lanka as Culture-Specific Psychotherapy*, Sri Lanka Studies 6, trans. M. H. Kohn (Amsterdam: VU University Press).

Wallace, A. F. C. (1958) 'Dreams and the Wishes of the Soul: A Type of Psychoanalytic Theory among Seventeenth Century Iroquois', *American Anthropologist*, 60, 234–48.

Wallace, P. (2003) *Chile and Scotland. Report on Glasgow Caledonian University (GCU) Research Collections Witness Seminar and Open Forum* (Glasgow: Glasgow Caledonian University). Available: http://www.gcal.ac.uk. Accessed: 18 October 2008.

Walsh, F. (2006) *Strengthening Family Resilience*, 2nd edn (New York and London: The Guilford Press).

Warburton, D. (ed.) (1998) *Community and Sustainable Development* (London: Earthscan Publications).

Warner, R. (1985) *Recovery from Schizophrenia. Psychiatry and Political Economy* (London: Routledge and Kegan Paul).

Watson, P. (1973) 'Psychologists and Race: The "Actor Factor"' in P. Watson (ed.) *Psychology and Race* (Harmondsworth: Penguin), pp. 13–19.

Watt, A. and Rodmell, S. (1993) 'Community Involvement in Health Promotion: Progress or Panacea? in A. Beattie, M. Gott, L. Jones and M. Sidell (eds) *Health and Wellbeing. A Reader* (Basingstoke: Macmillan), pp. 6–13.

Watters, C. and Ingleby, D. (2004) 'Locations of Care: Meeting the Mental Health and Social Care Needs of Refugees in Europe', *International Journal of Law and Psychiatry*, 27, 549–70.

Watts, A. (1962) *The Way of Zen* (London: Pelican Books).

Watts, A. (1971) *Psychotherapy East and West* (London: Jonathan Cape). First published by Pantheon Books, New York 1961.

Watts, A. (1995) *The Philosophies of Asia. The Edited Transcripts* (Boston, MA: Charles E. Tuttle).

Waxler, N. (1974) 'Culture and Mental Illness', *Journal of Nervous and Mental Illness*, 159(6), 379–95.

Waxler, N. (1984) 'Behavioural Convergence and Institutional Separation: An Analysis of Plural Medicine in Sri Lanka', *Culture, Medicine and Psychiatry*, 8(2), 187–205.

Waxler-Morrison, N. E. (1988) 'Plural Medicine in Sri Lanka: Do Ayurvedic and Western Medical Practices Differ?', *Social Science and Medicine*, 27(5), 531–44.

Weerackody, C. and Fernando, S. (2008) 'Field Report: Perceptions of Social Stratification and Well-Being in Refugee Communities in North-Western Sri Lanka', *International Journal of Migration, Health and Social Care*, 4(2), 47–56.

Weerackody, C. and Fernando, S. (2009) *Mental Health and Wellbeing. Experience of Communities Affected by Conflict and 2004 Tsunami in Sri Lanka* (Colombo, Sri Lanka: People's Rural Development Association (PRDA) and Oxfam America).

Wellman, D. (1977) *Portraits of White Racism* (Cambridge: Cambridge University Press).

Welwood, J. (ed.) (1979) *The Meeting of the Ways: Explorations in East/West Psychology* (New York: Schocken Books).

Wessels, M. and Monteiro, C. (2004) 'Internally Displaced Angolans: A Child-Focused, Community-Based Intervention' in K. E. Miller and L. M. Rasco (eds) *The Mental Health of Refugees. Ecological Approaches to Healing and Adaptation* (Mahwah, NJ: Lawrence Erlbaum), pp. 67–94.

West, C. (1994) *Race Matters* (New York: Random House).

West, M. (1979) 'Meditation', *British Journal of Psychiatry*, 135, 457–67.

Westermeyer, J. (1989) 'Paranoid Symptoms and Disorders among 100 Hmong Refugees: A Longitudinal Study', *Acta Psychiatrica Scandinavica*, 80, 47–59.

White, G. M. (1982) 'Ethnographic Study of Cultural Knowledge of "Mental Disorder"', in A. J. Marsella and G. M. White (eds) *Cultural Concepts of Mental Health and Therapy* (Dordrecht: Reidel), pp. 69–95.

WHO (World Health Organization) (1973) *Report of the International Pilot Study of Schizophrenia*, Vol. 1 (Geneva: WHO).

WHO (World Health Organization) (1975) *Schizophrenia: A Multinational Study. A Summary of the Initial Evaluation Phase of the International Pilot Study of Schizophrenia* (Geneva: WHO).

WHO (World Health Organization) (1977) *Apartheid and Mental Health Care* (Geneva: WHO).

WHO (World Health Organization) (1979) *Schizophrenia: An International Follow-Up Study* (London: Wiley).

WHO (World Health Organization) (1986) 'A Report on the Collaborative Study in Determinants of Outcome of Severe Mental Disorders', unpublished manuscript cited by Katz *et al.* (1988).

WHO (World Health Organization) (1988) *From Alma-Ata to the Year 2000: Reflections at the midpoint* (Geneva: WHO).

WHO (World Health Organization) (1993) *The ICD-10 Classification of Mental and Behavioural Disorders. Diagnostic Criteria for Research* (Geneva: WHO).

WHO (World Health Organization) (2000) *The World Health Report 2000. Health Systems: Improving Performance* (Geneva: WHO).

WHO (World Health Organization) (2001) *The World Health Report 2001. Mental Health: New Understanding, New Hope* (Geneva: WHO).

WHO (World Health Organization) (2002) *Working with Countries: Mental Health Policy and Service.* (Geneva: WHO).

WHO (World Health Organization) (2008) *Mental Health Gap Action Programme. Scaling up Care for Mental, Neurological, and Substance Use Disorders* (Geneva: WHO).

WHO Regional Office for South-East Asia (2008) *Broad Regional Strategy for Non-communicable Diseases and Mental Health; Mental Health and Substance Abuse* (New Delhi: WHO Regional Office for South-East Asia). Available: http://www.searo.who.int. Accessed: 15 September 2008.

WHO/UNICEF (1978) *Primary Health Care: The Alma Ata Conference* (Geneva: WHO).

Wickramage, K. (2006) 'Sri Lanka's Post-tsunami Psychosocial Playground: Lessons for Future Psychosocial Programming and Interventions Following Disasters', *Intervention: International Journal of Mental Health, Psychosocial Work and Counselling in Areas of Conflict*, 4(2), 167–72.

Wijesekera, N. (1989) *Deities and Demons Magic and Masks*, Part 2 (Colombo, Sri Lanka: Gunasena).

Williams, E. (1944) *Capitalism and Slavery* (Chapel Hill, NC: University of Carolina Press).

Wilmore, G. S. (1973) *Black Religion and Black Radicalism* (Garden City, NY: Anchor Books).

Wilson, D. C. and Lantz, E. M. (1957) 'The Effect of Culture Change on the Negro Race in Virginia, as Indicated by a Study of State Hospital Admissions', *American Journal of Psychiatry*, 114, 25–32.

Wing, J. K. and Haley, A. M. (1972) *Evaluating a Community Psychiatric Service* (London: Oxford University Press).

Wing, J. K. (1978) *Reasoning about Madness* (Oxford: Oxford University Press).

Wing, J. K., Cooper, J. E. and Sartorius, N. (1974) *Measurement and Classification of Psychiatric Symptoms* (London: Cambridge University Press).

Wirz, P. (1954) *Exorcism and the Art of Healing in Ceylon* (Leiden: E. J. Brill).

Wise, T. A. (1845) *Commentary on the Hindu System of Medicine* (London: Smith Elder).

Woodbridge, K. and Fulford, K. W. M. (Bill) (2004) *Whose Values? A Workbook for Values-Based Practice in Mental Health Care* (London: Sainsbury Centre for Mental Health).

World Bank (2008) *World Development Indicators 2008* (Washington, DC: World Bank). Available: http:www.worldbank.org. Accessed: 28 September 2008.

Yamamoto, J., James, Q. C. and Palley, N. (1968) 'Cultural Problems in Psychiatric Therapy', *Archives of General Psychiatry*, 19, 45–9.

Yamamoto, J., James, Q. C., Bloombaum, M. and Hattem, J. (1967) 'Racial Factors in Patient Selection', *American Journal of Psychiatry*, 124, 630–6.

Yancey, W. L., Erickson, E. P. and Julian, R. N. (1976) 'Emergent Ethnicity: A Review and Reformulation', *American Sociological Review*, 41, 391–402.

Young, A. (1995) *The Harmony of Illusions. Inventing Post-traumatic Stress Disorder* (Princeton, NJ: Princeton University Press).

Young, A. (1997) 'Suffering and the Origin of Traumatic Memory' in A. Kleinman, V. Das and M. Lock, M. (eds) *Social Suffering* (Berkeley and London: University of California Press), pp. 245–60.

Author Index

Subject Index